Kootenay Trips & Trails

Kootenay Trips & Trails

A Guide to
Southeastern British Columbia's
Kootenay–Columbia Region

MURPHY SHEWCHUK

Fitzhenry & Whiteside

Published in Canada by Fitzhenry & Whiteside,
195 Allstate Parkway, Markham, ON   L3R 4T8
Published in the United States by Fitzhenry & Whiteside
311 Washington Street, Brighton, MA   02135

Library and Archives Canada Cataloguing in Publication
Shewchuk, Murphy, author
Kootenay trips & trails : a guide to southeastern British Columbia's
Kootenay-Columbia Region / Murphy Shewchuk. -- First edition.

ISBN 978-1-55455-100-2 (softcover)

1. Trails--British Columbia--Kootenay Region--Guidebooks.
2. Kootenay Region (BC)--Guidebooks. I. Title. II. Title: Kootenay trips and trails.

FC3845.K7S54 2018   917.11'605   C2018-901873-9

Publisher Cataloging-in-Publication Data (U.S.)

Names: Shewchuk, Murphy, author.
Title: Kootenay Trips and Trails : A Guide to Southeastern British Columbia's
Kootenay-Columbia Region / author, Murphy Shewchuk.
Description: Markham, Ontario : Fitzhenry & Whiteside, 2018. | Includes bibliography and index. | Summary: "An illustrated guidebook to the back roads and trails of the Kootenay, British Columbia region including hiking, history, ecology, the environment, exploration, camping, and other outdoor recreation. Complete with maps" – Provided by publisher.
Identifiers: ISBN 978-1-55455-100-2 (paperback)
Subjects: LCSH: Kootenay Region (BC) – Description and travel. | Kootenay Region (BC) –
Outdoor recreation. | BISAC: TRAVEL / Canada / Western Provinces (AB, BC).
Classification: LCC F1089.K7S449 | DDC 917.1162043 – dc23

ONTARIO ARTS COUNCIL
CONSEIL DES ARTS DE L'ONTARIO

Canada Council **Conseil des Arts**
for the Arts **du Canada**

Fitzhenry & Whiteside acknowledges with thanks the Canada Council for the Arts and the Ontario Arts Council for their support of our publishing program. We acknowledge the financial support of the Government of Canada through the Canada Book Fund (CBF) for our publishing activities.

Design by Kerry Designs

Printed in Canada by Copywell.
2 4 6 8 10 9 7 5 3 1

To Katharine.

C O N T E N T S

Introduction

British Columbia is the custodian of some of the most spectacular wilderness remaining in the world, including the unique ecosystems of the Kootenay-Columbia basin.

However, there has been and continues to be degradation of these precious wild areas even by those who revere them. As more and more of us discover the wonders of our natural environment, it becomes increasingly important that each of us ensures it is protected and preserved so our children may also know its wonders.

Keep this in mind as you head out on the backroads and byways. Educate yourself to protect and preserve our natural areas. Remember to protect yourself as well, by learning about the nature of the area your trip or trail will take you into before you leave. Arm yourself with up-to-date maps, (and the tools and skills to use them), water, some sustenance, and suitable clothing.

Always let someone know where you plan to go and when you'll be back, and don't travel alone.

Water and waste.

Although it's essential to life, water can harm that life instead. No open body of water should be considered safe to drink without first treating it for invisible parasites and micro organisms which can otherwise cause mild to acute illness.

One of the most common causes of illness is the *Giardia lamblia* cyst, which multiplies in the intestinal tract of warm-blooded animals such as humans, and causes an illness often called beaver fever. The cysts are spread in water contaminated by the feces of infected animals or people and are present in more than 70 per cent of our watersheds.

To be safe, either boil your water for one minute before cooling and drinking it; treat it with four drops of iodine tincture per litre or four drops of pure household bleach per four litres of water, up to double that if cloudy; or filter it with a special system available in outdoor stores.

If using the iodine or bleach method, make sure you stir it in and let it sit for at least half an hour before drinking.

Cryptosporidium is resistant to chlorine, but boiling takes care of that. We can help prevent the spread of such internal infections by being responsible about disposal of our waste in the outdoors. Never use streams and lakes as a bath, toilet or sink.

Use the proper facilities provided whenever possible, but otherwise when hiking or camping in the back country, the ideal solution is to carry out all human waste.

If that goes further than your commitment to preserving the natural environment, do ensure you never urinate or defecate within 100 metres (110 yards) of open water. Instead, dig a small hole and replace the sod after you're through.

When camping, wash water should be disposed of in a hole, 25-30 centimetres (one foot) deep, at least 100 metres from any body of water. Create as little waste as possible. Always pack out what you pack in.

In wilderness areas, tread lightly in both the figurative and the literal sense, leaving no trace of your presence behind you. That way, both you and those who follow will enjoy fields of wild flowers, trees alive with birds and forests full of wildlife.

Leaving no trace begins with good planning before you depart, eliminating leftovers and reducing the garbage produced while on your trip.

Wild ways.

Wherever possible, use existing trails. Do not detour around muddy sections since the added traffic will break down the trail edge and widen it, or cause multiple trails which scar the natural areas that are the reason you go hiking.

Where trails don't already exist, select a route over the most durable terrain such as gravel creek beds, sandy or rocky areas. Whenever possible, avoid steep, loose slopes and wet areas.

Many plants die if they're stepped on and some soils will erode even after being trampled lightly.

When camping in a wilderness area, select a site that would be least damaged by your stay. Choose either high use sites already damaged or pristine sites in durable areas such as on rocky terrain or a gravel bar rather than the forest floor or sites with low growing shrubs.

Do not cut trees for firewood, furniture or boughs for beds. If you must have a fire, use an existing fire ring if possible, built on rocky or sandy soil away from trees, dry vegetation or roots. Use only as much dry dead wood as you need. Burn your fire down to ash before pouring water on it until it is cold enough for you to lay your bare hand on it. Leave no sign of your fire.

Remember that you are entering wild animals' homes when you're in the wilderness. Respect their space and minimize your intrusion on their lives. View them from enough distance that they are unaware of your presence.

Leave your pets at home.

Trail etiquette.

Trails are often used by hooves, feet and wheels, but by using common sense, communication and courtesy, conflict, danger and damage can be avoided.

Trail protocol suggests that the most mobile yields the right-of-way, but there are exceptions to the rule. Ideally, cyclists yield to everyone and hikers yield to horses. A loaded string of horses going uphill always has the right of way, and a cyclist climbing steeply will appreciate the same courtesy.

Hikers: If you encounter horse riders, your group should step off to the same side of the trail, the lower side if possible, allowing two to three metres for them to pass. If you come up on horses from behind, greet the riders before you pass so they're aware you're there before you startle either the animal or rider.

Mountain Bikers: Always anticipate a horse or hiker around a blind curve. Prevent the sudden, unexpected encounter possible from a bike's quick and silent approach. Yield to hikers and equestrians. Get off the bike and move to the lower side of the trail to let horses pass. When approaching from behind, speak so they know you're there. Learn to minimize damage to trails with techniques such as riding and not sliding, and cycle on designated trails. Meadows are easily damaged by bicycle tires. Stay off trails when they're wet and muddy since they'll become pathways for water erosion.

Horse Riders: Use an experienced, steady mount, and give clear directions to other trail users on how you would like them to stand clear. In steep, rough country, downhill traffic yields to uphill travellers, but use common sense. Whoever can pull off easiest should. Avoid soft and muddy trails.

Warn others of wire, potholes and boggy areas.

Above all, respect private property; "No Trespassing" signs; and leave gates as you found them.

GPS References

We have included Global Positioning System (GPS) latitude and longitude references for many points of interest in this book. The information has been taken directly from field data files generated by a variety of Garmin GPS receivers. In general, these references have been checked using Ozi Explorer, Garmin MapSource and Google Earth and should be accurate to within 15 metres. However, errors of up to 100 metres are possible as are errors in data entry. Tree cover, satellite configuration and equipment accuracy may also contribute to differences in readings. The GPS references should help in locating appropriate backroad and trail junctions etc., but should not be relied on to replace maps, a compass and good "bush" sense.

Important Notice!

Although every effort has been made to provide accurate information, road and trail conditions in this region are constantly changing. Consequently, neither the author nor the publisher can guarantee the continuing accuracy of this information.

We look forward to corrections and comments on ways that you think this book may be improved. Please write to the author in care of the publisher at the address listed in the front of the book.

Checklist for Camping

Back country camping can be a wonderful experience. However, it is often too easy to forget essential pieces of equipment until you are in the wilderness—then it is just too embarrassing to admit that the reason you are rubbing two sticks together is that you forgot the matches.

The following list of frequently used camping items (in alphabetical order) was provided by Jim Reid of the Coleman Camping Company. Use it when planning your next trip, and then adapt it to your own needs.

You may want to keep track of those pieces of equipment which you had and didn't need or needed and didn't have. This would help you on your future trips. Good camping.

- ☐ Air mattress
- ☐ Batteries
- ☐ Blankets
- ☐ Camera & Film
- ☐ Coffee pot
- ☐ Compass
- ☐ Cooking Utensils
- ☐ Cooler
- ☐ Dishpan & Pot Scrubbers
- ☐ Eating Utensils
- ☐ First Aid Kit
- ☐ Flares/Mirror
- ☐ Flashlight
- ☐ Folding Chairs or Camp Stools
- ☐ Folding Stands for Cooler or Stove
- ☐ Fuel
- ☐ Ground Cloth
- ☐ Hand Axe
- ☐ Ice or Ice Substitutes
- ☐ Insect Repellent
- ☐ Jug of Water
- ☐ Knife
- ☐ Lantern & Mantles
- ☐ Lighter-Disposable Butane
- ☐ Maps
- ☐ Matches & Waterproof Holder
- ☐ Pad, Pen or Pencil
- ☐ Plastic Zipper Bags
- ☐ Prescription Medicine
- ☐ Radiant Heater (cold weather)
- ☐ Rope, Cord or Wire
- ☐ Shovel-Small Folding Type
- ☐ Sleeping Bags
- ☐ Snakebite Kit
- ☐ Soap-Biodegradable
- ☐ Stakes
- ☐ Stove
- ☐ Sunglasses
- ☐ Suntan Oil or Lotion
- ☐ Tablecloth
- ☐ Tent & Poles
- ☐ Toilet Paper
- ☐ Toiletries
- ☐ Tool Kit, Hammer & Nails
- ☐ Towels-Paper & Bath
- ☐ Trash Bags
- ☐ Water Container
- ☐ Water Purification Tablets

Getting There–and Getting Back Using Maps, Simple Tools and GPS Units to Survive

Getting Lost Is an Epidemic

Scan the British Columbia newspapers; watch the TV news; search the Internet…

If you haven't been living in a cocoon, you will have seen the almost daily news of hikers, hunters and just plain walkers disappearing into the BC wilderness.

Some have come back on their own steam; some have been found by search and rescue teams and some have never returned.

Go Prepared To Return

While there are extenuating circumstances in every case, there are ways to use new (and old) technology to reduce your chances of becoming the next headline–or statistic.

Start At the Beginning

The first line of defence is mental preparation. Discard your know-it-all attitude and think in terms of a beginner. While you may be convinced that you know the terrain or you have read the signs or the maps, fatigue, panic or a touch of hypothermia–or hyperthermia–can undo all your previous knowledge. Without the aid of supplementary maps or technology or both, your name could be next on the headlines.

While it is hard to pack your memory in a backpack, you can take along some supplies to help restore it or, if that doesn't help you find your way back, to help you determine your location.

The supplies can be as simple as a water bottle and a windbreaker or rain jacket. Most of us can survive for days or weeks with very little food, but three or four days without water is the limit. Dehydration can cause a rise in blood pressure and body temperature. Fruit juice or milk can help replace water, but coffee, tea and alcohol can be counterproductive.

While you may have obvious concerns about the quality of the water you find in the backcountry, a doctor friend of mine is quick to remind me that it is easier to cure Giardia (beaver fever) than death by dehydration. To reduce the risk of water-borne problems, a variety of purification schemes are available, varying from tablets to hand-pump filters that fit in your water bottle.

If you find yourself suffering from cramps or unexpected fatigue, "Gastrolyte" (or equivalent, such as Hydralyte) rehydration salts can help re-establish your equilibrium. Although it is available off the shelf at most drugstores, check to make sure it won't interfere with any other medication you are taking. I learned about Gastrolyte on a trip to Costa Rica and now pack several packets in my kit and have used it frequently.

The windbreaker or rain jacket can help reduce the risk of hypothermia. Even on a +30° day, alpine mist or spray off the river rapids can quickly chill you. If you are averse to carrying a jacket, an extra-large orange garden bag can be rolled up small enough to fit in a pocket. In addition to protection, it can serve as a flag to attract help if you are in serious trouble.

A hat is also an important piece of equipment. It can protect you from the sun's heat and from the cold winds. It can serve to dip water from a stream or fan the embers of a reluctant campfire.

The rest of your clothing selection is extremely important. Shorts and T-shirt may be appropriate in a city park, but they don't offer much protection from bugs, branches and the weather when bushwhacking in the mountains. Good boots should also be a priority. The North Shore Search & Rescue recently asked hikers to warn fellow travellers about the perils of mountaineering in flip-flops.

Packing Paper

I have an extensive collection of federal and provincial topographic maps. As most of them do not appear to have been updated since the 1970s or 1980s, they are becoming less and less useful. Printed mapbooks and online maps are available and up-to-date for backroads and backcountry exploring.

The Mussio "*Backroad Mapbook*" series cover British Columbia and Alberta in a 1:200,000 scale. They are available in spiral bound paper editions and regional water-resistant printed sheets as well as a variety of digital editions that can be downloaded and used on your computer or printed to pack in your pocket.

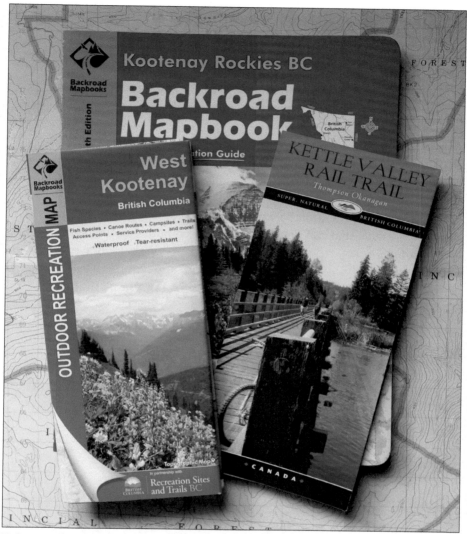

Various supplemental maps that are readily available. © Murphy Shewchuk

Local maps and brochures are often available from tourist centres for short distance hikes. At a recent stop at an info centre at Tumbler Ridge we found nearly a dozen one-page map-brochures of local attractions.

Hiking guidebooks often include maps and detailed descriptions. One of the best I have recently seen is "Canyon to Alpine", published by the Lillooet Naturalist Society. It describes 32 hikes in detail and includes maps and illustrations.

The website, MyTopo offers custom-printed Canadian topographic maps in a variety of sizes.

Paper requires protection. If you are planning a trip where you could experience adverse conditions, then protecting your vital information in plastic zipper bags or laminating your maps may be cheap insurance. Treat your maps like you would your cameras or sensitive electronics.

Incidentally, short of laminating it, you might want to take similar protective measures for the other kind of paper that is important for your personal comfort.

Digital Maps

Although paper maps are being continually updated, they aren't the only game in town—or on the Internet.

The previously mention Backroad Mapbook series is available in a variety of formats that can be viewed on your computer and tablet or loaded into your GPS or smartphone. They also have an app that will work on your IOS or Android device. The "BRMB Navigator" app requires a cell phone or network connection unless you do a bit of advance pre-planning and

Memory-Map Navigator on a laptop computer with a GPS attached. © Murphy Shewchuk

Google Earth satellite image with a GPS track. © Murphy Shewchuk

download the detailed maps for your planned travel area before getting out of range.

The Memory-Map Navigator app uses a different format of mapping. These "bit-map" maps can be used on your computer as well as mobile device and must be transferred in advance, but should work regardless of phone connection.

The Garmin Topo Canada map series is available on a DVD or MicroSD card to plug into your GPS. With Garmin MapSource or BaseCamp and the DVD version you can select the area you are planning to explore and print the necessary maps.

If you are looking for free downloadable maps, there are numerous sources. One of the most up-to-date is available through OpenStreetMap where digital maps can be selected from all over the world and downloaded for installation on your computer or GPS. They have pre-defined sets for each province, but if you don't mind waiting a few days, you can specify a set that includes more than one province or territory.

GPS File Depot is another online source of digital maps although their Canadian selection is limited.

There is a variety of software available to utilize the digital maps. In addition to Garmin MapSource and BaseCamp, there is Garmin nRoute which is no longer supported by Garmin but is still available from non-official sources. I have also used OziExplorer and Memory-Map Navigator. Both programs work with scanned (raster) digital maps, but cannot upload maps to a GPS receiver.

If you're exploring new territory, one important resource is Google Earth. You will need a decent computer and a network connection, but with a little experimentation, you can "fly" over your route. Much of British Columbia is illustrated with aerial photography with enough detail to identify the vehicle in your driveway. Note that the images are not "live" and occasionally may be several years old. I use it frequently to identify landmarks I have photographed and to plan my routes including snowshoe routes in the Kane Valley near Merritt.

Non-Electronic Tools and Gadgets

One of the best non-electronic pieces of gear to pack is a mirror compass. While few of us have taken the survival training needed to be proficient with a compass, it can still be helpful in maintaining your direction when heading for recognized landmarks. In my pre-GPS days, I used one frequently to find my way in mountainous, timbered terrain. The mirror may also prove to be a life saver if you are lost or injured and need to flash your location to a search aircraft.

A small key-ring magnifying glass could be useful if you need to remove a sliver or start a campfire.

My Victorinox Swiss Army sport knife is my constant companion. Though small enough to fit in my jean watch pocket, it has saved me in numerous emergencies, the latest being when a friend showed up with a bottle of wine and no corkscrew. On a more serious note, Mountain Equipment Co-op lists 40+ different knives and multi-tools to help you come back alive.

If you are carrying a day pack, you may also find room for survey ribbon, duct tape, a small folding saw, and cable ties (a.k.a. zap-straps). I've marked my route with pieces of survey ribbon on several bushwhacking adventures, removing it on my return trip. Duct tape and the folding saw came in handy to repair a broken ski pole on one winter trip into Little Douglas Lake. Duct tape has also repaired leaky boots and clothing tears. The folding saw has served to cut a walking stick, a splint and numerous branches along the ski trails.

I mentioned day pack earlier. My first serious day pack was made by a lady near Golden, BC for downhill ski patrollers. I have gone through several different types on various trips from New Zealand to the Arctic. I

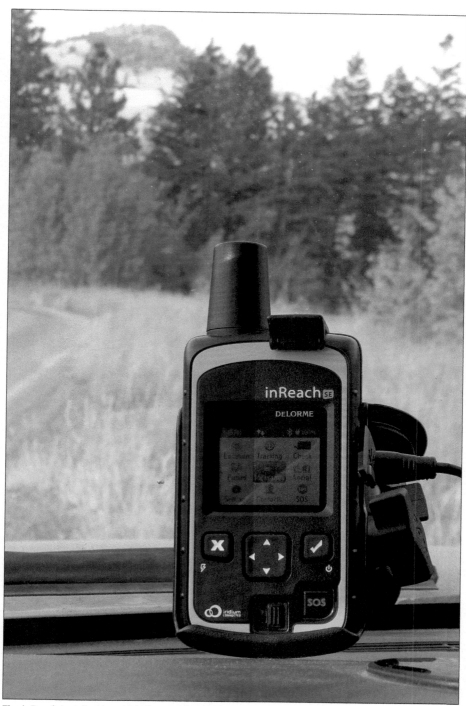

The inReach installed in vehicle for tracking via satellite. © Murphy Shewchuk

currently have several different packs to carry everything from camera gear to lunch and ski wax. With a chest strap, good shoulder straps and a vented back, they can be comfortable even on long walks.

GPS Units

The range of battery-operated gadgets that can help you find your way around in the backwoods is outstanding and increasing every day. My first of these was a Garmin GPS45 I bought in the mid-1990s. (Note: I

Qualcomm Globalstar installed in vehicle for communications via satellite. © Murphy Shewchuk

haven't any fiduciary interest in Garmin other than the money I have paid for GPS units.) I think it ended up in the recycle bin a long time ago to be replaced by newer units with more features. The race to outdo the competition and each previous model will never end, so with three handheld units and two vehicle units, I have decided to back off.

With thousands of GPS files and at least 100,000 km tracked, there are a few features that are at the top of my list when purchasing a new unit.

While you might think that accuracy should prevail, most modern GPS units (and smartphones) are accurate to within a few metres. If you are searching for a trail or backroad, this is probably more accurate than the best maps available.

Battery Life Is Important

Instead, my first consideration is battery life and battery variety. Any extra gadgets built into the GPS unit are likely to contribute to reduced battery life. While a camera might be nice, I have a number of cameras that are as good as the best GPS cameras. Being able to handle a variety of batteries means I can use rechargeable batteries when I have access to a charger, but I can put a couple of sets of quality alkaline batteries in my pocket to keep them warm or for emergency backup.

An important piece of extra insurance is a pocket portable charger. These are usually re-chargeable battery packs that can be charged from any 5 volt source and, with the appropriate cables, can be used to recharge your phone or other 5 volt digital device. A pocket unit I recently purchased weighs just 125 grams (4.4 oz.) and will theoretically supply two charges to my phone.

The ability to run the GPS unit and download data via a USB connection is also important. I can run my workhorse GPSMAP 76CSx off an inexpensive USB cigarette lighter adapter while driving or connect it to a tablet or netbook to give me a much larger moving-map display than readily available in consumer units. When I am taking a hike, I can clip the GPS to my backpack strap with the batteries still fresh. I can also use one of the numerous external battery packs while hiking. Note that while the external power source can take the load off the battery, I haven't found many handheld units that charge the internal battery while on a USB source.

Optional External Antenna

Because I am often travelling in a truck with a camper that can block the GPS signal from reaching the cab, the ability to attach an external antenna is very important. Many new models, though very sensitive and highly accurate, don't have external antenna jacks.

Well up on the list is the ability to upload maps or install memory cards containing detailed maps; the ability to store tracks and waypoints; a compass and an altimeter. Add holding brackets to firmly mount your GPS in or on your transportation choice and you should be well underway.

Automatic Tracking

While most GPS receivers can track your travels and display your position on a map, they do not transmit your location to anyone else.

The Garmin, InReach SE and the newer InReach Explorer are exceptions to this rule. My wife and I recently used the InReach SE satellite communicator to relay our position to family and friends while on a trip to the Arctic. With it programmed to automatically send a position every half hour, they knew roughly where we were in case of emergency.

While it doesn't give you voice contact, the Delorme handheld unit can be paired with your smartphone to send and receive text messages and to trigger an SOS with your position including time and elevation.

Talk to the World

While satellite phones have been around for more than a decade, they have recently become small enough and cheap enough to be considered a must-have tool for the avid outdoor person. Units from Iridium, Inmarsat, Globalstar and Thuraya weigh in at under half a pound and aren't much bigger than a smartphone. Basic unit prices and service plans vary as well as satellite configurations. Some offer data kits as well, but don't expect to be able to download movies.

They do have limitations in that they need to have a clear view of the sky. If you are using one in a vehicle you will likely need a car kit with an external antenna. If you are stuck in a canyon, coverage could be sporadic as the satellites line up overhead.

We used a Globalstar GSP-1700 on our Arctic trip and although coverage was sporadic at times, reception was clear when we had it.

Make It Home Alive

While there is often little you can do about external forces, advance preparation and modern technology can significantly reduce your chances of becoming the next headline or statistic.

Additional Information:

Backroad Mapbooks: www.backroadmapbooks.com
Garmin inReach: inreach.roadpost.ca
Garmin Open Street Maps: garmin.openstreetmap.nl
Globalstar: ca.globalstar.com/en
Google Earth: www.google.com/earth
Memory-Map Navigator: www.memory-map.com
MyTopo: www.mytopo.com
OziExplorer: www.oziexplorer.com

BOAT ENCAMPMENT

Located on the Big Bend of the Columbia River and now lying under the Mica reservoir, Boat Encampment was an important trans-shipment point where fur traders and travellers from Jasper House, having crossed the Athabasca Pass, boarded boats for Fort Vancouver. First visited by David Thompson who wintered there in 1811, Boat Encampment was for nearly 50 years an important transfer point on the express route from the Pacific Coast to Montreal and York Factory. It lost importance with the growth of Fort Victoria, advances in ocean transportation, and changes in the trading activities of the Hudson's Bay Company.

Situé dans le grand coude du Columbia sous le réservoir Mica, Boat Encampment était un important poste de transbordement des pelleteries, où les voyageurs venant de Jasper House s'embarquaient pour le fort Vancouver après avoir traversé le col Athabasca. Découvert par David Thompson qui y passa l'hiver de 1811, il fut aussi l'un des principaux postes de correspondance sur la route du Pacifique vers Montréal ou York Factory. L'émergence du fort Victoria, les progrès du transport océanique et les changements apportés à l'organisation de la Compagnie de la Baie d'Hudson lui valurent à peu près.

Historic Sites and Monuments Board of Canada Commission des lieux et monuments historiques du Canada

Boat Encampment Plaque located near the Columbia River/Kinbasket Lake north of Mica Dam.
© Murphy Shewchuk

The Kootenay-Columbia Region: Hugging the BC / United States Boundary

The Heart of South East British Columbia

The Kootenay and Columbia Rivers drain a significant tract of south central and eastern British Columbia. As the crow flies, it stretches over 370 km from Anarchist Summit, east of Osoyoos, to the BC/Alberta border in the heart of the Rocky Mountains. On a north-south tangent, the area stretches over 425 km from the BC/Washington boundary north to the head of Kinbasket Lake near Valemount.

Three Major River Systems

Kettle River

The region is drained on the west by the Kettle River. The main Kettle River rises in the heart of the Monashee Mountains east of Vernon. The West Kettle starts east Kelowna on the south slopes of Big White Mountain. They join at Westbridge and flow south and east to Midway before dipping down into Washington State. The Kettle River crosses north again into British Columbia at Grand Forks and flows east, crossing the border for the last time at Christina.

Kootenay River

On the east the region is drained by the Kootenay River. It rises in the Rockies south of Banff, and after joining the Vermillion River, flows south, narrowly missing joining the Columbia at Canal Flats, before continuing south into Montana. A major dam at Libby, Montana backs up the Kootenay approximately 100 km into Canada creating Koocanusa Lake as part of the Columbia River Treaty system. After looping south, the Kootenay flows north again, entering British Columbia south of Creston and creating 107-km-long Kootenay Lake northwest of Creston. Kootenay Lake drains west through Nelson and into the Kootenay River. After passing through a

Kettle River Canyon Creek BC Recreation Site. © Murphy Shewchuk

series of hydroelectric dams (some more than a century old), it empties into the Columbia River at Castlegar.

Columbia River

The Columbia River rises in Columbia Lake, just north of the previously mentioned Canal Flats and only a few km north of where the Kootenay River flows out of the Rocky Mountains. These few km have been subject to speculation ever since the 1880s when W.A. Baillie-Grohman proposed a canal to divert the Kootenay River into the Columbia. (More of the story can be found in the "Ancient Valley of the Ducks" chapter on the Creston Marsh.)

The Columbia flows north through Windermere Lake, creating a broad fertile valley as it winds slowly northwest through Golden to the head of Kinbasket Lake.

Kinbasket Lake (or Kinbasket Reservoir), was created by the completion of the Mica Dam in 1973, also as part of the Columbia River Treaty. Columbia Reach extends southeast from the dam 115 km almost as far as Golden and Canoe Reach extends north 100 km toward Valemount.

Generators at the Mica Dam have a capacity of 1,805 megawatts utilizing the energy in the Columbia River before passing it 130 km

Kootenay River in Kootenay National Park, BC. © Murphy Shewchuk

downstream where it is again trapped by the Revelstoke Dam a few km north of the city of Revelstoke. The resulting Lake Revelstoke extends upstream to the foot of Mica Dam. The Revelstoke Dam generating station is the largest in the system, utilizing the storage capacity of Kinbasket Lake and Lake Revelstoke to produce 2,480 megawatts with the potential to add another turbine.

The somewhat subdued Columbia River continues south through the city only to flow into the 230-km-long Arrow Lake—originally two lakes before the Hugh Keenleyside Dam was commissioned in 1968. Located about 10 km north of Castlegar, Keenleyside is primarily a flood control dam as part of the Columbia Treaty. The Columbia still isn't over its work. After combining forces with the Kootenay River at Castlegar, it flows south through Trail and into Washington State where more dams await it.

While exploring the area and working on various magazine articles, I noticed that looping flows of the Columbia and Kootenay River systems create a huge inland island that, before modern bridges, was only crossed by boat or over the soggy marshes of Canal Flats. An idle thought, but how much of an earthquake would it take to accomplish Baillie-Grohman's dream and shift the major flow north?

Columbia Lake, north of Canal Flats, is the source of the Columbia River. © Murphy Shewchuk

Several Regional Districts
Kootenay-Boundary
The area is administered by local governments within several Regional Districts. On the southwest, the Regional District of Kootenay-Boundary takes in much of the area from the height of land at Anarchist Summit east to the height of land on the Monashee Mountains with a jog east to Fruitvale. It extends north approximately 90 km. The terrain varies from dry valley bottoms to snowy mountain peaks. With headquarters in Trail, the RDKB encompasses 8,096 sq. km with a population of 31,000.

Central Kootenay
The Regional District of Central Kootenay has its headquarters in Nelson. It covers much of the area from the height of the Monashees east to the height of the Purcell Mountains.

In addition to two major mountain ranges, it encompasses two major north-south lakes. Arrow Lake (once two lakes) is the longer of the two at 232 km. Kootenay Lake, at 107 km is about half. Both lakes served as major paddlewheel steamer transportation routes in the late 1800s and early 1900s. Duncan Lake, at 45-km-long, is a reservoir lake while 38-km-long Slocan Lake is the smallest, and in my opinion, the prettiest of the major lakes.

Mount Dunkirk with Kinbasket Lake in foreground. © Murphy Shewchuk

Fisherman on Kettle River near Rock Creek, BC. © Murphy Shewchuk

East Kootenay

The Regional District of East Kootenay takes in the southeast corner of British Columbia between the Purcell Mountains and the crest of the Rocky Mountains. It extends from the US border north almost to Lake Louise. It is drained by the Kootenay River to the south and the Columbia River to the north. It is bisected, southeast to northwest, by the broad Rocky Mountain Trench. A striking physiographic feature, the Trench extends approximately 1,600 km from Flathead Lake, Montana, to the Liard River, just south of the BC-Yukon border near Watson Lake. On a trip to the Arctic a few years ago we noticed that the Tintina Trench near Dawson City is strikingly similar. Some suggest both sections of the trench were created by faulting that took place 150 to 200 million years ago.

The Regional District of East Kootenay has offices in Cranbrook and Invermere and a population of roughly 60,000.

Columbia Shuswap Regional District

The northern portion of what is generally known as the Kootenays comes under the jurisdiction of the Columbia Shuswap Regional District with offices in Salmon Arm. It takes in a broad pyramid-shaped region extending roughly from Chase in the west to Spillimacheen and Field in the east and north almost to Jasper. The Rocky Mountain Trench continues diagonally through the district.

The Columbia River was a water route during the fur trade, first explored by David Thompson in 1811 and 1812. He and his party over-wintered at the "top" of the Big Bend of the Columbia River in the winter of 1810-11 where they built a wooden boat to take them down the river the following spring. "Boat Encampment" became an important staging point for the fur trades. It remained on BC maps until it was flooded by the Mica Dam and disappeared under the Kinbasket Reservoir.

Those who drove the "Big Bend Highway" prior to the Rogers Pass being opened in 1962 may remember a small settlement at the location. Today the east portion of "Big Bend" is also inundated by Kinbasket Reservoir. The western portion, though flooded by Lake Revelstoke, has been rebuilt at a higher elevation to allow continuing access to Mica Dam. Finding remnants of Boat Encampment either requires a boat or a short hike from the Sprague Bay Recreation Site northeast of Mica Dam. See the "Big Bend Highway 23" chapter for details.

CPR tracks along the Columbia River near Radium Hot Springs. © Murphy Shewchuk

Lake Kookanusa / Kootenay River near Wardner Bridge. © Murphy Shewchuk

Canoe Reach

To add a bit of confusion, access to the north end of the Canoe Reach of Kinbasket Lake and the north end of the Columbia system is via Yellowhead Highway 5 or Yellowhead Highway 16. This entails travelling through the Thompson-Nicola Regional District or the Regional District of Fraser-Fort George to reach Valemount and the short drive south to Kinbasket Lake. Fortunately for all travellers, there aren't any customs checks or border stations between regional districts. Except for National Park gates, there also aren't any official stops between BC and Alberta—yet!

Roads Know No Boundaries

This entire preamble is to justify my decision to NOT classify the various roads and trails in this book by Regional District. Instead, I have chosen to include a selection of routes that will give you a taste of the Kootenays. I have also chosen to list them on a west to east basis starting in the southwest—with the exception of the C&W and KVR rail trails which make more sense (to me, at least) to describe them in the direction that the railroaders built and numbered them.

Additional Information

Regional District of Kootenay-Boundary
Web: www.rdkb.com
Regional District of Central Kootenay
Web: www.rdck.ca
Regional District of East Kootenay
Web: www.rdek.bc.ca
Columbia Shuswap Regional District
Web: www.csrd.bc.ca

Mica Dam on the Columbia River. © Murphy Shewchuk

Loading a pack Horse. PT07 courtesy of Nicola Valley Museum & Archives.

CHAPTER 1

Crowsnest Highway 3: The Southern Trans-Provincial Highway Background

STATISTICS

For map, see page 40.

Distance: 610 km: Osoyoos to Crowsnest Pass, Alberta via Highway 3.

Travel Time: Eight to ten hours.

Condition: Paved Highway.

Season: Maintained year around.

Map: British Columbia Highway Map.

Communities: Osoyoos, Grand Forks, Castlegar, Creston, Cranbrook & Fernie.

Crowsnest Highway 3

While the west end of the British Columbia portion of Highway 3 starts near the outskirts of Hope, I have covered much of the Hope to Princeton section in *Coquihalla Trips & Trails* and the Princeton to Osoyoos section in *Okanagan Trips & Trails*.

The section covered in this book starts (or ends) at the junction with Highway 97 in Osoyoos and continues east to the Alberta border at Crowsnest Pass–thus the name and subtitle.

It would take most of the book to do a serious description of each of the communities along the route, leaving little room for the back roads and trails that I have found so interesting. Instead, I will touch on the communities and the points of history and interest that help make up the special mosaic that holds the region together.

Historic Southern Trans-Provincial Route

While it could hardly been called a "highway" when Edgar Dewdney

NOTE: For Reference Only.
Carry topographic maps.
See text for detailed listing.

completed the trail from Osoyoos to Wild Horse Creek in 1865, it was the
first land route to cross British Columbia, and like the railways that followed
half a century later, it was built as a reaction to concerns about an American
takeover.

Edgar Dewdney (November 5, 1835–August 8, 1916)

Highway 3, The Crowsnest Route, is a memorial to a young engineer
who came to Canada in 1859. An Englishman from Devonshire, 24-year-
old Edgar Dewdney arrived in Victoria with little more than a letter of
introduction to Governor James Douglas. To keep himself alive during his
first few months in the west, he found work cutting hay and surveying for
the Royal Engineers. Then the discovery of gold in the Similkameen River
and Rock Creek prompted Governor Douglas to build a trail to the mines
through British territory. In 1860-61, the Royal Engineers surveyed a route

Columbia River south of Trail, BC. © Murphy Shewchuk

from Fort Hope to Vermilion Forks (Princeton). Edgar Dewdney and Walter Moberly won the contract to build the Hope-Princeton Trail and completed it in 1861.

Destination: Wild Horse Creek

When gold was discovered in Wild Horse Creek a few years later, Edgar Dewdney was given the job of continuing the trail into the Kootenays. Fighting half a dozen mountain ranges, numerous rivers and countless bogs, Dewdney and his crew that included four former Royal Engineers set out from what is now Osoyoos in May 1865.

The surveyors led the way, crossing over Anarchist Summit to Rock Creek where a gold rush was waning, and continuing east down the Kettle River Valley to the Midway area before temporarily leaving the Kettle. Their route took them northeast up Boundary Creek to what is now Greenwood, then over the mountains to Grand Forks, then via the Kettle River to Christina Lake where the Rossland Range of the Monashee Mountains proved to be a formidable obstacle.

The surveyors split up; Edgar Dewdney headed one group searching for a route via the north end of Christina Lake, Lower Arrow Lake and Kootenay Lake. The second group under former Royal Engineer George Turner headed east just north of the United States Boundary over what is now Santa Rosa summit.

Dewdney determined that the northern route had too many large lakes to be a viable wagon road. His group decided on the route via the Santa Rosa to Fort Shepherd near present-day Rossland. From there they went up the Pend d'Orielle River to Salmo and across the Nelson Range via Kootenay Pass. They headed down Summit Creek to the present Creston Valley.

The swampy south end of Kootenay Lake was a challenge. They continued east across the Purcell Mountains via Yahk and the Moyie River to the Cranbrook area and "Galbraith's Ferry" now Fort Steele. Dewdney had completed the survey in a month and he now hired crews to build the "waggon" road. By September, 1865 pack trains were travelling the trail: they had completed the 590-km-long trail in seven months at a cost of $75,000.

Dewdney was only 28 when he built the trail, but he was well on the way to a successful business and political career. His hard work and ambition took him through provincial and federal politics to the position of Lieutenant-Governor of British Columbia before he retired in 1897.

A Quarter Century of Activity

The wagon road to the Rockies and the Alberta border was completed later in 1865, and it served as a vital route for Canadian commerce for the next 25 years. The railways gradually supplanted the wagon road, first the Canadian Pacific Railway in 1885 and then the Columbia & Western (1896) and theKettle Valley Railway (1915). Numerous smaller, often short-lived, railway lines filled in the gaps between paddle-wheel steamer ports on the large lakes and the mining communities that supplied the much sought-after riches of the region.

Revenge is Sweet

The railways took the traffic off the wagon road and, in many instances, buried the road under a layer of ballast and twin ribbons of steel. But if turnabout is fair play, then the Crowsnest Highway has come out the winner. Portions of the KVR were abandoned in 1961 after a disastrous washout in the Coquihalla Pass. The last train from Okanagan Falls to the

CPR Caboose at Midway, BC © Murphy Shewchuk

CPR mainline at Spences Bridge rolled over the KVR tracks in 1989. The section of the C&W Railway from Castlegar to Midway is now part of the Trans-Canada Trail as is most of the KVR grade from Midway to Hope.

Rails to Trails

Now much of the 650 km railway grade from Hope to Castlegar is part of the Trans Canada Trail. While wagons and mules aren't the primary mode of transportation, it is a further step back. I think Edgar Dewdney would be pleased that his trail is still all-Canadian.

Cascade Gorge on Kettle River west of Christina Lake, BC, Canada. © Murphy Shewchuk

Crowsnest Highway 3: The Southern Trans-Provincial Highway Part 1: Osoyoos to Christina Lake

STATISTICS

For map, see page 40.

Distance: 610 km: Osoyoos to Crowsnest Pass, Alberta via Highway 3.

150 km: Osoyoos to Christina Lake.

Travel Time: Two to three hours.

Condition: Paved Highway.

Season: Maintained year around.

Map: British Columbia Highway Map.

Communities: Osoyoos, Midway, Greenwood, Grand Forks & Christina Lake.

Osoyoos Start

The British Columbia Visitor Centre @ Osoyoos is a good place to start your exploration of the southern Kootenay region. The Centre is at the junction of Highway 97 and Crowsnest Highway 3 with enough parking to get safely off the highway to collect your up-to-date maps and information. It is open daily during the summer months and Monday to Saturday from mid-November to the end of March. A nearby service station may also be a good place to top up your fuel supply.

If you need a break before heading east, sẁiẁs Provincial Park (formerly Haynes Point) offers 41 campsites and an extended beach and nature walk on a spit of land that juts across Osoyoos Lake about three km south of the junction. The Okanagan Indian Band (OIB) and BC Parks jointly manage the park. If the provincial park is full the OIB also manages Nk'Mip RV Park & Campground on the east end of Osoyoos. With 400 sites, yurts, a nearby resort, winery and spa; and the Nk'Mip

Cascade Gorge on Kettle River west of Christina Lake, BC, Canada. © Murphy Shewchuk

Desert Cultural Centre they should have most of your bases covered.

Highway 3 winds through the busy downtown where Osoyoos Lake and a host of tourist attractions beckon. In the summer months the fruit stands near the east end of the strip provide prime fodder for a healthy diet.

Anarchist Mountain

The view to the east from downtown Osoyoos is of an almost barren mountainside dotted with the white domes of private observatories. Laced across this rocky slope is the grey looping ribbon of Highway 3.

Sculpture at Osoyoos Information Centre. © Murphy Shewchuk

The 30 km climb from downtown to the ridge at Anarchist summit will take you up nearly 1,000 metres with much of the climb in the first 20 km. This is no place for doubtful power going up and definitely no place for doubtful brakes coming back down.

The "Anarchist" of Anarchist Mountain was Richard G. Sidley, a wild Irishman who arrived in the district around 1895. He was appointed J.P., postmaster and Customs Officer for the community, but his extreme political views ultimately cost him these appointments. Despite his falling out with the officials, his name and nickname remain

Camping at Schulli Resort on Christina Lake, BC, Canada. © Murphy Shewchuk

on Sidley Mountain and Anarchist Mountain.

Anarchist Summit also marks the boundary between the Okanagan and Kettle River drainages, and the start of what is known as BC's Boundary District.

Rock Creek Canyon Bridge

Roughly seven km east of the summit, Highway 3 crosses the Rock Creek Canyon Bridge. Though possibly not the longest at 286 metres, at 91 metres above Rock Creek, it is probably the highest. If you are interested in a bit of backcountry exploring or winter adventure, Mount Baldy Road, at the west end of the bridge, will take you north to the local ski hill. Continuing the loop west on Camp McKinney Road will take you past the local ski trails and back down to the Okanagan Valley at Oliver.

Conkle Lake Loop

If you are looking for an off-highway campground, Johnstone Creek Road, another four km down the hill, will take you 25 km north to 34-unit Conkle Lake Provincial Park. The road is, according to BC Parks, considered "unsuitable for motorhomes, vehicles towing trailers or low-clearance vehicles." We have driven a VW Van and a truck camper in there a few times only to discover small motorhomes and small holiday trailers—so you take your chances. The beach can be a welcome break on a hot day and there is an interesting trail to a hidden waterfall.

An alternate route out will take you north and east to the Kettle River near Rhone. Both routes are rough gravel roads with narrow sections.

See *Okanagan Trips & Trails* for more information on Mount Baldy and Conkle Lake.

Johnstone Creek Provincial Park

If you aren't interested in spending an hour on a gravel road, Johnstone Creek Provincial Park is nestled in a treed glade only a minute or two off the highway. With only 16 campsites, it may pay to check it out early on a summer day. Note that while reservations don't apply, the gate is locked during the off-season.

Rock Creek

Depending on when you take this trip, you may notice charred hillsides on the last few km to Rock Creek. A fire that was believed started in early August, 2015, by a tossed cigarette destroyed 30 homes and caused millions of dollars in damage before it was brought under control.

Rock Creek was the location of several gold rushes during the late 1850s

Osoyoos from Highway 3 viewpoint on Anarchist Mountain. © Murphy Shewchuk

and early 1860s. It was also on the route of the Kettle Valley Railway, now part of the Trans-Canada Trail. In addition Rock Creek is also the junction for Highway 33 to Kettle River Park and north to Kelowna. See the "West Kettle Route-Highway 33" and "Up the Kettle River without a Paddle" chapters for details.

Following the Kettle River

The highway to Midway generally follows the edge of the hillside overlooking farms and ranches along the Kettle River. Midway was the Mile 0 point on the Kettle Valley Railway. The Midway Museum, located along the highway, contains local history plus artifacts from the railway, including a CPR caboose.

Smelter Row

The Kettle River dips down into Washington State and Highway 3 climbs up Boundary Creek to Greenwood. A close look at the debris on the northwest side of the road will reveal that it is not all gravel. The black slag from Boundary Smelter (1901-1907) hangs down the bank near the KVR tracks eight km from Midway. Across the highway is a pullout and Stop-of-Interest sign marking the smelter and Boundary Falls where there was a dam and

Jewel Lake from Jewel Lake Provincial Park. © Murphy Shewchuk

Carlyle, a guide on the Castlegar to Beaverdell leg of a Trans Canada Trail bike trip, here on the C&W Rail Trail above Christina Lake. © Murphy Shewchuk

generating station to supply electricity to the short-lived smelter.

Boundary Creek Provincial Park, located less than a km south of Greenwood, offers 17 campsites and is open mid-June to mid-September.

Drinking water and flush toilets are available as are trout in the nearby creek. You will need a fishing license for the trout.

The British Columbia Copper Company smelter was located at Anaconda on the southwest outskirts of Greenwood. The 36-metre-high stack is a prominent landmark as you make the final approach to the city. The smelter was blown in on February 18, 1901 and operated steadily until 1912 before a shortage of ore slowed it down. It closed permanently in November 1918. The former site is now the City of Greenwood's Lotzkar Park.

Greenwood

Greenwood, incorporated in 1897, flourished with the smelters and the nearby copper mines and nearly died when the last one closed. While the World War II Japanese Internment is not a bright spot in Canada's history, it was the savior of Greenwood as more than 1,100 Japanese Canadians were housed there.

Heritage hotel on Copper Street in Greenwood, BC, Canada. © Murphy Shewchuk

The colourful history is too long to adequately describe here, but the century-old buildings located throughout the city are well worth exploring. There is a RV parking lot near downtown to make your walking tour easier. When you are done, the Copper Eagle Cappuccino & Bakery can provide some delectable goodies to take your mind off your feet. If you need more serious fare, there is the Pacific Grill next door and Deadwood Junction at the south end of the city. It also sells antiques and local art.

The Greenwood Museum and Visitor Centre is located at the north end of the main drag. Across Copper Avenue (Highway 3) is My Udder Store, an ice cream shop, and O'Hairi Park with a tribute to the Japanese Canadians. There is more camping in the centre and north end of the city.

Phoenix Road

Greenwood Street, near downtown, heads east and appears to disappear into the woods as it climbs up the hill. It becomes Phoenix Road after the first switchback. No place for a big motorhome or RV trailer, Greenwood Street is nevertheless the start of an interesting 18-km backroad that

BC Copper Co. stack at Greenwood, BC, Canada. © Murphy Shewchuk

could take you up to an historic mine site and out to Highway 3. See the "Phoenix Road" chapter for details.

The Climb to Eholt

The Trans-Canada Trail crosses Highway 3 at the north end of Greenwood and the highway begins a steady climb up Eholt Creek to the pass at Wilgress Lake.

The highway leaves Boundary Creek just before the start of the climb.

Grand Forks C&W Railway station, now a neighborhood pub. © Murphy Shewchuk

If you are looking for a pleasant place to camp, away from the summer heat, Jewel Lake, 13 km from the highway and at an elevation of 1,145 metres, is an excellent candidate. There is also a network of backroads that can take you north up Boundary Creek to Burrell Creek and back down to Grand Forks. See the "Granby Loop" chapter for details.

Eholt

Highway 3 climbs to Eholt and Wilgress Lake before starting the descent to Grand Forks. During the copper smelting heyday, Eholt was an important junction for a spur line carrying copper ore from Phoenix to the Granby Smelter at Grand Forks. Now the siding is a pit stop on the Trans-Canada Trail with access to the highway. If you are a determined bushwhacker, there is a narrow backroad that could take you 10 km west to the west end of Jewel Lake. We did it a decade ago and haven't tried it since.

Downhill to Grand Forks

While the climb up to the summit parallels the old KVR tracks in many places, the road down the east side follows the former Vancouver, Victoria & Eastern Railway grade that also carried Phoenix ore to the smelters. The highway dips down to within a couple hundred metres of the US boundary then continues northeast into Grand Forks.

At the risk of being considered selective, I would like to say that Grand Forks has a full selection of services and accommodations. In addition to motels, hotels and RV parks, there is a community campground near downtown and a fine museum on Reservoir Road near the west end of the city. The Boundary Museum and Interpretive Centre was originally located near the downtown but moved to the Fructova School in 2009. The Fructova Heritage Site also contains numerous artifacts related to the Doukhobor involvement in the community.

The Granby Consolidated Mining & Smelting Company operated a smelter north of Grand Forks from 1900 to 1919 producing two huge mountains of slag. Pacific Abrasives has been processing the slag since 1999 for use in Roxul Rockwool insulation products.

Granby Road, at the east end of downtown, heads north up the Granby River. It is paved for 43 km with a possible return via North Fork Road at 16 km. See the "Granby Loop" chapter for details.

Follow the Kettle River to Christina Lake

Highway 3 parallels the north side of the Kettle River eastward to Christina Lake. The former Columbia & Western Railway (now the Trans-Canada Trail) runs between the highway and the river for most of the way. Also on the river side are a variety of agriculture undertakings including a tree nursery and a meandering section of river known as the Boothman Oxbows.

On the north side of the highway, roughly halfway between Grand Forks and Christina, is the relatively new Gilpin Grasslands Provincial Park. The 912 hectare park was established in 2007 to protect the grassland ecosystem and species-at-risk including bighorn sheep. While hiking and cycling is

Phoenix Cemetery on Phoenix Road near Greenwood, BC, Canada.r. © Murphy Shewchuk

permitted, the only motorized access is the Gilpin Forest Service Road.

There aren't any fees or facilities at the park. BC Parks advises a pack it in—pack it out policy and watch for rattlesnakes.

Access to U.S.A.

Highway 395 heads south near the western outskirts of Christina, following the Kettle River south to Franklin D. Roosevelt Lake and the Columbia River. On the way to the border the highway crosses the Kettle River at Kettle Falls and the C&W Railway/Trans-Canada Trail. There is a small parking area just south of the river crossing and a set of stairs heading up to a trail along the cliff where you can get a top-down look at the canyon–with caution.

Katharine on Kettle River C&W Railway Trestle west of Christina Lake, BC, Canada.
© Murphy Shewchuk

The railway right-of-way isn't nearly as challenging although you might easily miss the trail crossing. Look for a small square building on the right and a small parking area on the left of Highway 395, 1.4 km south of the junction with Highway 3. If you park on the left (east), you can ride your bike down the railway grade southeast for a km to one of the longer bridges on the C&W/TCT. On the right (west), the grade climbs up and crosses the Kettle River on the Cascade Gorge Trestle 1.3 km west of Highway 395 before continuing west to Grand Forks and Midway. See the "Columbia & Western Railway Trail" chapter in the Rail Trails section for details about the route.

There is access to Cascade Cove RV Park just north of the junction to Highway 395. They offer tent camping spots as well as RV hookups.

Christina Lake

The community of Christina is located at the foot of the lake a few minutes east of the junction. Christina Lake Prov. Park is located one km off the highway to the west. There is beach access, parking and a change house, but no camping. Santa Rosa Road, to the right (east) a few hundred metres north of the Christina Creek Bridge leads up the C&W/TCT. If you are interested a backroad adventure, you could consider taking the Old Cascade Highway all the way to Rossland. "Highway" is a drastic misnomer as, if it is open at all; it is only likely to be passable in the dry summer months. Check with the staff at the Wildways Adventure Sports store just off the highway near the north end of town. See the "Old Cascade Highway" chapter for details about the road.

Sandner Frontage Road provides access to a small supermarket and other services on the east side of the highway while Bakery Frontage Road provides access to (you guessed it) a bakery, food services, and lakeshore camping at Schulli Resort.

There is also lake access and camping at the Texas Creek campground at Gladstone Provincial Park. The access road is off Highway 3, five km north of the bakery and it's another five km to the campground. There is also boat access camping farther up Christina Lake.

Stump Woman, Zuckerberg Island, Castlegar, BC, Canada. © Murphy Shewchuk

CHAPTER 3

Crowsnest Highway 3: The Southern Trans-Provincial Highway Part 2: Christina Lake to Crowsnest Pass. Alberta

STATISTICS

For map, see page 60.

Distance: 610 km: Osoyoos to Crowsnest Pass, Alberta via Highway 3.

                466 km: Christina Lake to Crowsnest Pass, Alberta.

Travel Time: Eight to ten hours.

Condition: Paved Highway.

Season: Maintained year around.

Map: British Columbia Highway Map.

Communities: Christina Lake, Castlegar, Creston, Cranbrook & Fernie.

Christina Lake Starting Point

I covered a few points of interest about Christina Lake in the previous section. Now it is time to continue east. The highway climbs quickly up to Bonanza Pass, gaining 1,000 metres in 25 km. It climbs another 50 metres before it reaches the Paulson Summit. On the way it crosses Paulson Bridge, which at 258 metres long and 84 metres high, offers serious competition to the 91-metre-high Rock Creek Canyon Bridge. The view below is McRae Creek and the C&W Rail Trail.

Nancy Greene Lake

From what used to be known as the Blueberry-Paulson Pass, the highway has a somewhat easier descent to Nancy Greene Lake, where there is a small BC Parks campground as well as a parking area and beach. A five-km-trail around the sub-alpine lake provides a few photo-ops and good exercise for

NOTE: For Reference Only.
Carry topographic maps.
See text for detailed listing.

humans and dogs. See the BC Parks web page for details.

If you are interested in diversity, Highway 3B leaves the Crowsnest Highway just east of the lake and heads south to Rossland and Trail. You can wind through Trail and continue east on 3B through Montrose and Fruitvale to rejoin Highway 3 west of Salmo.

Castlegar

Meanwhile, Highway 3 follows Blueberry Creek east to the Columbia River at Kinnaird Bridge, half a km south of downtown Castlegar and the mouth of the Kootenay River. The city claims to be the West Kootenay commercial service centre—numerous visits to the area have prompted me to agree.

Castlegar was an important hub for the Columbia & Western Railway during the silver mining heyday and is now the eastern

Tin Cup Rapids, Columbia River, Millennium Park, Castlegar, BC, Canada.
© Murphy Shewchuk

terminal of the C&W Rail Trail. See the "Columbia & Western Railway Trail" chapter for details.

It was also an important Doukhobor community and the Doukhobor Discovery Centre on Heritage Way is well worth a visit. It may take a bit of sleuthing to find, but the Zuckerberg Island Heritage Park near the junction of 9th Street and 7th Avenue is also worth exploring.

After visiting Zuckerberg Island you could head a bit farther north to Millennium Park at 5th Street and 2nd Avenue. The outdoor pools and facilities there could be a welcome break on a warm day.

Options abound at Castlegar. You can take Highway 3A north to the junction of 3A/6 at South Slocan and continue north on Hwy 6 to New Denver or east to Nelson and Kootenay Lake. As this is supposed to be a description of attractions along the Crowsnest Route, we will continue east from the Kinnaird Bridge and climb up the side of Aaron Hill on our way to the junction with 3B and Salmo.

Stone Mural at Salmo, BC, Canada. © Murphy Shewchuk

Salmo

Salmo was also an important mining town in the first half of the 20th Century. The Hudson's Bay Mine (a.k.a. HB Mine) was first staked in 1910. The lead-zinc-silver ore was shipped to the smelter at Trail. The tailings dump near the highway was part the Cominco operation that was worked sporadically between 1912 and 1978, producing over 6.6 million tonnes of ore.

Salmo is also the southern terminal of the 48-km-long Nelson Salmo Great Northern Rail Trail (a.k.a. Burlington Northern Rail Trail) that continues north through Ymir. Additional up-to-date information is available in the Nelson Mountain Bike Guide and from Trails BC at http://www. trailsbc.ca/ .

It is worth detouring half a km north on Highway 6 to check out the Village of Salmo stone murals. While many other BC communities have painted murals, the Kootenay Stone Masonry Training Institute has done one better in five murals that are certainly unlikely to fade in our lifetime.

Kootenay Pass

From Salmo, the highway winds south and then east before climbing up Stagleap Creek to Kootenay Pass (a.k.a. Salmo-Creston Summit or Kootenay

Cedar Waxwing at Creston Valley Wildlife Management Area , Creston, BC, Canada.
© Murphy Shewchuk

Skyway) at 1,775 metres. Today's highway follows much the same route as Edgar Dewdney's crew carved across the Selkirk Mountains over a century ago. According a highway profile, it is a 6.6% grade up the west side and 7.4% to 5.1% down the east side to the Kootenay River at Creston. A bit of a strain if you are piloting an RV, but darned hard work if you are pedaling a bicycle.

Creston Marsh

No trip along Highway 3 is really complete without a stop at the Creston Valley Wildlife Management Area (a.k.a. Creston Marsh). Fortunately it is the first major road when you emerge from the Summit Creek canyon on your way down from Kootenay Pass. The headquarters are located along West Creston Road, less than a km south of Highway 3. The history of the 7,000 hectare Ramsar recognized wetland goes back to the 1880s. See the "Ancient Valley of Ducks" chapter for details.

Creston

The Town of Creston is primarily located on the east side of the Kootenay River. If you are following the highway from west to east as described here, you may notice, as I have, the downtown grain elevators. Their colourful

Gourds at a Creston Fruit Stand, Creston, BC, Canada. © Murphy Shewchuk

history goes back to 1935 and 1936. They were built to accommodate the grain expected once the marsh was reclaimed. Unfortunately for the elevator operators and farmers, but fortunately for the wildlife, much of the marsh remains un-reclaimed. A 50-page booklet *"A History of Creston's Downtown Grain Elevators"* is available from the Creston Museum. It sheds more light on the story of these magnificent wooden structures–a rapidly disappearing part of Canadian heritage.

Creston has a variety of services including a few of the usual fast food places and slow food places downtown and a fruit stand or two on the eastern outskirts. If you are remotely interested in beer, Creston is the home of Columbia Brewery and Kokanee beer.

The Road to Yahk

Highway 3 continues east following the Goat River and Kitchener Creek upstream to a low pass before descending to the Moyie River and the junction with Highway 95. To the south is the Kingsgate border crossing and to the north is Yahk where there are a few services and a BC Parks campground on the banks of the Moyie River.

I made the rash assumption that Yahk referred to the Asian animal that looks like a cross between a longhorn bull and a bison. Akrigg's *1001 BC Place Names* enlightened me. According to G.P.V & Helen B. Akrigg, the name is derived from the word "yak" meaning "bow", a name which the Kootenay Indians (a.k.a. Ktunaxa or Kutenai) applied to the Kootenay

River which first flows south, then west, then north. They also suggest that by extension the word could be applied to the country contained within the "bow" of the Kootenay. Some derive the name from "a'k," meaning "arrow."

Moyie Lake

Highway 3/95 now continues north, following the Moyie River to 13-km-long Moyie Lake. Eagle's Nest RV Resort is at the south end of the lake. The settlement of Moyie is located about halfway up the lake. As you approach the community from the south, you may notice the remnants of the St. Eugene Mine on the hillside. According to history, a Ktunaxa Indian, Pierre, discovered a rich galena outcrop here in 1893. By 1907 it was described as "... the most important silver-lead mine in Canada." By 1920, Moyie's glory days were over and it was practically a ghost town. Take time to stop and meander through the town. St. Peter's Catholic Church could prove an excellent photo subject in the late afternoon light.

Moyie Lake Provincial Park, at the north end of the lake, has a day-use area and a 111 site campground set in the trees. The north end of the lake can be windy and on our last visit we watched a kite surfer frequently getting airborne as he traversed the end of the lake.

Cranbrook

Highway 3/95 continues north another 30 km to Cranbrook, the largest city in the East Kootenay. You have a couple of options to take a break at a

Moyie Lake, west of Cranbrook, BC, Canada. © Murphy Shewchuk

Peter Boulton, an avid Cranbrook cyclist, on the Chief
Isadore Trail east of Cranbrook. © Murphy Shewchuk

major intersection at the south end of the city. If you are interested in camping or a lakeshore picnic on the beach, Jim Smith Lake Provincial Park is located about 4.5 km north on Jim Smith Lake Road. It has a boat launch, 35-unit campground and a beach. The lake is located 150 metres above the valley floor so it could be a bit cooler in summer. South of the highway is the Elizabeth Lake Sanctuary and picnic area. In addition to the tables, it has a trail through the marsh with floating piers ideal for relaxing or wildlife photography.

A Cranbrook must-see is the award-winning Canadian Museum of Rail Travel. It is located on the northwest side of the highway near the downtown. With vintage restored deluxe passenger cars dating back to 1886, here is your chance to view how the upper crust travelled over a century ago.

If you are still looking for a place to camp, the Mount Baker RV Park is located within walking distance of most of the downtown attractions.

Important Junction

Read the road signs carefully at the north end of the city. Highway 95A will take you north to Marysville and Kimberley and on to Highway 93/95 south of Wasa. Highway 3/95 continues northeast to another junction where you could head north to Fort Steele and, if you are persistent, Radium and Banff. What is now Highway 3/93 on my map continues southeast crossing the Kootenay River / Koocanusa Lake near Wardner. It then continues southeast to the junction with Highway 93 which goes south to the BC-Montana border crossing at Roosville.

Elk River to Fernie

Highway 3 now follows the Elk River northeast to Fernie. If you are interested in skiing, Fernie Ski Hill Road, five km south of the city, leads west to Fernie Alpine Resort. With 10 lifts and 142 runs, it should challenge every member of the family.

With a population of 5,000, Fernie is the largest city on the western slopes of the BC Rockies. If you are still looking for a place to camp, Mount Fernie Provincial Park is located about a km west of the highway near the south entrance to city. There are services along the highway and skiing in the mountains, but for the serious urban photographer the century-old brick buildings are a downtown attraction.

Coal Towns

Coal was the raison d´être for Fernie dating back to the 1890s when prospector William Fernie founded the Crows Nest Pass Coal Company. Now Teck Coal Limited operates major open-pit coal mines farther to the northeast near Sparwood and Elkford. The Fording River operation, 29 km northeast of Elkford, ships over eight million tonnes of steelmaking coal annually to the bulk terminals in the Vancouver area.

If you are interested in some backcountry exploring, Elk Lakes Provincial Park lies 103 km north of Sparwood on Highway 43 and Elk River Forest Service Road. See the "Elk River Forest Service Road" chapter for details.

It is another 20 km south east to the BC-Alberta border at Crowsnest Pass. On the way you might notice the remnants of Natal, one of the original coal mining communities of the Elk Valley.

If you need a break from driving, there is an excellent little campsite at the east end of Island Lake, about two km east of the border.

KVR Bridge over Kettle River – Kettle River Provincial Recreation Area. © Murphy Shewchuk

CHAPTER 4

West Kettle Route—Highway 33: Kelowna to Rock Creek

STATISTICS

For map, see page 70.

Distance: 129 km, Hwy 33, Rutland to Rock Creek.

Travel Time: Two to three hours.

Elev. Gain: 880 metres.

Condition: Paved throughout, some steep grades.

Season: Open year around.

Topo Maps: Kelowna 82 E/NW (1:100,000).
Penticton 82 E/SE (1:100,000).
Grand Forks 82 E/SE (1:100,000).

Backroads Mapbook: Thompson Okanagan BC.

Communities: Kelowna, Beaverdell & Rock Creek.

Placer gold, an abandoned railway, fishing lakes, and a ski resort that rivals Europe's best may appear to be an unusual combination, but Highway 33 provides access to all of them and much more. Add a winding, paved road that is a motorcyclist's dream and you've got plenty of reasons to get out of town when the true "back" roads are too muddy or icy to appeal to the passenger side.

This 129-km-long highway links the central Okanagan with the Boundary Region. On the way, it passes through the West Kettle River valley—a dry, timbered region rich in both scenery and history. This is a quiet part of the province; still largely unspoiled by modern hustle and bustle.

The north end of Highway 33 begins at its junction with Highway 97 in Rutland, a Kelowna community. (Just a word of warning, the next gasoline service station is at Beaverdell, 79 km down the road.) It ends at Rock Creek, at the junction with Crowsnest Highway 3 near the Canada-U.S.A. boundary, 52 km east of Osoyoos.

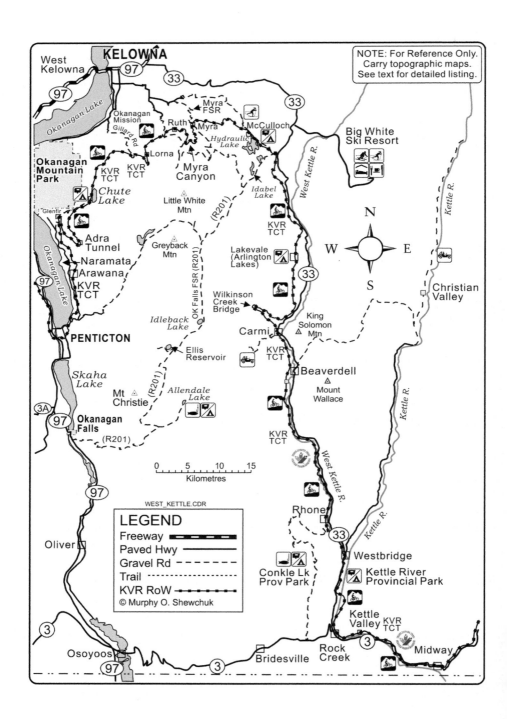

Follows Mission Creek

Highway 33 passes through the heart of Rutland before beginning a steady southeast climb out of the Okanagan Valley. Rangeland, scrub brush and pine forests gradually replace the orchards that have helped make the Okanagan Valley famous.

After allowing one last glimpse of the sprawling city below, the road opens to a view of the timber-lined canyon of Mission Creek. Originally named Riviere L'Anse du Sable by the fur traders, Mission Creek was a busy gold placer creek for a short time in the mid-1870s. According to historian N.L. "Bill" Barlee, Dan Gallagher, the last of the old prospectors, eked out a living on the creek until the 1940s.

Heading for the High Country

Philpott Road, at Km 20.4, presents an opportunity to detour north into the uplands east of the Okanagan Valley's Lake Country. There are at least a dozen lakes in the high country, and if you are easily distracted, you could continue north all the way to Lavington.

Skier at Big White. © Murphy Shewchuk

KVR Bridge over Kettle River - Kettle River Provincial Recreation Area. © Murphy Shewchuk

Three Forks Road, at Km 23, may be of more interest to backcountry snowmobilers in winter and backcountry hikers in summer. Motorized vehicles are not permitted on the hiking trails. According to BC Parks, 12,000 hectare Graystokes Provincial Park was established in 2001 to protect an extensive complex of swamps, meandering streams and meadows as well as wildlife habitat. It is about 18 km to the park info sign and another 10 km to Graystoke Lake. Check out the BC Parks website for details.

Approximately 24 km east of Kelowna, the highway crosses Mission Creek and enters the Joe Rich Valley. During the period between the two World Wars, the remarkably rich black soil of the valley supported a lettuce market gardening industry. E.O. MacGinnis started the lettuce farming and made a fortune before everybody got into it, says one old-timer. The Joe Rich Community Centre marks the heart of the former market gardening enclave.

Big White Ski Resort

Less than 10 minutes beyond the Joe Rich Valley community center, a junction marks the paved road that leads 24 km east and up to Big White

Canoeist on Arlington Lake, BC Arlington Recreation Site. © Murphy Shewchuk

Ski Resort. From a start in the early 1960s, Big White has become the closest a westerner can get to a European ski experience. It is a ski village in the mountains, equipped with private chalets, condominium style apartments, and a hotel complex with ski-to-your-door accommodations. A choice of restaurants, discos, lounges and a grocery store help round out the facilities. Oh yes! Chair lifts and T-bar lifts, numerous downhill runs plus cross country ski trails on top of 12 metres of average snowfall help complete the requirements for a memorable ski holiday.

West Kettle Valley

Just beyond the Big White junction is the Rock Creek—Kelowna Summit. At an elevation of 1265 meters (4,159 feet) it marks the divide between the Okanagan and West Kettle drainage basins. The summit also marks a change in the scenery from the narrow valley of Mission and Joe Rich creeks to a broader, drier valley, lightly timbered with aspen and pine.

Five km past the summit (Km 37.6), there is another major junction, this time to the right. The well-maintained Okanagan Falls Forest Service Road continues south past Idabel Lake to Okanagan Falls.

A secondary road parallels the former Kettle Valley Railroad bed as far as McCulloch Station before the railbed strikes across the mountainside to Penticton and the road winds down the mountainside to Kelowna. If you are searching for a spot to camp or fish, the Hydraulic Lake / McCulloch Reservoir complex has both. There is a large BC Recreation Site on the lake, approximately 5.5 km northwest of the junction with Highway 33.

If self-propelled travel is more your style, the Kelowna Nordic Ski Trails base is located on the north side of McCulloch Road and just past the junction to the BC Rec Site. With over 70 km of trails, there is plenty of variety for all ages. In summer, the Mildred Wardlaw Nature Trails (part of the same system) attracts birdwatchers and nature enthusiasts.

Kettle Valley Railway

Under the direction of Chief Engineer Andrew McCulloch, construction of the Kettle Valley Railway (KVR), a Canadian Pacific Railway subsidiary, was begun in the summer of 1910. By the end of 1913, tracks had been laid from Midway in the Boundary region to Mile 83, a short distance west of McCulloch Station. This long-awaited Coast-to-Kootenay railway was finally completed through the Coquihalla Canyon (north of Hope) on July 31, 1916.

Steam buffs will undoubtedly remember the Kettle Valley Railway as one of the last bastions of "real" railroading. With speeds that varied from 25 km per hour (15 mph) on the tortuous mountain grades to 90 km per hour (55 mph) on the flat valley floors, steam led the way. The Mikados, the Consolidations and a few old Ten-Wheelers pulled passengers and freight over some of the most difficult terrain in North America. In its heyday, the steam-driven cylinders powered the eastbound Kettle Valley Express from Vancouver through Hope, Penticton, Rock Creek, Midway and on to Nelson in 23 hours. In another five hours, the "Express" had arrived at Medicine Hat, Alberta.

A large washout permanently closed the Coquihalla section of the KVR in 1959 and the last passenger run from Penticton to Midway took place in 1964. Since then, despite protests and suggestions that the route could be operated as a tourist attraction, the tracks have been removed on the Penticton-Midway section, as well as the Coquihalla and most of the route between Okanagan Falls and Spences Bridge.

Arlington Lakes

Lakevale, the second KVR station southeast of McCulloch summit, was originally named Arlington Lakes in 1915 after the three lakes located three km west of Highway 33. According to one source, it was soon renamed

Cyclists at Arlington Lake KVR Water Tank foundation, BC, Arlington Recreation Site.
© Murphy Shewchuk

to Lakevale to avoid confusion with a station by the same name on the Esquimalt & Nanaimo (E&N) rail line on Vancouver Island.

If you are interested in fishing, camping, or cycling the KVR from a lakeshore base camp, watch for the "Arlington Lakes" sign on a gravel road on the west side of Highway 33, approximately 57 km south of the junction with Highway 97 in Kelowna. There is a supervised BC Recreation Site on the southernmost of the three lakes with a total of 23 vehicle access camping sites. Camping fees apply from mid-May to the end of October.

The old KVR grade goes through the rec site. The remains of the water tank foundation are clearly visible and the old railway pump house was still there in June, 2011.

Carmi

Back on Highway 33, about 73 km south of Kelowna, the paved road passes the remnants of the former community of Carmi. There is little left to indicate that, in 1914, Carmi had two hotels, two stores, a shoe shop, a resident policeman and jail, and a railroad hospital. The railway and a gold mine were the source of income in Carmi. When the mine closed in 1936, the town was dealt a severe blow. The closure of the railway finished it off.

Columbia Ground Squirrel at Kettle River Provincial Recreation Area. © Murphy Shewchuk

More Upland Lakes

Six km south of Carmi, on the outskirts of Beaverdell, the East Beaver Creek Road begins a winding route eastward around Curry Mountain to Christian Valley. If you're interested in a little backcountry exploring, there is a network of logging roads and a dozen BC recreation sites in the mountains between Beaverdell and Christian Valley. The Boundary Forest District Recreation Map has the details–or check out www.sitesandtrailsbc.ca/.

Fingers of Silver

There have been silver mines on Wallace Mountain, to the east of Beaverdell, since the 1890s. The first claim was staked on the mountain in 1889, but was apparently allowed to lapse. In 1896, a flurry of staking took place and the West Kettle River soon saw three new communities, including Carmi, Beaverton and Rendell. Later Beaverton and Rendell, only a short distance apart, were united under the name of Beaverdell.

Several mines operated profitably during the first half of the twentieth century. The Bell Mine, for instance, produced 350,000 ounces of silver between 1913 and 1936. The Highland Bell Mine, the site of more recent activities, was formed in 1936 through the amalgamation of the Bell and the Highland Lass claims. The silver was in veins "like the fingers on my hand," remembered miner Charlie Pasco of the day in 1945, when he first came to work for the old Highland Bell.

Beaverdell Hotel

The Beaverdell Hotel, built in 1901, was one of the oldest operating hotels in British Columbia, and a museum piece until fire destroyed it in the early morning hours of Monday, March 28, 2011. It was certainly one of the more colourful places to visit in the community, particularly on a Friday or Saturday night. It was also undoubtedly the most photographed attraction along the West Kettle route.

More Distractions

Approximately 30 km south of Beaverdell, Blythe-Rhone road crosses the West Kettle River and winds north to the old to the old KVR station of Rhone. Little over a km north of the junction, a serious backroad leads southwest to Conkle Lake Provincial Park. If you still haven't found your ideal camping and fishing lake, you could take the gravel road 21 km southwest to Conkle Lake. Motorhomes and vehicles pulling large trailers aren't recommended on this road.

The West Kettle River and the Kettle River join at Westbridge (Km 115.5). A secondary road follows the Kettle River northward, past the settlement of Christian Valley, eventually joining Highway 6 near Monashee Pass, east of Lumby.

Kettle River Recreation Area

The Kettle River Recreation Area campground is located seven km south of where Westbridge is located. Set in the pines at a bend on the west bank of the Kettle River, this picturesque spot contains nearly 90 campsites, plus picnic tables and an opportunity to swim, fish or cycle. The area is also ideal for the artist or photographer. In the summer months, the nearby irrigated hay fields are lush green, while outside the range of the sprinklers, the foliage is typical of the interior semi-desert plateau country.

Rock Creek

Rock Creek is the southern terminus of Highway 33 and the end of the 129-km drive from Kelowna—plus side trips, of course. Rock Creek was also the

Camping at Kettle River Provincial Recreation Area. © Murphy Shewchuk

best-known placer gold creek in the Boundary region of British Columbia. Discovered in 1859 by Adam Beam, the creek was worked extensively from 1860 to 1864. At the peak of activity at least 500 miners scoured its gravels. Historians estimate that well over 250,000 ounces of gold—then worth $16 per ounce—was recovered from the creek before the paydirt played out and the miners moved north to the Cariboo. The creek saw limited action again during the recessions of the 1890s and 1930s. With the present price of gold, there may again be prospectors searching for the elusive Mother Lode.

Today, Rock Creek is the center of a busy agricultural community. Patient ewes and prancing lambs liven up the fields in the spring, while the yellow arrow-leaved balsamroot brightens the open slopes.

Go East

Midway, 19 km east of Rock Creek on Crowsnest Highway 3, is well worth the visit regardless of your ultimate direction. The Kettle River Museum, located at Mile 0 of the KVR, is an excellent source of information on the history of the Kettle Valley and the Kettle Valley Railway.

The West Kettle Route—Highway 33—seems left out of the hustle and

Carlyle on C&W Rail Trail at Paulson Bridge east of Christina Lake, BC, Canada. © Murphy Shewchuk

bustle of today. But, if you are interested in a skiing holiday, or a camping, fishing or back-country exploring vacation, this may be an advantage—not a disadvantage.

<hr/>

Additional information

BC Parks
Web: http://www.env.gov.bc.ca/bcparks/
BC Recreation Sites and Trails
Web: http://www.sitesandtrailsbc.ca/
Books:
"Kettle Valley Railway Mileboards: a historical field guide to the KVR" by Joe Smuin.
"McCulloch's Wonder: the story of the Kettle Valley Railway" by Barrie Sanford.

GPS References for major points of interest

Ref: WGS 84 - Lat/Lon hddd.ddddd

Allow +/- 100 metres due to data conversions

WPT	Km	Description	Latitude	Longitude	Elev.
001	0.0	Hwy 97 & 33 in Kelowna	N49.88909	W119.42078	372 m
002	20.4	Jct to Philpott Rd	N49.86454	W119.18907	840 m
003	23.0	Jct to Three Forks Road	N49.86755	W119.15351	796 m
004	24.0	Joe Rich Hall	N49.86435	W119.14041	825 m
005	33.0 J	ct to Big White Ski Area	N49.80258	W119.09082	1175 m
006	34.7	Summit	N49.78975	W119.09398	1242 m
007	37.6	Jct to Thunder Mtn Raceways	N49.76816	W119.11336	1219 m
008	39.0	Jct to McCulloch Road	N49.75765	W119.12652	1178 m
009	0.8	201 Rd OK Falls FSR	N49.76107	W119.13318	1200 m
010	4.3	Jct to Kettle Valley Rec Site	N49.77715	W119.16830	1239 m
011	4.6	McCulloch Nordic Ski Trails	N49.77931	W119.17050	1253 m
012	4.5	Trans Canada Trail - KVR	N49.77690	W119.17060	1250 m
013	4.6	Kettle Valley Recreation Site	N49.77650	W119.17171	1255 m
014	56.8	Jct to Arlington Lakes	N49.61844	W119.06272	967 m
015	4.0	Arlington Lakes Rec Site	N49.60411	W119.08681	1057 m
016	66.6	Hall Creek Rest Area	N49.53570	W119.07751	868 m
017	71.3	Wilkinson Creek	N49.50590	W119.12007	844 m
018	72.6	Carmi & West Kettle River	N49.49532	W119.12277	831 m
019	80.5	Beaverdell Hotel	N49.43579	W119.08782	791 m
020	103.4	Blythe-Rhone Road North End	N49.26520	W119.01795	692 m
021	109.2	Rest Area	N49.21696	W119.01404	656 m
022	110.6	Blythe-Rhone Road South End	N49.20666	W119.00524	646 m
023	1.3	Conkle-Ripperto Cr FS Road	N49.21128	W119.01721	643 m
024	2.9	Rhone Station	N49.22576	W119.01847	653 m
025	115.3	Westbridge	N49.17039	W118.97547	625 m
026	122.4	Jct to Kettle River Park	N49.11193	W118.99444	640 m
027	129.0	Rock Creek Jct Hwy 33 & 3	N49.05762	W119.00018	606 m

Winnifred Falls, Kettle River. © Murphy Shewchuk

CHAPTER 5

Up the Kettle River without a Paddle: Rock Creek to the Monashee Summit

STATISTICS

For map, see page 84.

Distance:	Approximately 126 km Highway 3 at Rock Creek to Highway 6 at Monashee Summit. Additional 26 km to Holmes Lake.
Elev. Gain:	Approximately 770 metres.
Travel Time:	Four to five hours.
Condition:	Mostly gravel, some rough sections.
Season:	Best in dry weather-closed in winter north of Christian Valley to Highway 6. Keefer Lake Road maintained in winter.
Topo Maps: (1:50,000)	Osoyoos, BC 82 E/3. Greenwood, BC 82 E/2. Almond Mountain, BC 82 E/7. Christian Valley, BC 82 E/10. Damfino Creek, BC 82 E/15. Creighton Creek, BC 82 L/2. Eureka Mountain, BC 82 L/1.
Backroads Mapbook:	Thompson Okanagan BC. Kootenay Rockies BC.
Communities:	Rock Creek and Lumby.

The Kettle River is truly an international waterway. It starts high in the Monashee Mountains surrounding Keefer Lake, 70 km east of Vernon, and winds its way southwest to Rock Creek, 50 km east of Osoyoos, before swinging east and dipping down into the USA at Midway. It loops through Washington State before returning north at Grand Forks. It then winds east through BC's Boundary District to Christina Lake before making the final trip south to the Columbia River.

The Kettle River was an integral part of the life of the Interior First

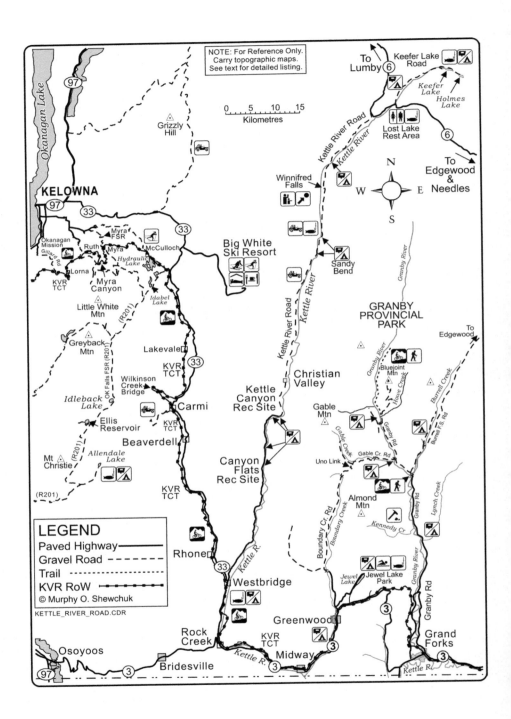

NOTE: For Reference Only.
Carry topographic maps.
See text for detailed listing.

Okanagan Lake

97

To Lumby

Keefer Lake Road

6

Keefer Lake

Holmes Lake

Kettle River Road

Lost Lake Rest Area

6

To Edgewood & Needles

Grizzly Hill

0   5   10   15
Kilometres

KELOWNA

97

33

Winnifred Falls

Myra FSR

Okanagan Mission

Ruth   Myra   McCulloch

Gillard Rd

Lorna

Hydraulic Lake

KVR TCT

Myra Canyon

33

Big White Ski Resort

Kettle River

Sandy Bend

N
W   E
S

GRANBY PROVINCIAL PARK

Granby River

Little White Mtn

Idabel Lake

Greyback Mtn

Idleback Lake

Lakevale

KVR TCT

33

Kettle River Road

Kettle River

Christian Valley

Bluejoint Mtn

Howe Creek

To Edgewood

Burrell Creek

Wilkinson Creek Bridge

OK Falls FSR (R201)

(R201)

Carmi

Ellis Reservoir

KVR TCT

Kettle Canyon Rec Site

Gable Mtn

Gable Creek

Granby Rd

Burrell S. Rd

Beaverdell

Mt Christie

Allendale Lake

(R201)

KVR TCT

Canyon Flats Rec Site

Uno Link

Gable Cr. Rd

Almond Mtn

Kennedy Cr.

Granby Rd

Lynch Creek

LEGEND
Paved Highway ────
Gravel Road − − −
Trail ·················
KVR RoW •─•─•─•
© Murphy O. Shewchuk

KETTLE_RIVER_ROAD.CDR

Rhone

33

Kettle R.

Boundary Cr. Rd

Boundary Creek

Jewel Lake

Jewel Lake Park

Granby River

Westbridge

Greenwood

Granby Rd

Rock Creek

KVR TCT

Kettle R.

Midway

3

3

Grand Forks

Osoyoos

97

Bridesville

3

Kettle R.

3

Nations long before European fur traders ventured westward two centuries ago. It is a life-giving river, providing water for fish; navigation; hydro-electric power; irrigation; mining; and recreation.

Sections of the historic Dewdney Trail; the equally historic Columbia & Western Railway and Kettle Valley Railway; and the present Crowsnest Highway 3 follow the Kettle River Valley as it winds through cities and towns on both sides of the boundary.

For the backroads enthusiast, there is a little known route that follows the Kettle River northeast from Rock Creek to the summit of the Monashee Mountains. This 150-km-long route is an explorer's paradise with numerous recreation sites, dozens of fishing holes and more opportunities to avoid work and civilization than any poor slacker can handle.

Colourful History

According to the Akriggs in *1001 British Columbia Place Names*, the Kettle River was known as "Ne-hoi-al-pit-qua" to the Natives and Colville River to the first white fur traders. The "Kettle" reference appears to date back to 1825 and may to have been prompted by the round holes, shaped like cauldrons, which current-borne rocks had carved in the river bottom at Kettle Falls, near Christina Lake.

Rock Creek Gold

Rock Creek became the best known placer gold creek in the Boundary region of British Columbia during the 1860 gold rush. Discovered in 1859 by Adam Beam, the creek was worked extensively from 1860 to 1864. See pages 77 and 78 for more detail

Rock Creek Starting Point

With the junction of Highway 3 and 33 at the Km 0 reference, follow two-lane highway 33 north along the valley floor, but don't forget to top up the grub box and fuel tank. (The service station just south of the junction also serves a well-stacked ice cream cone.) The first potential diversion is Kettle River Recreation Area at Km 6.5 km. The park has group camping, a picnic area and 87 vehicle campsites. The river is noted for its kayaking, canoeing and tubing, while there are some good swimming holes near the Kettle River railway bridge. The BC Parks website and brochures provide additional information on park facilities and reservations.

Rock Creek Fire

A forest fire that was believed to have been started by a tossed cigarette on August 13, 2015 forced the temporary evacuation of Rock Creek, Westbridge and Kettle River Recreation Area. The fire spread to over 40 square km and destroyed over 40 homes and buildings and a number of recreation vehicles at the recreation area. By mid-summer 2016 many of the homes had been rebuilt and the campground was reopened with little obvious damage.

Westbridge

Westbridge, at Km 13.5, was originally a railway community. The first school was built near here in 1921 and the schools were moved to various locations up the West Kettle River and Christian Valley Road, depending on the number of students living nearby.

This was the days before buses. A letter from Miss I. Savard, a teacher in the school year 1925/26, describes conditions in the Westbridge little one-room school and indeed for many other one-room schools:

"In 1925/26, there were ten pupils from grade one to grade eight. Seven of them lived about two miles up the Christian Valley road and every school day, sun, rain or snow, they trudged to school—no mean feat. The other three were the children of the railway section man, very bright children.

"The pupils and I learned a lot for we were all hard workers. But, oh how much they missed; no music, no library, no sports and no companionship of others in their own age group.

"Westbridge consisted of a rather attractive hotel and post office combined, the tiny schoolhouse and the home of the section foreman, that was all...."

In more recent history, the Westbridge General Store and Post Office was located in the "V" at the junction of Highway 33 and Christian Valley Road. The store, empty at the time, burned to the ground in 2005. A new Westbridge store opened on the south side of the bridge in 2008.

Christian Valley Road a.k.a. Kettle River Forest Service Road

The junction of Highway 33 and Christian Valley Road also marks [0 Km] of the Kettle River Forest Service Road. (Note that I've used square brackets to indicate the roadside km markers.) This is decision making time. Double-check your fuel and supplies for its 113 km north to Highway 6 and another 30 km west or 50 km east to the nearest fuel stop.

The wide open fields near Rock Creek give way to forests interspersed with hayfields and farms, but the Kettle River is never very far from view

KVR Bridge over Kettle River - Kettle River Provincial Recreation Area. © Murphy Shewchuk

to the east. The first river access is near Km 15 and the next access is at Fiva Creek Road (Km 21).

HÜMÜH Buddhist Monastery

A bridge across the Kettle River at Km 40.5 [27 Km] also provides access to the HÜMÜH Buddhist Monastery located on the east side of the Kettle River approximately three km to the south. The Hümüh Skycliffe property is open to visitors on Sundays with a service at 9:45 a.m. followed by a self-guided tour of the monastery grounds. For reservations and more information, call 1 800 336-6015 or visit their website at www.humuh.org.

Canyon Flats Recreation Site

The first two of several BC recreation sites lie along the Kettle River just north of the Kettle River Forest Road [30 Km] marker. Canyon Flats, at 43.7 km north of Rock Creek, is only a few hundred metres east of the road. It is a potential put-in for kayaking down the river. The junction to the Canyon Creek Rec Site is at Km 44.5 and it, too, is only a couple hundred metres east of the main road.

The pavement ends at the junction with the Fourth of July Forest Service Road, a few hundred metres farther north [32 Km]. The main road climbs

Arrowleaf Balsamroot wildflowers in an old burn. © Murphy Shewchuk

to the west and away from the river for the next eight km, dropping down to river level near Km 52 and the junction to Kettle Bench Recreation Site. This is a relatively open site along the river with pools and rapids to attract fishers and tubers or kayakers. If you are interested in exploring a little farther off the main road, there are also rec sites at Thone Lake, Sago Creek and Buck Lake. You should do some advance research on the BC Rec Sites website (http://www.sitesandtrailsbc.ca/) or carry a copy of the Thompson-Okanagan Backroads Mapbook. If you aren't keen on roaming the hills, there is another small rec site alongside the main road at State Creek (Km 59.5).

Christian Valley

While there are farm buildings and cultivated fields near the 50 Km roadside marker (approximately 63 km north of Rock Creek), there isn't much else to mark the community of Christian Valley, named after Joseph Christian, a trapper who was the first settler here.

Schooling was also difficult here for the early settlers. An account by Mrs. Alice Christian appeared in the Second Boundary Historical Report:

"By this time (1915) it became very important that we have a school. I taught our children and then we hired Mrs. Dacre privately.

Mrs. Dacre had come into the valley, hoping to get a permit to teach. However, she was told that there were too many teachers out of employment to grant her request. Soon our request for a school was granted. We gave a piece of land and built a log schoolhouse. The Department gave desks, etc., and of course, a teacher. She was Miss Edith Lettice, a middle-aged gentle-woman from Victoria. She stayed one year."

End of "Public" Road

Christian Valley Road ends near Km 72 (60 Km on the roadside markers), but the route north continues as Kettle River Forest Service Road. Although it may look as well travelled, don't take the Rendell Creek FS Road to the right, particularly if Highway 6 is your ultimate destination. The area highway contractor maintains the road to this point and it should be passable winter and summer. However it may be closed to the north in winter, depending on the logging activity.

Damfino Creek Recreation Site

There are campsites on both sides of Damfino Creek and both sides of Kettle River FS Road at Km 70 [68 Km]. Although tables are limited, there is room to spread out. It is about 200 metres down to the Kettle River, but the trek could be worth the effort for a bit of stream fishing.

The main road continues northeast for the next 10 km, generally high above the river, before it drops down to river level at Km 91 [79 Km] near the Sandy Bend Rec Site. This is a small rec site with an easy trail down to the river where the back eddies and a pool can be particularly inviting in hot weather. If you are interested in huckleberries, saskatoons or bunch berries (ground dogwood) mid-August could be good time to check out the slopes on the west side of the road.

Countdown to Highway 6

A bridge across the Kettle River at near Km 92.5 [80 Km] marks the start of the roadside marker countdown to the Monashee Summit. There is also a small rec site near the bridge.

The road has been rough in places for the past 20 km and can be the same for the next 15 to 20 km—don't count on travelling much more than 30 kph in this section.

There are more camping possibilities at Mohr Creek (Km 96.5) and at Winnifred Falls (Km 106). The waterfall is well worth the stop. The trail is fairly steep in places and there aren't any guard rails so caution is essential. Winnifred Creek flows to the southwest at this point so mid-afternoon may provide the best light to photograph the waterfalls.

Bruer Creek Rec Site

It is interesting to note that the BC Rec Sites website lists the Bruer Creek site at Km 111.5 [67 Km] as only having one campsite while there appears to be room for half a dozen vehicles even if the occupants snore. If you desperately want privacy, there is an opening or two in the trees across the road and to the north another few hundred metres.

Worth noting is that all the sites along this route are user-maintained.

Be prepared to pack out ALL your garbage and be sure you have plenty of essential supplies such as toilet paper.

Highway 6

The Kettle River FS Road crosses the river at the Bruer Creek rec site (Km 111.5) and swings generally northeast on the final 15 km to Highway 6. The road is wider here and is likely to be better maintained because of more recent logging in the area.

The junction with Highway 6 (Km 126.5) or [58 Km] marks another decision point. You can head west to Cherryville, Lumby or Vernon or east to Edgewood, Needles and Nakusp.

Follow the Kettle to the Source

If you are still looking for more Kettle River backcountry to explore, follow Highway 6 east for 6.5 km to the Lost Lake Rest Area and the junction of Keefer Lake FS Road. Keefer Lake Road crosses the Kettle River near the Monashee-Kettle Rec Site, 1.6 km to the north. It then swings eastward, crossing the Kettle again before reaching a junction approximately 14 km from Highway 6.

The road straight ahead continues about 700 metres east to Keefer Lake Wilderness Resort.

Keefer Lake Wilderness Resort

Wilderness is the key word here. Although the resort offers boats, campsites, hot showers, cabins, and wall tent accommodations, the store has a limited stock and, most important of all, there is no cell phone or TV reception. To further enhance the feeling of isolation, the resort doesn't accept credit or debit cards. You'll need to pack along cash or your cheque book. A deck of

Keefer Lake, Kettle River. © Murphy Shewchuk

cards and a cribbage board or a good book may be needed to tide you over
smart phone withdrawal.

In a recent interview, resort host Bob Horkoff gave me a bit of background
to the local lake names. He said that Charles Keefer was a Government Agent
who was involved with railway surveys in the 1890s. Horkoff also mentioned
that the first crown lease on Keefer Lake was obtained by Henry Catt and
Alec Monroe in 1949. Arthur Holmes, after whom Holmes Lake was named,
was involved with mica mining in the 1920s.

Holmes Lake and the end of the road

Back at the junction at the west end of Keefer Lake, the road to the north
crosses the Kettle River and then winds through the trees north of Keefer
Lake to a clearing east of Holmes Lake. There isn't any obvious lake access
along the north shore of Keefer Lake, but there is a small rec site on a knoll
north of the road at Holmes Lake. A short steep trail provides access to the
boat launch and beach at Holmes Lake. For most RV drivers, the road ends
in a clearing at the height-of-land about a km east of the Holmes Lake rec
site and 19.5 km from Highway 6. There are some skid roads and trails
beyond this point, but I haven't explored them yet.

Additional information

BC Parks

Web: http://www.env.gov.bc.ca/bcparks/

BC Recreation Sites and Trails

Web: http://www.sitesandtrailsbc.ca/

Backroad Mapbook:

Thompson Okanagan BC

GPS References for major points of interest

Ref: WGS 84 - Lat/Lon hddd.ddddd

Allow +/- 100 metres due to data conversions

WPT	Km	Description	Latitude	Longitude	Elev.
K01	0.0	Jct Hwy 3 & Hwy 33	N49.05723	W118.99988	620 m
K02	6.5	Kettle River Park Entrance	N49.11201	W118.99462	641 m
K03	13.2	Westbridge Gen Store	N49.16767	W118.97863	643 m
K04	13.5 [0 Km]	Christian Vly Rd & Kettle River F.S. Rd	N49.17030	W118.97481	632 m
K05	21.3	Fiva Creek Road & Bridge	N49.23061	W118.92882	640 m
K06	40.3	Jct. Hümüh Monastery	N49.38264	W118.87698	680 m
K07	43.2	Jct. Canyon Flats Rec Site	N49.41246	W118.86738	693 m
K08	44.5	Jct Canyon Creek Rec Site	N49.42004	W118.86797	693 m
K09	44.7	4th of July F.S. Rd	N49.42083	W118.86898	702 m
K10	52.1	Jct. Kettle Bench Rec Site	N49.48155	W118.84788	721 m
K11	53.6	Jct. Kettle Canyon Rec Site	N49.48008	W118.82788	723 m
K12	59.5	Jct. State Cr Rec Site	N49.52663	W118.81905	747 m
K13	62.9 [50 Km]	Christian Valley	N49.55456	W118.80720	749 m
K14	72.0	Jct. Rendell Creek FS Rd	N49.63201	W118.77649	808 m
K15	80.1	Damfino Creek Rec Site	N49.70135	W118.77104	848 m
K16	91.2	Sandy Bend Rec Site	N49.78703	W118.71529	931 m
K17	92.4	Kettle R. Crossing Rec Site	N49.79678	W118.71430	936 m
K18	96.3 [81 Km]	Mohr Cr Rec Site	N49.82898	W118.70087	965 m
K19	105.6	Winnifred Falls Rec Site	N49.90811	W118.69303	1040 m
K20	111.2 [67 Km]	Bruer Cr Rec Site	N49.95395	W118.67812	1055 m
K21	126.0	Jct. Kettle River FS Road & Hwy 6	N50.04924	W118.55796	1141 m
K22	132.5	Lost Lake Rest Area	N50.06257	W118.48828	1234 m
K23	134.0	Monashee Kettle R Rec Site	N50.07564	W118.48443	1226 m
K24	146.2	Jct. Keefer Lake Resort	N50.12987	W118.36322	1345 m
K25	151.2	Holmes Lake Rec Site	N50.11758	W118.30734	1372 m
K26	152.2	End of Road	N50.11550	W118.29473	1391 m

Gravestone at Phoenix Cemetery. © Murphy Shewchuk

CHAPTER 6

Phoenix Road: Exploring one of Boundary Country's richest mining areas.

STATISTICS
For map, see page 96.

Distance: 18 km, Greenwood to Hwy 3 via Phoenix.
Travel Time: One hour or less under good conditions.
Elev. Gain: 650 metres (2,130 feet).
Conditions: Paved from Greenwood to mine site, gravel east to Hwy 3.
Season: Maintained year-around.
Topographical Maps: Grand Forks, BC 82 E/SE (1:100,000)
Backroad Mapbook   Kootenay Rockies BC. Thompson Okanagan BC.
Communities: Greenwood and Grand Forks.

Back Country Explorers Dream
British Columbia's Crowsnest Highway 3 carves an inverted "U" as it winds its way east from Midway through Greenwood and on to Grand Forks. Inside this inverted "U" is a 200-km-square section of the Kettle Forest with a maze of backroads, abandoned railway grades, and cycling, hiking, snowmobiling and skiing opportunities. Breaking up the landscape is a handful of knolls that reach close to 1,600 metres (5,250 ft.) in altitude.

Greenwood
The city of Greenwood began with the dreams of Robert Wood, who arrived in 1895. It grew with the discovery of several important copper deposits in the area. In the early 1900s, the BC Copper Company built a smelter near the southwest corner of town to process ore from the Motherlode mine, four km to the west. The Anaconda smelter operated until November 26, 1918, when depressed copper prices, strikes in the Crowsnest coalfields (coking coal was used in the smelting process) and a shortage of copper ore forced its closure. The giant BC Copper Company brick smokestack, built in 1904,

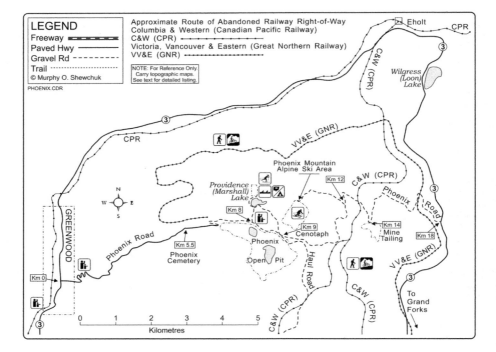

LEGEND
Freeway ▬▬▬▬
Paved Hwy ─────
Gravel Rd ────────
Trail ··············
© Murphy O. Shewchuk
PHOENIX.CDR

Approximate Route of Abandoned Railway Right-of-Way
Columbia & Western (Canadian Pacific Railway)
C&W (CPR) ·─·─·─·─·─·
Victoria, Vancouver & Eastern (Great Northern Railway)
VV&E (GNR) ·······················

NOTE: For Reference Only.
Carry topographic maps.
See text for detailed listing.

is clearly visible as you approach Greenwood from the south. It is now part of Lotzkar Park and can be reached via the bridge across Boundary Creek at Washington Street.

Greenwood was saved from becoming a ghost town in 1942 when 1,200 Japanese were evacuated from the coast and took up residence in many of the substantial, but empty, buildings.

Today the City of Greenwood has a look of renewed hope. The wide main street is a picture from the past with snippets of the present thrown in. The Copper Eagle cappuccino bar and bakery on Copper Street (Highway 3) is a good place to stop for a break. A little farther north is an "original" hardware store that has everything you could possibly want. Throughout the city are many fine restored wood and brick buildings, some close to a century old. Check out the Greenwood Museum and take the city walking tour. Good shoes, fresh batteries in your camera and a couple of hours are essential.

Phoenix Road

Phoenix Road, the main route east across the mountain, leaves Highway 3 as Greenwood Street in the heart of Greenwood. It is maintained year-around, providing ready access to the heart of the area. Although paved for

View from Marshall Lake Cross Country Ski Trails hut at Phoenix. © Murphy Shewchuk

the first six km, the initial switchback climb is steep enough to test most vehicles, particularly motorhomes and vehicles pulling trailers.

Kilometre references for this description are based on the west junction of Phoenix Road and Highway 3 in Greenwood as Km 0 [18]. For the sake of those who might be approaching the area from the east, I've marked the key distances from the east junction of Phoenix Road and Highway 3, south of Wilgress Lake, in square brackets.

Phoenix Cemetery

The little cemetery, nestled in the trees to the south of Phoenix Road near Km 5.5 [12.5], had its beginnings in September, 1901, when Phoenix Aldermen Marshall, Roy and Clark where appointed to establish a site for a city cemetery.

By February, 1902, the site had been found and approved by the government— just in time to receive its first customer, one Clyde Peel Crawford.

While some feel uncomfortable meandering through a cemetery, I've found the experience to be quite educational. The grave markers often reveal the source of present-day names of landmarks and geographical features. Because Phoenix had such a short life, this link with the past is not nearly as apparent. What is apparent is that many of those interred here also had a relatively short life. A group of graves dating around 1911 included many relatively young people of Swedish, Welsh, Italian and Russian descent. With an estimated 4,000 people living and working in Phoenix at that time, mine accidents could account for some of those deaths. It is also possible that residents succumbed to disease as happened in the influenza epidemic of 1918-19.

The infamous flu epidemic took its toll. R.M. Simbreck, in an article in the Boundary Historical Society 10th Report, records that he was able to confirm a total of 91 burials in the cemetery. One quarter of those died in November, 1918. Many of the 22 people buried then were young children.

Open Pit Mine
A wide spot in the road near Km 7.5 [10.5], provides a view of the tailing lake and the remnants of the Phoenix open pit mine.

Phoenix: Arizona or Egypt?
Phoenix residents once proudly proclaimed their city to be the highest in Canada. They also claimed to have started professional hockey and originated skiing in BC I'm sure others may question all three claims as they question the source of the name.

Some suggest that it was named after a mining community in Arizona while others claim it came from the mythical Phoenix of Egypt. This legendary bird is said to set fire to its nest when old and perish in the flames, only to rise again from the ashes with renewed vitality. While the Phoenix mining operations did experience a Phoenix-like rebirth, the town name came from one of the many claims that were staked on the ore body. Swiss-born Robert Denzler, who staked the Phoenix claim in the early 1890s, is no longer around to answer the question.

Two Railways into Phoenix
It didn't take long for the outside world to recognize the profits to be made from supplying transportation to this mountain-top city. The Canadian Pacific Railway had acquired the Columbia and Western Railway and the Trail smelter early in 1898 and began a rapid push westward. On September 18, 1899 the first official train travelled the line to Grand Forks. From Grand Forks the line looped northwest to Eholt and a 16 km C&W spur line was constructed south to Phoenix. With some stretches of 5.5 per cent grade this was no ride for the faint hearted, particularly when carrying a load of copper concentrate to smelters at Grand Forks or Greenwood.

Greenwood Post Office, constructed in 1913, is located on South Government Street.
© Murphy Shewchuk

The C&W Railway hold on the Phoenix railway traffic did not go unchallenged. The period between 1896 and World War One was one of intense competition (sometimes including violence) between various railway interests. The CPR's Thomas Shaughnessy dominated the Canadian corner of the ring and James J. Hill, a disgruntled former CPR director, fought the CPR at every turn from the American corner. J.J. Hill's determination bordered on madness, but through the acquisition of the Vancouver, Victoria & Eastern Railway charter, he was able to push a line north from Washington State. The VV & E reached Phoenix in 1905 over a much better grade—the general route of much of the present Highway 3 descent from Wilgress Lake to Grand Forks.

First Incarnation Ended In 1919

The Granby Consolidated Mining and Smelting Company, the BC Copper Company and the New Dominion Copper Company all had operating mines at the Phoenix camp. The city boomed with tennis courts, a theatre, a brewery and 17 saloons. It also had a fine hospital, said to have been designed by F.N. Rattenbury, who also designed Victoria's legislative buildings.

Phoenix Cenotaph. © Murphy Shewchuk

The residents of Phoenix contributed greatly to World War One, both in men and financial aid. However, when the war ended, the demand for copper dropped. With falling prices, a spent ore body and a shortage of skilled workers, the last straw was a strike in the Crowsnest coalfields. In 1919, the Granby Company shut down operations and a year later, the City of Phoenix was down to two residents.

With the spirit of its namesake watching over the proceedings, a short-lived attempt to revive Phoenix began in 1936. World War Two squelched this attempt, and it wasn't until 1955 that new techniques and rising copper prices permitted the Phoenix to rise from the ashes. The city disappeared in the onslaught of explosives and monster shovels. A little over two decades later, all was again quiet. The Phoenix is again at rest, but with a total of over $1 billion in gold, silver and copper already wrested from the ground, a recent drilling program in the area suggests the mining men haven't given up completely.

Open pit lake at Phoenix Mine. . © Murphy Shewchuk

Phoenix Cenotaph

The Phoenix cenotaph, at Km 9 [9], was originally erected in honor of the Phoenix men who served in the First World War. The cenotaph is one of the few remaining landmarks of the city of Phoenix—and it has been moved from its original site. The remains of the city of 4,000 disappeared into the gaping maw that lies across the road.

The cenotaph also marks an important four-way junction. To the south, a network of roads can take you to the US border, Grand Forks or back to Greenwood. You may also be able to find remnants of the old railway beds both north and south of the mine site. However, the sure way east is to keep to the left just past the cenotaph and start the steady descent to Highway 3.

Marshall Lake Road

If you are looking for a place to camp, wet a fishing line, or strap on a pair of cross-country skis, a gravel road leads northwest from the cenotaph to Marshall (Providence) Lake. The Forest Recreation Site on the north shore of the lake, near the foot of the old Phoenix ski hill, could be a good base to explore the area.

Note that if you haven't visited the area in a while, the Marshall

Lake dam was decommissioned in 2013 resulting in a significantly lower waterlevel. A large dock has been installed since then, but it may take a while for the shoreline vegetation to return.

Marshall Lake is also a base for local cross-country ski trails with a history that goes back to when all skis looked much like today's cross-country skis.

Old Phoenix Ski Hill

What's left of the old Phoenix ski hill is a strong indication of its simplicity. A post near the top appears to have served as the head of a rope tow. And those who liked to schuss the run could probably count on the ice of man-made Marshall Lake to serve as a run-out. With a base elevation of 1,400 metres (4,590 ft.) and a close proximity to the city of Phoenix, the ski hill supported some serious skiers.

One of these was Engwald (Minnie) Engen, a native of Norway, who, in 1907, left his job as a railway brakeman in Grand Forks to take up mining at Phoenix. Engen honed his skills on the local hill and was soon competing in Rossland for the Jeldness Cup, the symbol of Canadian skiing supremacy. He won the national title and held it for seven years.

Alpine Skiing

The last major Phoenix Road side-trip before Highway 3 is near Km 12 [6]. It's less than two km west to the Phoenix Mountain alpine ski hill. A far better hill than the one at Marshall Lake, it has a vertical difference of 240 metres (800 ft.) and nine runs serviced by a T-Bar and a rope tow.

As Phoenix Road continues the descent, it passes the remains of a mine tailing pond near Km 14 [4] and crosses the old Vancouver, Victoria & Eastern Railway right-of-way just before reaching Highway 3 near Km 18 [0].

While the drive over the mountain could take you less than an hour, if you choose to explore the country at that speed, you may as well stay on the blacktop of Highway 3. Allow yourself at least a weekend if you want to savor a bit of the mining history that was a century in the making.

Additional information

Phoenix Mountain Alpine Ski Society
Box 2428, Grand Forks, BC V0H 1H0
Office phone: 250-442-5870
Mountain phone: 250-444-6565
Fax: 250-442-5090
Email: skiphoenix@gmail.com Web: http://www.skiphoenix.com/
Phoenix Mountain Alpine Ski Society.

BC Parks
Web: http://www.env.gov.bc.ca/bcparks/ BC Recreation Sites and Trails
Web: http://www.sitesandtrailsbc.ca/

Backroad Mapbook:
Thompson Okanagan BC

Books & Pamphlets:
Heritage Cemeteries in British Columbia edited by John D. Adams (1985).
Various Boundary History Society Reports.
McCulloch's Wonder by Barrie Sanford (2011).
History Still Standing: A Guide to the Historical Mine Sites of the Boundary Country.
Phoenix Forest and History Tour.

GPS References for major points of interest
Ref: WGS 84 - Lat/Lon hddd.ddddd
Allow +/- 100 metres due to data conversions

WPT	Km	Description	Latitude	Longitude
P01	0 [18]	Hwy 3 & Greenwood St.	N49.08850	W118.67736
P02	5.5 [12.5]	Phoenix Cemetery	N49.10201	W118.62724
P03		End of Pavement	N49.10399	W118.61415
P04	7.5 [10.5]	View of Open Pit Mine	N49.10347	W118.60616
P05	9 [9]	Cenotaph & Marshall Lk Rd	N49.09955	W118.59130
P06		Marshall Lake Rec Site	N49.11554	W118.59998
P07	12 [6]	Phoenix Mtn Ski Hill Rd	N49.10790	W118.58563
P08		Phoenix Mtn Ski Hill	N49.10905	W118.58563
P09	18 [0]	Phoenix Rd & Hwy 3	N49.10337	W118.52892

View of Grand Forks from historic Doukhobor House. © Murphy Shewchuk

CHAPTER 7

Granby Loop: Grand Forks to Greenwood via Granby River and Boundary Creek

STATISTICS

For map, see page 106.

Distance: Approximately 100 km, Grand Forks to Greenwood.

Travel Time: Four to six hours. Allow a day or two extra for side trips.

Conditions: Partly paved, mostly gravel with some steep sections.

Season: Summer road—may be closed in winter.

Topo Maps Grand Forks, BC 82 E/SE. (1:100,000)
Upper Kettle River, BC 82 E/NE.

Backroad Mapbook

Kootenay Rockies BC.
Thompson Okanagan BC.

Communities: Grand Forks and Greenwood.

Backroads and Mountain Trails

There is a network of backroads that can take you on an inverted-U shaped summer trip from Grand Forks to Greenwood. It will probably take a day longer than Highway 3, but the opportunities for back country exploring, rock hounding and hiking are worth it. Allow a few days, if you can, to take in a detour to the new Granby Provincial Park or to explore many of the backroads and savor the history of the region.

You'll be on your own as far as services are concerned. There are a several British Columbia recreation sites, but Granby Provincial Park is largely undeveloped and likely to stay that way for some time. The pass between Gable Creek and the headwaters of Boundary Creek is at an elevation of 1,500 metres (4,920 feet) so it could have a short open season.

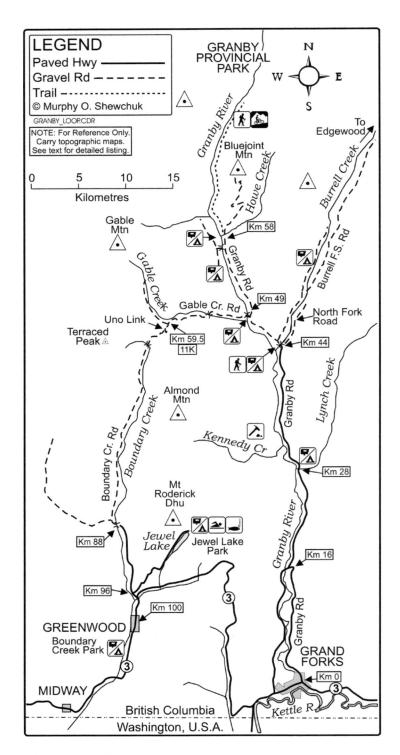

LEGEND
Paved Hwy ———
Gravel Rd — — —
Trail ·············
© Murphy O. Shewchuk

GRANBY_LOOP.CDR

NOTE: For Reference Only.
Carry topographic maps.
See text for detailed listing.

0   5   10   15
Kilometres

GRANBY
PROVINCIAL
PARK

N
W   E
S

To
Edgewood

Granby River

Bluejoint
Mtn

Howe Creek

Burrell Creek

Gable
Mtn

Km 58

Granby Rd

Burrell F.S. Rd

Gable Creek

Gable Cr. Rd

Km 49

North Fork
Road

Uno Link

Terraced
Peak

Km 59.5
11K

Km 44

Almond
Mtn

Granby Rd

Lynch Creek

Kennedy Cr

Boundary Cr. Rd

Boundary Creek

Mt
Roderick
Dhu

Km 28

Jewel
Lake

Jewel Lake
Park

Km 88

Granby River

Km 16

Km 96

Km 100

③

GREENWOOD

Boundary
Creek Park

③

GRAND
FORKS

Km 0

③

MIDWAY

British Columbia
Washington, U.S.A.

Kettle R.

Cabin near Boundary Creek Forest Service Road. © Murphy Shewchuk

Grand Forks

The Grand Forks area, at the junction of the Kettle and Granby rivers, was the seasonal home of Interior Salish Indians long before the fur traders passed through in the early 1800s. In the mid-1800s, when the fur trade waned and the gold rush started, it became part of the east-west route across southern BC.

Lieutenant H.S. Palmer of the Royal Engineers made the following observations on October 2, 1859. "At the confluence of three valleys occurs a large open plain, three miles by two, designated in the plan 'La Grande Prairie'. ... Little snow falls here in winter and its sheltered position renders it an excellent 'guard' for cattle and horses during that season."

The Dewdney Trail, built from Rock Creek to Wild Horse Creek in 1865, passed through this grassland, carrying the traffic that opened up the Boundary region. The first settlers moved into the area in the 1880s, raising fine beef that they herded westward over the Dewdney Trail to Fraser River steamers at Hope each fall.

Grand Forks City was incorporated on April 15, 1897, the year of Queen Victoria's Diamond Jubilee. Shortly after incorporation, the Granby Mining and Smelting Company began construction of a copper smelter at Grand

Granby River from Hummingbird Bridge. © Murphy Shewchuk

Forks. From 1899 to 1919, the smelter was the prime employer in the valley, with both the Canadian Pacific Railway and Great Northern Railway hauling in ore from the nearby mines.

Granby River

The aboriginal people knew the Granby as the Inchwointon River. It was part of the territory of the Kettle, Colville, and Lakes people of the Interior Salish group. The valley served as part of the Native trade route to the Arrow Lakes and the Okanagan Valley, near present-day Vernon. Fur traders changed the name to the North Fork of the Kettle River. The name was changed again when the Granby Mining and Smelting Company (which incidentally took its name from Granby, Quebec) moved into the region.

When the smelter was constructed at Grand Forks in 1899, a dam was built across the river, a short distance upstream, to supply water and hydro-electric power. Smelter Lake flooded about 300 hectares (750 acres) of the valley bottom. The dam remained until the winter of 1947-48 when it was removed just in advance of the province-wide flood of 1948—although unfortunately, not far enough in advance to save Grand Forks from serious flooding when debris blocked the dam gates.

Logging Truck on Granby Forest Service Road. © Murphy Shewchuk

Granby Road

Highway 3 crosses the Granby River on the eastern edge of downtown Grand Forks. Highway 3 and Granby Road, near the Omega II Restaurant just east of the bridge, is the Km 0 reference for this backroad adventure. Roadside km markers also prove useful for waypoints and will be referred to where appropriate. Be forewarned: Grand Forks is your last chance to stock up on fuel and supplies.

Black Slag

The pyramids of black granulated glass-like material near Km 1.5 are remnants of some thirteen million tons of slag created by the Granby Smelter operation. In recent years, the mountains of slag have been turned into sandblast grit and insulating material–with the proceeds going to revitalize Grand Forks' public buildings.

The remains of the previously mentioned Granby River dam can be seen to the left near Km 3.2.

Hummingbird Bridge

If you are cycling or only interested in a leisurely day trip, there is an opportunity to cross the Granby River on the Hummingbird Bridge near Km 16 and return to Grand Forks via the west side of the river. This route will take you through the short-lived town of Niagara and back into town via Donaldson Drive.

Hot Air Line

Much of the first 30 km of Granby Road follows the original Republic & Grand Forks Railway route. The railway company, formed in 1900, was dubbed the "Hot Air Line" after delays in construction, but it did reach as far north as Lynch Creek (Km 28) before World War I. In 1918, it was extended three km farther north to serve the Rock Candy Mine at Kennedy Creek. (The "Rock Candy" name came from the beautiful purple, green and blue colours of the fluorite ore.)

The railway served the many mines and lumber outfits of the "North Fork" region until 1935. The rails were removed a year later and the right-of-way became part of the road north. If you started late or aren't in a rush, there is a British Columbia recreation site on the north bank of Lynch Creek.

Burrell Creek

Granby Road takes a sharp turn to the left at the end of pavement and the "28 Mile Bridge" (Km 44). If the meadows above the canyon at the bridge across Burrell Creek look as though they may have been flooded, that's because they were. A dam was built here in 1936 to supplement the water storage for Smelter Lake and the hydro-electric plant then supplying Grand Forks with power. Nature did not cooperate and within a few years the city gave up on generating its own power and signed a contract with West Kootenay Power and Light.

The Granby-Burrell recreation site near the bridge could prove to be an interesting base for a little river fishing. Beyond the bridge, the signs mark this as the Granby Forest Service Road.

Burrell Creek Road

While not part of this route description, Burrell Creek Forest Service Road

Burrell Creek dam site near Km 44. © Murphy Shewchuk

Fisherman on Jewel Lake. © Murphy Shewchuk

to the right near Km 45 could take you 70 km north to Edgewood on Lower Arrow Lake. We made this trip without difficulty in late August a few years back.

If you are interested in a hike along the river, the Grand Forks Secondary School has been rehabilitating a nearby section of the old Granby Trail. There is a place to park alongside Granby Road about 200 metres past the Burrell Creek F.S. Road junction. The easy three-km-long trail provides scenic riverside views and plenty of rest stops.

Gable Creek Road

The next major junction is Gable Creek Forest Service Road, to the left near Km 48.5. If you are in a hurry to get to Greenwood, go left here. If not, keep to the right on Granby FS Road and watch for a picnic site on bend in the Granby River near the 52K marker. The rapids here could be an interesting spot to test your kayaking skills.

Continue north to the 58K marker on Granby Road and take Bluejoint Lookout F.S. Road to the right. It is about 15 km to the lookout on 2326 metre (7,630 foot) Bluejoint Mountain, but the last few km could be a tough climb.

Granby Provincial Park

The southern access to the recently established 41,000 hectare (101,000 acre) Granby Provincial Park is via a rough road or trail that leaves Bluejoint Lookout Road about two km from Granby Road. For most travelers, the best bet is to park near the Howe Creek Bridge and walk or bicycle down to the old access road and then four km up that road to the trailhead.

The Granby Trail is a relatively easy walk along the river, offering scenic canyon views; fishing opportunities, sandy beaches, and some excellent examples of old growth stands of cedar and hemlock. Some of the trees are up to 40 metres high and over 300 years old.

The park also provides important habitat for mountain goat and a regionally significant grizzly bear population. Some environmentalists suggest that Granby grizzlies may be distinctive because they have adapted to the harsh, dry conditions of the Southern Interior. Generally, they may be smaller in size and their food sources and home ranges wider because there are no salmon runs on the Granby River. There have been some suggestions that these bears may be genetically unique because of their isolation from other grizzly populations.

There is considerable concern that Granby Park and the new 39,000 hectare (97,000 acre) Gladstone Provincial Park, to the east at the head of Christina Lake, may not provide a large enough base for the approximately 50 grizzlies that roam the area. Without carefully planned logging and controlled access in the adjacent drainages, these shy animals could face extinction.

Gable Creek Road, again

Meanwhile, back at Km 48.5 and the Gable Creek F.S. Road. The climb north from Grand Forks (elev. 516 m) to Gable Creek (elev. 760 m) has been gradual, but that changes on the next 15 km to the headwaters of Boundary Creek. But first there is a switchback descent to the Granby River before the steady climb west. Again diversions abound. You can explore 8-Mile Creek; Almond Mountain; or West Almond Mountain F.S. Roads before reaching the important Uno Creek Road (Uno Link) near the 11K marker. (Boundary Creek F.S. Road on some maps.) On any of these narrow logging roads, weekends are safest, but extreme caution is necessary every day of the week.

It's a four km switchback climb up Uno Link road to the summit of the pass (Km 64 from Grand Forks) and the junction with Boundary Creek F.S. Road at an elevation of about 1,500 metres (4,920 feet). Take the road to the left at the junction at the 4K marker. We found an open field just south of the crest and enjoyed a warm mid-July lunch break amid singing birds and subalpine wildflowers.

From here it's a steady descent on the 35 km run to Highway 3 at Greenwood. We passed at least half a dozen side roads before reaching the pavement near the south boundary of TFL 8 (Km 88). The forest road gives way to farmland, then the permanent mark of a pioneer community in the form of the Greenwood Cemetery. A few moments later and you should be at the Jewel Lake Road junction (Km 96-if my calculations are correct).

Jewel Lake from Jewel Lake Provincial Park. © Murphy Shewchuk

Jewel Lake

If time permits, Jewel Lake is well worth the 10 km climb back up into the mountains. There is a resort on the north shore of the lake as well as a provincial park campground on the east end of Jewell Lake.

The Twelfth Report of the Boundary Historical Society has an intriguing story about "Lord Pelly of Jewel Lake" that is too long to recite here except to say that this scion of British aristocracy built a cabin at the west end of the lake in 1899. From a fishers' perspective, an even more interesting story is one by Myler Wilkinson that was published in the October/November 1982 edition of *BC Outdoors* magazine. Mr. Wilkinson's story recounts reports of world record Kamloops trout being caught in Jewel Lake in 1913. Although the method of capture seems debatable (a gaff hook), the 25.4 kg (56 pound) adult male would have been a load for anyone's creel. His 21.8 kg (48 pound) mate was no slouch either. There were more reports in the 1930s and '40s of fish over 23 kg (50 pounds) being taken. Unfortunately, local fishers will assure you that this is no longer the norm at Jewel Lake.

Greenwood

It's a one km drive to Highway 3 and then another three km south to downtown Greenwood, completing this 100 km loop backroad. If you were a crow, the distance from Grand Forks is a bit over 18 km, but think of all the fun you would have missed.

Additional Information:
Boundary Museum and Interpretive Centre
Fructova Heritage Site
6145 Reservoir Road Grand Forks, BC V0H 1H5
Web: http://boundarymuseum.com/
Greenwood Museum and Visitor Centre
Greenwood Heritage Society
PO Box 399,
214 South Copper Avenue, Greenwood, BC V0H 1J0
Web: http://www.greenwoodmuseum.com/

Hiker on Dewdney Trail near Old Cascade Highway. © Murphy Shewchuk

CHAPTER 8

Old Cascade Highway: Christina Lake to Rossland via the Santa Rosa Summit

STATISTICS

For map, see page 118

Distance: Approx. 62 km, Hwy 3 in Christina to Hwy 22 at Rossland.

Elev. Gain: 1234 metres.

Travel Time: Three to four hours.

Condition: Some rough gravel sections, closed in winter.
May be closed due to washouts or mudslides.

Season: Mid-July through October.

Topo Maps: Grand Forks, BC 82 E/SE (1:100,000).
Trail, BC 82 F/SW (1:100,000).

Backroad Mapbook: Kootenay Rockies BC.

Communities: Grand Forks, Christina Lake and Rossland.

There's history in the mountains of south central British Columbia. If you care to go looking for it, you can find sections of an historic trail that has changed little since it was first built nearly 150 years ago.

A Trail to the Goldfields at Wildhorse Creek

You don't have to be an ardent hiker to follow in the footsteps of Edgar Dewdney and the miners who trudged across the southern Monashee Mountains to the gold fields of Wild Horse Creek in the 1860s. You can, with a little care in your choice of vehicle and the season you travel, parallel the last major untouched sections of the trail that helped keep central British Columbia Canadian.

The first "Dewdney Trail" was from Hope to Princeton, roughly paralleling the present route of Highway 3. This was a major effort for man

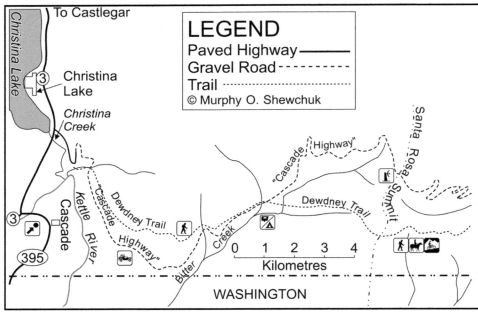

and beast when Edgar Dewdney and Walter Moberly opened it in 1860, but it was little more than a training ground for what lay ahead in 1865.

Reports of rich gold diggings in Wild Horse Creek (north of present-day Cranbrook) had drifted back to Governor Seymour of the Crown Colony of British Columbia. With a treasury deep in debt from building the "Cariboo Waggon Road" from Yale to Barkerville, the Governor faced a difficult decision. He could ignore Wild Horse Creek and risk losing the Interior to American interests or he could increase debt and create a trade route north of the 49th parallel that would insure a British presence and, he hoped, bring more duties and taxes into the treasury.

Edgar Dewdney was Assigned the Task

The Crown Council chose to compromise. In April, 1865, Edgar Dewdney was assigned the task of opening up a mule trail through unmapped territory from "Sooyoos Lake" in the south Okanagan valley to Wild Horse Creek. Just to make it more challenging, the assignment also included the suggestion that it be done at maximum haste and minimum cost. Dewdney met the challenges of spring snow packs and floods, summer windstorms, ill-informed guides and the worst that the mountains could present. With the able assistance of two scouts, Howell and Turner, and as many as 300 workers (many of them disgruntled miners), he completed the task.

Perhaps the best (and most understated) description is in excerpts from

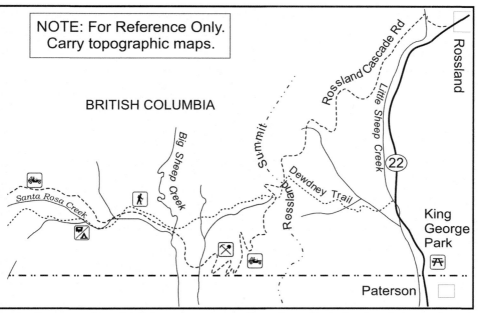

NOTE: For Reference Only.
Carry topographic maps.

BRITISH COLUMBIA

Rossland Cascade Rd

Little Sheep Creek

Rossland

Big Sheep Creek

Summit

Dewdney Trail

Rossland

22

Santa Rosa Creek

King George Park

Paterson

his letter to the Chief Commissioner of Lands and Works dated December 20th, 1865:

"Sir:

"I have the honour to inform you that in accordance with instructions received from His Excellency the Governor, I left New Westminster on the 12th of April 1865, in charge of a party to explore the country between Sooyoos Lake, and Wild Horse Creek, for the purpose of deciding upon the best line for a Mule Trail between those two points, and also to superintend its immediate construction as well as other works more fully described in my letter of instruction dated 10th April 1865.

"My operation commenced at Sooyoos Lake, from which place I set out with my party on the 13th May.

"I had previously visited Mr. Angus McDonald of the Hudson Bay Company at Colville, to obtain from him information regarding the different routes I proposed exploring, and which I heard he was acquainted; from him I received much valuable information.

"In my previous reports from Fort Sheppard and Kootenais Lake, dated respectively May 28th and June 2nd, I described what my success had been in following what I supposed to be, the line indicated by Mr. McDonald, viz, up Boundary Creek to its Forks, thence Eastward to the Inchivomiton, (or north fork of Kettle River) crossing about ten miles from its mouth then through a divide at the north side of the largest mountain in that neighbourhood, called McDonald's Mountain, to the Columbia River.

"You will find I was unsuccessful in this section.

"Had I found on the East side of the Columbia, a practicable line for a road to Kootenais in connection with this, I should have made a further exploration of McDonald's Pass.

"On my arrival at Kootenais Lake from the Columbia River... I was in hopes I had succeeded, but subsequent examinations convinced me that no feasible divide existed by which a trail could be continued, without following the Lake to its northern end, and about 20 miles up the stream flowing into it from the North west, then striking across the old Indian trail to the headwaters of the Columbia.

"As I mentioned in my report of June 20th, I considered this a long and expensive line—and one that would not have carried out the object of my expeditions. I consequently gave up all idea of it, and proceeded southward to the lower end of the Lake.

"Here I instructed Mr. Turner to return to the Columbia and examine the valleys through which the Hudson Bay Co. had constructed a rough trail, and through which I was informed horses had travelled the previous year, and also if favourably impressed with it to blaze that line at once.

"I, with the remainder of my party, continued to explore the country between the East side of the Lake, and the valley of the Mooyie along which the old trail to Wild Horse Creek runs.

"I considered this in every respect fit for a road, being almost level, and with good feed.

"I arrived at Wild Horse Creek on the 13th June, and as I was satisfied, that the only continuous line of communication between Sooyoos Lake and Kootenais, north of the 49th parallel, and south of the upper end of the Arrow Lakes was as follows, I determined to commence work at once.

"Starting from Sooyoos Lake, I follow generally the old trail to Boundary Creek, crossing it about 3 miles from its junction with Kettle River, thence to the Columbia, via the trail known as McKay's, but making such deviations as were necessary to avoid bad grades; this section I estimate at 110 miles.

"I crossed the Columbia about two miles above the Boundary Line, and keeping down its East bank half a mile, left it and continued up

Christina Crest Trail at Santa Rosa summit. © Murphy Shewchuk

the Pende d'Oreille and Little Salmon Rivers, then down the valley of Summit Creek to Kootenais Lake; this section I estimate at 64 miles.

"Here I met with the only difficulty on the whole line, which was, to determine at which point it was most advisable to establish a crossing.

"The Valley of the Kootenais is here about three miles in width, and at high water is almost entirely overflowed, and I found that the high water crossing which I had been informed, and which I was depending, was a few hundred yards below the Boundary line; after several days search I was compelled to adopt the present one which will require rather a large outlay to make it a convenient and permanent crossing...

"On leaving Kootenais Lake, I follow up Goat River about twenty miles, and leaving it turn eastward along occasional meadows to the trail on the Mooyie River which I join about eight miles north of the Boundary Line, and continuing along the old trail, reach Wild Horse Creek in an estimated distance of one hundred miles from Kootenais Lake."

Communications antennae at Santa Rosa summit. © Murphy Shewchuk

196 Miles of Trail at $254.00 per Mile

Dewdney went on to list the distances of various sections of the 196 miles of trail he had constructed that summer, including a 50 mile section from Christina Creek to the Columbia River. The total cost of the road, including exploration, was $53,400.00. With the $3,600.00 in exploration work subtracted, he had succeeded in building a mule trail across southern British Columbia for the princely sum of $254.00 per mile.

The Wild Horse Creek gold rush was already in decline when Dewdney finished his trail, and the hoped-for rush to the Big Bend of the Columbia River turned out to be a flop. Two decades later, much of the trail through the West Kootenay area was virtually impassable, but the section between Rossland and Christina remained an important thoroughfare until the C&W Railway reached the town of Cascade, on the Kettle River south of Christina Lake.

Cascade City

The "cascade" in the Kettle River that prompted the construction of Cascade City in the late 1890s is about all that is left of a hydroelectric dam and powerhouse and a community that boasted 14 hotels and numerous brothels. The city had a very short life: The C&W Railway arrived in August, 1899; a fire destroyed much of the town at the end of September, 1899; and a second fire effectively finished it off in 1901. The powerhouse lasted another 20 years–the remnants of the Kettle River dam and diversion ditches can be seen near Cascade Falls, just off the C&W Railway grade / Trans Canada Trail west of Highway 395. The Christina Lake Golf Club's 18-hole golf course sits on much of what was the original townsite.

Cascade Highway Completed In 1922

Around 1905, West Kootenay Power and Light built a transmission line over the Santa Rosa and the Dewdney Trail became the power-line tote road. In the early 1920s, a public road was constructed between Rossland and Cascade. Although it crossed the Dewdney Trail at several locations, it did little damage to the original trail. Because of the settlement of Cascade City at its western terminus, it became known as the "Cascade Highway". The term "highway" should be taken with more than a grain of salt as anyone who travelled it between 1922 and 1962 will tell you.

It's half a century since the Cascade Highway was relegated to backroad status. The route fell victim to progress and was replaced by the Blueberry-Paulson section of Highway 3 through Bonanza Pass. Travellers through southern British Columbia can make the 73 km trip from Christina to Castlegar in about an hour. The drive from Christina to Rossland via Bonanaza Pass and Nancy Greene Lake could take even less time at today's highway speeds.

If time isn't your main concern, step back into the past and allow at least half a day to drive the old Cascade Highway–with lots of time to smell the roses.

Starts Off In the Community of Christina Lake

When approaching the route from the west on Crowsnest Highway 3, look for the Santa Rosa Road about 0.3 km east of the Christina Creek Bridge (about 25 km east of Grand Forks). Signs here when we last travelled through stated "No Through Road–Maintained for 22 km". Depending on the season and the amount of maintenance done east of the Santa Rosa summit, this could be true. Take along enough fuel to backtrack if necessary and enough common-sense to recognize an impassable road before you have to dig yourself out.

Note: A check with Josh Strzelec of Wildways Adventure Sports in the summer of 2018 indicated the road was open.

Crosses the Old Columbia & Western Railway Grade

With the Santa Rosa Road junction at Highway 3 as km "0", follow the road southeast as it begins climbing away from the Kettle River valley and crosses the former Columbia & Western Railway (C&W) grade at Km 1.4.

Driven by the rich deposits of gold, silver, lead and copper in the Kootenay-Boundary area, the 1880s and 1890s saw massive railroad development in Western Canada and the US North West. The frantic pace of rail building was helped by the intense rivalry between American and Canadian railway interests. The original railway charter between Castlegar and Grand Forks was sought in 1896 by Frederick Augustus "Fritz" Heinze–an American–who wanted to build a railway from what is now the City of Trail to Penticton. He was rebuffed by Ottawa but in 1898 he convinced the CPR to share a half-interest in constructing the rail line and on September 18, 1899 the first train rolled into Grand Forks on the C&W rail line.

The C&W rail line allowed the CPR to reach the Boundary district and score a huge win with the businesses and residents of the region in the historical battle between the CPR and the Burlington Northern Railway to build the first Coast to Kootenay rail line.

When railway freight traffic declined, the line was abandoned and it

Cascade Gorge on the Kettle River near Christina Lake. © Murphy Shewchuk

is now part of the Trans Canada Trail across southern British Columbia. A kiosk near the crossing provides background information on the railway and details about the Trans Canada Trail connection to Castlegar.

Spectacular Views

The pavement ends a few hundred metres beyond the old C&W and the gravel road eastward begins. There are a few narrow sections along here, but where there is a safe pull-out, stop to enjoy the view of Christina Lake and the Kettle River valley, both westward toward Grand Forks and south into Washington State.

The road passes under the West Kootenay Power (now FortisBC) high voltage line at Km 6.5 as it dips south almost to the boundary before climbing steadily northeast along the mountainside. The Dewdney Trail climbed even more steeply, taking somewhat of a shortcut to the north of the road.

The old Cascade Highway crosses the Dewdney Trail near Km 14. The crossing was also the location of the Trout Creek Recreation site. Don't count on doing any fishing, but there is a pleasant, shady spot to take a lunch break. The Dewdney Trail is well marked and Trout Creek could be a good base from which to explore parts of it.

Santa Rosa Road crosses the Dewdney Trail a couple more times before winding northeast to the headwaters of Bitter Creek and the Santa Rosa summit near Km 23 where there is ample room to park and explore the ridges.

Santa Rosa Summit

It's only a short one km rough road south along the ridge to a communications site that affords an excellent view of the area. The microwave towers and the nearby logging are the main reason the road is maintained to the summit.

Christina Crest Trail

A signpost on the north side of the parking area marks the start of the Cristina Crest Trail. According to local information, "It follows the ridge line from the Santa Rosa summit to Mt. St. Thomas and is a multi-day hike or a long day biking. Be prepared for a rugged backcountry experience and bring water as none is available along route. This trail boasts alpine meadows and rock bluffs with panoramic views in all directions, including spectacular views of Christina Lake and Big Sheep Creek valleys."

It is 14.6 km to the peak of Mount St. Thomas. If you are a serious mountain bike rider, you could continue north to Crowsnest Highway 3. Check with Wildways Adventure Sports in Christina Lake for details.

Switchback Descent

The Santa Rosa Forest Road sign marks the route westward toward Rossland. Check your brakes here because you'll soon begin a switchback descent from the 1,600 metre summit that will quickly indicate why few travellers looked forward to the old "Cascade Highway". This is a backroad trip that can be made by car in the best of weather, but a creek crossing at Km 30 and a muddy section at Km 32 could be challenging if you head out too early or too late in the season. The Santa Rosa BC Rec Site at Km 34 offers access to the Dewdney Trail which, since Trout Creek, ran considerably south of the Cascade Highway. Continue on the low road (to the left) at the junction just past the recreation site.

Big Sheep Creek

The Big Sheep Creek bridge near Km 38 marks the return to "maintained" roads. A sign near the bridge clearly states that "the road beyond this point westerly will not be maintained from November 15, 1966–proceed at your own risk." After a short jaunt across the valley floor, the road makes a switchback climb north-eastward to the crest of Ivanhoe Ridge. We counted 15 switchback turns in the ascent–and we might have missed a few while gawking at the old mine dumps near Km 45.5.

Velvet Mine

Mining exploration on the west slopes of Mount Sophia goes back to the 1890s with the Velvet claim staked in 1896 by Olaus Jeldness. Various mining companies have sporadically worked the Velvet and adjacent Portland claims for nearly a century. According to the BC Ministry of Energy mining reports "From 1901 to 1964, 88,833 tonnes of ore produced 620,785 grams gold, 664,359 grams silver, 1,154,104 kilograms copper, 37 kilograms lead, and 25 kilograms zinc."

Also according to the report, mining and diamond drilling continued into the 1980s. "In August 1982 it was reported that 1,000 tons grading 5.48 grams per tonne gold and other commodities were shipped to the H.B. Mill of David Minerals Ltd. in Salmo."

Seven Summits Alpine Ridge Trail.

If you are interested in hiking, horseback riding or a mountain bicycle

Seven Summits Trailhead sign near Rossland. © Murphy Shewchuk

adventure, a widening of the road and signposts at Km 50.6 (approximately 12 km southwest of Highway 22 at Rossland) mark the start of the 30 km ridge ride north to Nancy Greene Pass on Highway 3. The Seven Summits trail heads north and across the road, the Dewdney Trail continues east on a switchback descent to Highway 22 approximately seven km south of Rossland or three km north of the Paterson border crossing.

Rossland

The Old Cascade Highway (now Rossland-Cascade Road) gives way to pavement near Km 62, a few hundred metres before the junction with Highway 22 and 3B at the outskirts of Rossland.

If you're trying the trip from the Rossland end, watch for "Rossland-Cascade Road" or "Santa Rosa" signs south of the Rossland Museum and Le Roi Mine historic site.

Additional Information

Christina Lake Chamber of Commerce

1675 Highway 3 Christina Lake, BC V0H 1E2

Tel/Fax: (250) 447-6161

E-mail: info@christinalake.com

Web: www.christinalake.com

Kootenay Columbia Trail Society

PO Box 1179

Rossland, BC V0G 1Y0

Tel: (250) 362-5095 Web: www.kcts.ca

Wildways Adventure Sports

Highway 3

Christina Lake, BC, Canada V0H 1E2

Tel: (250) 447-6561

E-mail: adventures@wildways.com

Web: www.wildways.com

GPS References for major points of interest

Ref: WGS 84 - Lat/Lon hddd.ddddd

Wpt	Km	Description	Latitude	Longitude	Elev.
C01	0.0	Hwy 3 and Santa Rosa Rd	N49.04402	W118.20536	465 m
C02	1.4	TCT C&W Rail Grade	N49.03356	W118.19800	519 m
C03	6.3	Cross under power line	N49.01065	W118.18067	874 m
C04	10.0	10 km marker	N49.00535	W118.14553	961 m
C05	13.6	Cross Dewdney Trail	N49.02209	W118.11444	1021 m
C06	22.8	Santa Rosa Summit, Christina Crest Trail to North	N49.02994	W118.05378	1589 m
C07	1700 m	Santa Rosa MW Site,	N49.02445	W118.05948	1699 m
C08	23.2	38 km marker - counting down	N49.02827	W118.05038	1589 m
C09	28.5	Viewpoint	N49.02553	W118.02217	1266 m
C10	30.6	Hunter's Creek	N49.02652	W118.01563	1134 m
C11	32.0	30 km marker	N49.02533	W117.99976	1043 m
C12	32.4	Could be slippery in wet weather.	N49.02309	W117.99556	1016 m
C13	33.4	Powerline, Jct. we were on "Santa Rosa FSR (Old Cascade Highway)"	N49.02079	W117.98528	948 m
C14	33.8	Jct. keep right	N49.01850	W117.98130	921 m
C15	34.1	Santa Rosa Rec Site & Dewdney Trail	N49.01831	W117.98474	902 m
C16	35.8	Mudslide area.	N49.01873	W117.96660	815 m
C17	37.6	Big Sheep Creek	N49.01441	W117.94534	704 m
C18	39.8	Jct. Rossland Cascade Rd, go right.	N49.00704	W117.92635	714 m
C19	45.6	17 km marker & Velvet Mine site.	N49.01302	W117.91518	1050 m
C20	50.6	Record Ridge Trailhead & Dewdney Trail.	N49.02996	W117.89683	1388 m
C21	62.6	Jct. Rossland Cascade Road & Hwy 22	N49.07857	W117.82160	1068 m

Canal Flats between Kootenay River and headwaters of Columbia River. © Murphy Shewchuk

CHAPTER 9
Ancient Valley of Ducks: Creston Valley Wildlife Management Area

Once Threatened Marshland Is Now an Important Stop for Wildlife and People

Travellers, especially those from outside British Columbia, often feel as if they are riding a natural roller coaster as they follow Crowsnest Highway 3 through the Kootenays. Dipping, climbing and swooping from one spell-binding scene to another makes it easy to miss important signs and intersections. But despite that, up to 35,000 visitors a year manage to find their way off the highway and explore a Kootenay River marsh that once faced total destruction.

Approaching Creston from the west, British Columbia's Crowsnest Highway makes a long, steep downhill run from the 1,774-metre summit of the Kootenay Skyway to one of the most productive wetland complexes in the BC Interior. The downhill run is symbolic of the fate that Creston Marsh faced for more than half a century.

The Creston Valley story starts high in the Rocky Mountains southeast of Golden with the first trickle of the Kootenay River. The river carves a meandering, international route southward through the Rocky Mountain Trench and into Montana before making a wide loop through Idaho and northward into BC From the Canada-US boundary, the Kootenay River continues northward to Kootenay Lake before draining into the Columbia River near Castlegar. Through thousands of years of meandering, the river created a 70-km-long swamp, eight to ten km wide, that extended from Bonners Ferry, Idaho, past Creston's doorstep, to Kootenay Lake. Waterfowl congregated here in great numbers, especially in spring and fall.

Native people followed the last retreating ice age into the region thousands of years ago, living off the wildlife and adapting their way of life to the marsh.

Fur Trader David Thompson explored the Kootenay system between

Eastern Kingbird at Creston Valley Wildlife Management Area. © Murphy Shewchuk

1807 and 1811. The establishment of the boundary in 1846, between what is now Idaho and British Columbia, helped open the valley to settlers.

First Efforts to Drain the Marsh Began In 1880s

While the Creston marshes served the Kootenay First Nation and complicated the 1860s construction of the Dewdney Trail to the Kootenay gold fields, it wasn't until the mid-1880s that anyone actually tried to do anything about the marsh itself. It was then that W.A. Baillie-Grohman began his Canal Flat project north of Cranbrook. Baillie-Grohman intended to divert the upper Kootenay River into Columbia Lake and the Columbia River, in an effort to reduce downstream flooding on the Creston Marsh. Unfortunately for him the Canadian Pacific Railway, whose tracks along the Columbia would have faced flooding, had the project halted. Nevertheless, Baillie-Grohman pursued his plan to reclaim the Creston Marshes for more than a decade before returning to England in 1898, broke and disheartened.

Although Baillie-Grohman gave up, the threat to the Creston marshes continued. Others picked up the shovel where Baillie-Grohman dropped it and by 1927, the Creston Reclamation Co. Ltd. was intent on "opening up every acre of these 30,000 acres on each side of the (border) line."

From the first reclamation efforts in 1884 until the West Kootenay Power hearings in 1942, the marshes were repeatedly under siege. And if the Kootenay had not been an international river, the marshes would almost certainly have been lost. Hearings were frequently held to determine the effects of reclamation and hydro-electric projects on vested interests on both sides of the international boundary. But it wasn't until Nelson resident J.J. (Mickey)

Female Red-winged Blackbird. © Murphy Shewchuk

McEwen presented a brief at the 1942 hearing that wildlife interests were heard. McEwen's presentation on behalf of the region's fish and game clubs prompted the International Joint Commission (IJC) to postpone their decision until wildlife studies could be completed.

CWS, DU and Rod and Gun Clubs Oppose Draining Marsh

Dr. James Munro of the Canadian Wildlife Service (CWS) was commissioned to study the marsh, and when he presented his findings in November, 1947, the stage was set for a major confrontation. Provincial and federal government departments and a host of business groups supported further reclamation. Against the application was the CWS, Ducks Unlimited (DU) and numerous rod and gun clubs from BC and Idaho. The IJC delayed their decision and the flurry of briefs that followed further heightened the controversy surrounding the marshes. Then, in August 1949, the IJC gave the Creston Reclamation Company permission to dike off 3,200 acres on the south end of Duck Lake, a relatively small, shallow body of water that bordered on the south end of Kootenay Lake. The reclamation company later decided that the land allotment wasn't adequate and controversy erupted again. The Creston Board of Trade supported complete reclamation of Duck Lake while the BC Game Commission opposed it. The conflict boiled over into the BC legislature with the Minister of Agriculture and the Attorney General taking opposite sides. Hearings followed in 1950 and the IJC approved a plan that would see the Creston Reclamation Company drain the south end of Duck Lake and renounce all claims for the remainder of the lake. A year or two later, Dr. Munro issued his report detailing a plan for the development of a Duck Lake wildlife management project, which would eventually serve as the basis for today's agreement.

Tempers Cooled—Then the Fight Was On Again

Tempers cooled. Then in 1954 the Duck Lake Dyking District applied for an additional 1,500 acres of marshland—and the fight was on again. Mickey McEwen had led the battle to save the marsh for more than a decade and was wearing down. McEwen asked Frank Shannon, a geologist at the nearby Bluebell Mine, to head the Duck Lake preservation fight. Shannon accepted the challenge, beginning a battle that would consume him too, for more than a decade.

Six more years passed. The Creston Wildlife Management Area was delineated by the BC Wildlife Federation and the West Kootenay Association of Rod and Gun Clubs when they jointly applied to purchase all Crown lands surrounding Duck Lake for wildlife conservation. Although their offer was rejected, their concerted lobbying continued through numerous hearings, studies and surveys before the Creston Valley Wildlife Management Act was passed in March, 1968.

"We all breathed a sigh of relief," says Frank Shannon. "It was finally

Footbridge at Creston Valley Wildlife Management Area. © Murphy Shewchuk

Painted Turtle at Creston Valley Wildlife Management Area. © Murphy Shewchuk

over after 26 years. Through those years there were many people who worked hard and long to make this become a reality."

A few years after the act was passed, Frank Shannon retired from his job at the Bluebell and moved to Summerland in BC's south Okanagan Valley. His retirement from the Creston arena was somewhat short-lived, though. In January, 1978, at the age of 67 years, he was pressed back into action as the public representative on the Creston Valley Wildlife Management Authority (CVWMA), a post he held for nearly a decade more.

The Drainage Dikes Were Converted To Enhance Wildlife Habitat

The formal creation of the wildlife management area in 1968 was the end of the war to save the marsh and the beginning of major efforts to turn the flood plain into productive wildlife and waterfowl habitat.

With almost 17,000 acres (7,000 hectares) of priceless wetlands under their protection, the CVWMA faced a monumental task. The continuing support of Ducks Unlimited, BC Hydro, Terasen Gas, local and regional wildlife groups and various federal, provincial and local government grants has made the task a little easier. The dikes that were intended to drain the marshes have been expanded and modified to control the wide seasonal variations in water levels

Cedar Waxwing at Creston Valley Wildlife Management Area. © Murphy Shewchuk

and create much-needed nesting and brood rearing habitat.

Not Just Ducks

Duck Lake, the focal point of much of the battle to save the marsh, is not only home to waterfowl. A whole range of animal life forms from leopard frogs and western painted turtles, to fish; to playful river otters and majestic elk make the lake home. In fact, where some once visualized cultivated land, a significant bass recreational fishery has developed, attracting fishers from western Canada and the US with catches occasionally reaching four kilograms.

The Creston Valley Wildlife Management Area is home to over 265 bird species, 50 mammal species, 30 fish, reptile and amphibian species, plus thousands of invertebrate and plant species. The Valley is a migration corridor for Tundra Swans, Greater White-fronted Geese, and other waterfowl and is the largest regional locale for wintering birds of prey in the interior of the Province. In British Columbia the Creston Valley Wildlife Management Area is considered second only to the coast as a flyway route for numbers of migrating waterfowl that follow it twice yearly.

People Benefit, too!

While the prime focus is the development and maintenance of wildlife habitat, this could not be sustained without considerable long-term public support. To maintain that support, the CVWMA has a continuing public education role that has attracted international attention.

The Creston Valley interpretive centre was constructed and recently renovated to serve as an introduction to the marsh. Renovations included steel support beams, roof extensions and a wheelchair friendly walkway. The centre is usually open Tuesday to Saturday from mid-May to mid-October. Guided canoe tours are offered from the centre during the summer months. There is also a 20-minute boardwalk loop trail that includes two viewing towers; one three-stories high.

For the serious naturalist, birdwatcher or hiker, the 32 km of dikes that control the marsh also serve as trails that are open year around and can occupy visitors for hours, days or weeks. Up-to-date hours of operation, plus various maps and publications are available at the interpretive centre or online at http:// www.crestonwildlife.ca/ .

The financial spinoff to the Creston Valley may be difficult to measure, but is surely significant. As part of the International Selkirk Loop and the Two Nation Birding Vacation, a birding and ecotourism experience, the CVWMA is a major destination and attraction for people traveling through southeastern BC. The centre hosts numerous special events, workshops and conferences which also bring visitors to the valley.

International Recognition

The Creston Valley Wildlife Management Area (CVWMA) was the first and is now the second largest wildlife management area in the Province of British Columbia. It's area averages 20-km-long by 3.4 km wide and consists of one 1,500 ha lake and 17 marshes, plus a section of the Kootenay River and adjoining mountain slopes.

Because of the site's importance, it was designated in 1994 as an internationally significant wetland (Ramsar Site). The CVWMA was also recognized by Birdlife International as an Important Bird Area (IBA) because it regularly supports over 100,000 water birds during migration periods. Single day concentrations are spectacular, occasionally exceeding 40,000 individuals. As well, the CVWMA has been designated an Important Amphibian and Reptile Area (IMPARA) in Canada by the Canadian Amphibian and Reptile Conservation Network.

Cattle and rainbow at Creston Valley Wildlife Management Area. © Murphy Shewchuk

The CVWMA was chosen as a 2009 Rand McNally Best of the Road Editor's Pick and featured in the 2009 Rand McNally Road Atlas.

Getting There

At 1.2 km, the section of West Creston Road to the red-roofed CVWMA interpretive centre is probably the shortest "backroad" I've covered in this book. West Creston Road heads south off Highway 3 about 8.2 km west of the junction of Highway 3 and 3A or about 10 km west of downtown Creston.

If you are travelling from the west, West Creston Road is the first major junction when you enter the Kootenay River valley approximately 34 km east of the Kootenay Pass Stagleap Summit.

Additional Information:
Creston Valley Wildlife Management Area
PO Box 640
Creston, BC V0B 1G0
Administration: (250) 402-6900
Wildlife Centre: (250) 402 6908
Wildlife Interpretation Centre
1760 West Creston Rd
West Creston, BC
Web: http://www.crestonwildlife.ca/

RAMSAR?
Named after the Iranian city of Ramsar where the Convention was signed in 1971, the Ramsar Convention on Wetlands of International Importance is an international treaty geared toward the conservation and protection of wetlands around the world. The List of Wetlands of International Importance as of 2018 include 2,306 Ramsar Sites that comprise over 2.1 million square kilometres (810,000 sq mi).

Cyclist on Kimberley–Cranbrook Trail. © Murphy Shewchuk

CHAPTER 10
Kimberley, Cranbrook, Fernie & Area Trails
Rail Trails & Greenways

STATISTICS

For map, see page 144.

Distance: 28 km: Kimberley to Cranbrook Rails to Trails. 43.4 km: Cranbrook to Wardner Destination Trail.

150 km: Wardner to Round Prairie, north of Elkford.

Travel Times: Variable.

Conditions: Variable: gravel roads and trails, paved trails and city streets.

Season: Primarily summer with X-C skiing and snowshoeing in winter.

Elev. Gain: Variable—see text for details.

Map: British Columbia Highway Map.

Backroad Mapbook: Kootenay Rockies BC.

Communities: Kimberley, Cranbrook, Wardner, Elko, Fernie, Sparwood and Elkford.

The Kimberley-Cranbrook trail is a paved rail trail while the Chief Isadore Trail, formerly Cranbrook to Wardner Trail is one of BC's longest greenway trails with a mixture of old rail beds, backroads and newly built trail. At the time of writing, both trails are part of the BC portion of the Trans Canada Trail (a.k.a. The Great Trail) route through the East Kootenay region. The route from Wardner to Elkford follows a network of forest roads, new recreation trails and heritage trails. North of Elkford, the route starts off as a recreation trail, but then continues as the forest road to Elk Lakes Park and the Alberta Border.

Silver, Lead and Zinc

Galena ore has been instrumental in the early development of many

Kootenay communities from mines of the Silvery Slocan to the Mighty Sullivan. The North Star Mine near Kimberley, discovered in 1892, is one of the properties that brought the area to prominence. The story is that Joe Bourgeois, a mine-finder of note, met a group of Native Americans, on a huckleberry picking outing. One woman reported picking up some heavy, bright stones. Bourgeois followed the woman's directions to rich mineral ledge and staked the first North Star claims.

Shortly after the news of the rich discoveries got out, a party of four prospectors explored farther afield and discovered the ore body that was to become the basis for the Sullivan Mine.

To keep the story short, the rich deposit helped spur the development of sternwheel steamer traffic and railways to carry the ore to smelters, initially in Great Falls, Montana, but later in Nelson and Trail. It also prompted the development of Kimberley as a major mining community, and later, as a fertilizer supplier.

Betty Oliver has lots more information on the Kimberley Keepers website at http://kimberleykeepers.ca/ .

North Star Rails to Trails

The foundation of the present trail was a CPR spur line running from Cranbrook to the North Star and Sullivan mines. It was built in 1899 and transported millions of tons of lead and zinc ore to the smelters before the mines closed in 2001.

The rail spur was no longer used after the closing of the mine. Local residents with vision successfully lobbied to obtain the property. Construction of the North Star Rails to Trails began in the spring of 2009 and opened in the fall of 2010. The trail winds generally southeast through Marysville and Wycliffe to Cranbrook. The Cranbrook trailhead is off Collinson Road, northwest of the junction of Highways 95A and 3/95. The Kimberley trailhead is near the Aquatic Centre and the junction of Archibald Street and Rotary Drive.

The average cyclist can ride from one end to the other in less than two hours. Given it's an old railroad line, the grade is typically less than three percent.

Fernie Trans Canada Trail Pavilion unveiling in 2005. © Murphy Shewchuk

The trail is used by cyclists, runners, walkers, and those on roller blades. Motorized vehicles and horses are not permitted. The season starts once the snow has cleared which is typically mid-April. Users may encounter patches of snow in the shady sections early in the season.

The City of Kimberley plows half of the trail during winter within city limits—approximately eight km. The other half is self-tracked and is left for X-C skiers to use. The trail is very popular with thousands of users every year.

There are detailed maps of the trail and the various trailheads and accesses on the North Star Rails to Trails website at http://www.northstarrailtrail.com/.

Cranbrook to Wardner Destination Trail

The 43.4 km "Chief Isadore Trail" as it became known at the official opening in 2017, is broken down into 11 components. Rail trail sections, new trail sections, legacy Cranbrook sections, short road sections, a trail in Highway 3 right-of-way section and abandoned road sections designated as trail. It is considered to be a hybrid gravel trail; half rail trail; half 1.2 metre wide single track.

The Cranbrook trailhead is at the City of Cranbrook Visitor Centre. From there it is a short ride to the Isadore Canyon trailhead. The Isadore Canyon Rail Trail is roughly 13 km long. The Mayook Trail climbs southwest and then continues southeast to bypass private property. There are access points at Pritchard Road and Ha Ha Road. From Ha Ha Road the trail runs south of Crowsnest Highway 3/93 before using the Wardner Rail Trail and the highway right-of-way. It leaves the highway right-of-way and follows parts of Wardner Road to the southern terminus at Wardner Community Park. There are trail access points at Tokay Hills Forest Service Road and Wardner Road.

Each section has discreet references and GPS information on the Trailforks website. There is also usually up-to-date information posted on the Chief Isadore Trail Facebook page as well as updates on their website.

Fernie Trail Alliance

The Elk Valley Community Trail is a work in progress, but at the time of writing significant progress had been made between Elko and Round Prairie, just north of Elkford. The "trail" utilizes utility access roads, forest roads and specially built trail sections.

Numerous communities and community groups are involved in the work as well as the Nature Conservancy of Canada and private landowners. A cooperative community partnership with the District of Elkford, District of Sparwood, and the Fernie Trails Alliance was established to support the construction of the 150 km trail.

The Elk Valley Community Trail

Extending from Round Prairie north of Elkford to Elko in the south, the trail has connected the local trail networks with some of the missing links to create this continuous route through the Rocky Mountains.

In Elkford, eight km of new trail has been built to the north, so travelers can enjoy the "Mountain Walk" on the route to Elk Pass on the BC Alberta border. To the south, the Sulphur Springs Trail has a new 12-km section, joining up low traffic forestry roads to Line Creek.

The Sparwood section begins at Line Creek, where the route follows the Lower Elk Valley Road, before departing onto an open meadow trail along the Elk River for three km. It meets up with Wilson Creek, and then the trail further extends onto Sparwood's Cypress Trail. Here pedestrian/cycle crossings of the Elk River and the CPR tracks are provided by the Iron Rails Bridges.

The trail continues through Sparwood and under Crowsnest Highway 3, where new trail has been constructed around the Golf Course and Mountain Shadows Campground. The original 32-km Coal Discovery Trail between Sparwood and Fernie has had major enhancements to grades, bridges and signage as part of the project. This trail section passes through the historic Hosmer mining ruins, where old coke ovens and other mine workings can be observed and appreciated.

Arriving in Fernie, the Elk Valley Trail descends into town to join the existing community trails, and leads to the Aquatic Centre Trail Hub, adjacent to the historical downtown, where supply restocking and accommodation can be found.

South of Fernie, the route follows the Coal Creek Heritage Trail to where it crosses Coal Creek. Twenty-five km of quality single track ascends to panoramic viewpoints, lush creek crossings, and meandering mountainside magnificence. The remainder of the route to Elko primarily follows forestry roads from Cokato to Silver Springs Lakes. The Trans Canada Trail continues to where it joins the Cranbrook to Wardner Destination Trail.

The Elk Valley Trail network provides the missing link between the Trans Canada Trail's High Rockies Trail in Alberta's Kananaskis Country and Wardner near the Kootenay River.

Mount Fox on the BC-Alberta Border near Elk Lakes Park.© Murphy Shewchuk

See the "Elk River Forest Service Road" chapter for information on the route from Elkford to Elk Lakes Park and Elk Pass.

❧

Acknowledgements:

Special thanks to Chris Newel–North Star Rails to Trail; Al Skucas–Trails, BC Rockies Region and Terry Nelson–Fernie Trails Alliance for supplying the material for this chapter.

❧

Additional Information:

Chief Isadore Trail

Web: http://c2wtrail.ca/ (Under construction at the time of writing.)
Facebook: https://www.facebook.com/Cranbrook-to-Wardner-Destination-Trail-1502088490009857/

Fernie Trails Alliance

Web: http://www.fernietrailsalliance.com/
Facebook: https://www.facebook.com/Fernie-Trails-Alliance-136085899841404/

NorthStar Rails 2 Trails

PO Box 122,
Kimberley BC V1A 2Y5
Email: northstarrailtrail@gmail.com
Web: http://www.northstarrailtrail.com/
Facebook: https://www.facebook.com/NorthStarRails2Trails

Trails Society of British Columbia (Trails BC)

1247 Charter Hill Drive
Coquitlam BC V3E 1P1
Email: trailsbc@trailsbc.ca
Web: http://www.trailsbc.ca/

Cranbrook to Wardner Trail

Web: http://www.trailsbc.ca/tct/east-kootenay/cranbrook-wardner
Facebook: https://www.facebook.com/Chief-Isadore-Trail-1502088490009857/

Trailforks

Web: https://www.trailforks.com/

Elk River Sunrise near Elk Lake Provincial Park, north of Elkford, BC. © Murphy Shewchuk

CHAPTER 11

Elk River Forest Service Road: Trails, Lakes and Mountain Peaks

STATISTICS

For map, see page 152.

Distance: 34 km, Sparwood to Elkford.
69 km, Elkford to Elk Lakes Park

Travel Time: Two to three hours.

Elev. Gain: Approximately 585 metres.

Condition: Gravel road with some rough sections

Season: May be closed in winter, slippery when wet.

Topo Maps: Crowsnest, BC 82 G/10 (1:50,000)   Tornado Mountain, BC 82 G/15
Fording River, BC 82 J/2
Mount Head, BC 82 J/7
Mount Rae, BC 82 J/10
Kananaskis Lakes, AB 82 J/11

Backroads Mapbook: Kootenay Rockies BC

Communities: Sparwood and Elkford.

If you are interested in getting up in the world or looking for a cool retreat on a hot August day, the Elk River Forest Service Road in the Rockies north of Sparwood and Elkford could be an excellent place to start. Add the scenic beauty of Elk Lakes Provincial Park; an opportunity to camp at half a dozen rec sites; and a chance to pedal your bike or hike along the Trans Canada Trail or Great Divide Trail and you could be gone a week or more.

Terex Titan

The starting point of the backroad into the Rockies is on Crowsnest Highway 3 at Sparwood, about 20 km west of the BC Alberta border and

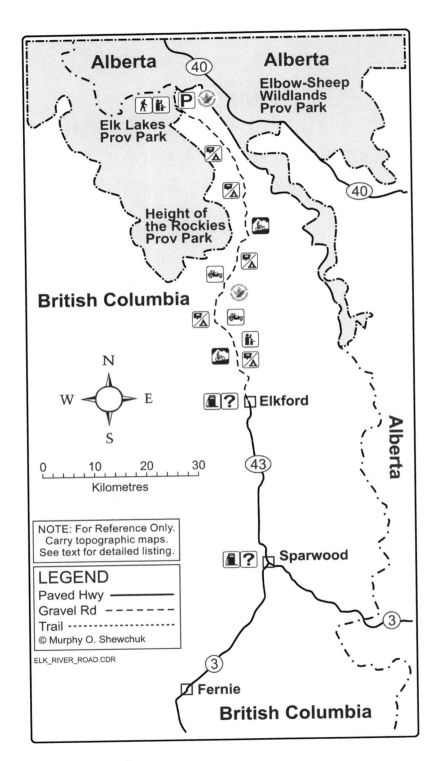

Alberta

⑩40

Alberta

Elbow-Sheep
Wildlands
Prov Park

⑩40

Elk Lakes
Prov Park

Height of
the Rockies
Prov Park

British Columbia

N
W — E
S

Alberta

Elkford

0   10   20   30
Kilometres

⑬43

NOTE: For Reference Only.
Carry topographic maps.
See text for detailed listing.

LEGEND
Paved Hwy ———
Gravel Rd – – – –
Trail ·················
© Murphy O. Shewchuk

ELK_RIVER_ROAD.CDR

Sparwood

③3

Fernie

British Columbia

Lower Elk Lake with Mount Elkan near the center. © Murphy Shewchuk

Crowsnest Pass. Highway 43 heads north a few hundred metres east of the Sparwood Info Centre and the giant Terex Titan haul truck.

This huge ore truck certainly gives credence to the chorus line "Give me forty acres and I'll turn this rig around" in the Willis Brothers popular 1964 song (Earl Green / John William Greene). Only one Terex 33-19 "Titan" was ever produced by General Motors. It first went into service in California in 1975 and took up duties at Sparwood in 1978. While in active service it regularly hauled loads exceeding 350 short tons (320 tonnes). The Titan was retired in 1993 and after restoration it sits on display just off Highway 3 in Sparwood.

Foothills Prairie

Highway 43 crosses the Elk River on the outskirts of Sparwood and then heads north on what is the BC version of a foothills prairie. Grain fields and farms mark a sharp contrast to what you see on the approach from Fernie or Crowsnest Pass. The broad prairie narrows as you get closer to Elkford. The last stop for fuel and supplies is on the north side of Elkford about 35 km from Highway 3. There is also a well-stocked Information Centre in Elkford with maps and local history material.

At an elevation of 1,300 metres or 4,265 feet above sea level, Elkford

Upper Elk Lake Panorama with Mount Castelnnau and Mount Fox in background. © Murphy Shewchuk

claims to be BC's highest community. Pioneer Gold Mines in the Coast Range where I grew up in the 1950s would have given Elkford a run for the prize. Their Top Townsite was 1,280 metres (4,200 feet), but Pioneer is little more than a ghost town now.

Elk River Forest Service Road

Highway 43 ends near the junction of Alpine Way (left) and Fording Road (right) with service stations on either side. Elk River Forest Service Road takes over, continuing north across Boivin Creek and generally follows the west side of the Elk River upstream. Just to add a bit of confusion, the roadside markers appear to start at 100 at the Alpine Way/Fording Road junction. As it is tricky to reset your odometer to 100 km, I will consider this junction as Km 0 and make additional references where appropriate.

Krivensky Farm

The pavement soon gives way to a winding gravel road with a few potholes

and dusty sections. The older maps show a recreation site along the Elk River at Krivensky Farm, near Km 10. Although there were vehicles parked at both the north and south ends of a large green field when we visited in a recent August, the BC Sites and Trails website doesn't list it.

Coal Mines

Coal mining in the Elk Valley goes back at least a century and a viewpoint near Km 12 presents an opportunity to see the vastness of the operation. Teck's Greenhills mine produces approximately five million tonnes of steel-making coal annually. The Fording River operation, a little farther north and east, produces nearly double that amount.

The Blue Lake rec site sign near Km 21 marks a short diversion into a small treed two-campsite lake. At the time of writing, all of the recreation sites along the Elk River Forest Road were free, user maintained, and clean. Remember to bring your own toilet paper and pack out ALL your garbage.

Unless yours is an exceptional family, your mother isn't going to drop by to clean up after you.

Access Management
Signs and a map near Bingay Creek (Km 22) serve to advise travellers of vehicle restrictions in the Upper Elk Valley and Fording River drainages.

Forsyth Creek and Connor Lakes
A junction near Km 29 marks the route up Forsyth Creek to the rec site which serves as a staging area for the trail into Height of the Rockies Provincial Park and Connor Lakes. It is about six km to the park boundary and another five km to the Connor Lakes rec site.

Except for a few km near Elkford, the road as far as the 130 km marker was well maintained. It had been recently upgraded with gravel and crushed rock. Beyond this point it is wise to expect slippery sections and lots of potholes. Worth noting is that much of the road is one-lane and really not practical for a large motorhome or a large RV trailer.

Also worth noting is that cell phone reception can be spotty to this point and non-existent farther north.

Weary Creek
The Weary Creek Rec Site at Km 45.5 marks the crossing of the upper Elk River from west to east. The small treed rec site is on the river's edge near the 146 km marker if you are using these for reference.

Kananaskis Power Line and Great Divide Trail
The main road passes under the Kananaskis Power Line another km to the north. This 138 kilovolt line links TransAlta's Pocaterra hydroelectric plant in the Kananaskis Valley with Natal Substation near Sparwood. The 15 megawatt Pocaterra plant first went on stream in 1955 and served as a major power source for the Calgary area. As the load grew it was supplanted by larger hydro and coal-fired power plants.

The line initially served to supply the mines of the Elk Valley but as that load also grew, it has been relegated to a secondary intertie between the BC Hydro and TransAlta systems.

The Great Divide Trail is a rather circuitous route that runs from Kakwa Provincial Park in the north to Waterton in the south. The Great Divide Trail Association website (www.greatdividetrail.com) describes the trail as "wandering through the vast wilderness of the Canadian Rocky Mountains for more than 1200 km... It is not officially signed and not always even an actual trail, sometimes merely a wilderness route, inspiring modern-day adventurers to walk the same paths of the original explorers to the area.

Weary Creek Recreation Site Elk River near Elk River Forest Service Road north of Elkford , BC, Canada. © Murphy Shewchuk

A journey on the Great Divide Trail promises to be demanding but on the GDT you'll discover a definitive wilderness experience in one of the most magnificent settings on Earth."

The trail follows the Kananaskis Power Line north into the upper Elk Valley and continues along the forest road to the Elk Lakes before crossing over the divide into Alberta.

Important Junction

It is worth remembering your northward route at the powerline road junction. The route continuing north to Elk Lakes Park follows the powerline much of the way, but on your return trip you should keep to the right (west) at this junction or you could end way off course in the middle of the open-pit coal mines.

Horses on Road

This is no road for speeding at the best of times, but just to add to the complications, watch for horses on the road in the neighbourhood of the Elk Valley Bighorn Outfitters base camp near Km 52.

Riverside recreation site near Km 57 (157 on the roadside markers) is another small sheltered spot for a break. Tobermory Creek Rec Site five km farther north (Km 62) has several tables alongside the road and in the cleared right-of-way, and a cabin that could serve as a welcome shelter for self-propelled travellers.

Upper Elk River

Upper Elk River recreation site (Km 63.5) has served as our base for hikes into the park. The tables back on a relatively open lodgepole pine forest with the meadows to the north providing unobstructed views the Elk River and Mount Aosta. Trails through the forest lead to the outhouse and several oxbows in the river.

I suspect that kids would love to explore the trails, but if you bring them camping here, be prepared for warm days and cool nights. At an elevation of 1,700 metres (5,580 feet) you can expect frost any time of the year. (In an early August visit, the daytime high was about +25°C, but it dropped down to 0°C at night, while a few days later we were driving through Kelowna at +40°C.)

Elk Lakes Provincial Park

For the motorized user, Elk River Forest Service Road ends at the Elk Lakes Provincial Park parking lot at Km 68.3 and an elevation of 1725 metres. A gated road to the right (north) just before the parking lot marks the continuation of the powerline route through Elk Pass.

Elk Lakes Park and neighboring Height of the Rockies Park protect 71,532 hectares of mountain wilderness located along the Great Divide on the British Columbia-Alberta boundary. These BC parks border on Banff National Park and Peter Lougheed Provincial Park to the north in Alberta. Important features include 26 peaks over 3,000 metres, over 60 alpine and subalpine lakes, 25 glaciers, extensive alpine meadow areas, valley bottom meadows, and several old growth stands.

Easy Hikes

While there isn't a vehicle campsite at the park and motorized vehicles aren't permitted on the trails, there, is an easy 1.2 km walk to Lower Elk Lake with a backpackers campground at the lake. It is roughly 1.3 km farther to Upper Elk Lake.

Check the BC Parks website for up-to-date information and maps for this and the numerous other trails in the park.

The terrain surrounding Lower and Upper Elk Lakes has been

Elk River Forest Service Road north of Elkford , BC, Canada. © Murphy Shewchuk

compared to the spectacular scenery of Lake O'Hara in Yoho National Park. To the south is 2,994 metre (9,823 foot) Mount Aosta and to the north is 2973 metre (9,754 foot) Mount Fox. To the west lie the massive Pétain, Castlenau and Elk glaciers and 2,760 metre (9,056 foot) Mount Elkan.

Many of the prominent features in the area were named after European World War I commanders and heroes. For example, Emanuele Filibertol (Duke of Aosta) was the commanding general of the Third Italian Army during WW I. Philippe Pétain was a WW I French General who reached the distinction of Marshal of France.

Elk Lakes Cabin

If you are looking for accommodations at the park, there is a cabin a few hundred metres from the parking lot that can be rented .The Elk Lakes cabin was built in 1992 to house BC Parks Rangers. In 2003, BC Parks issued a request for proposals for the operation of the cabin for public use. The Alpine Club of Canada (ACC) was awarded operation of the cabin as part of its extensive alpine hut system, and began operating it in the summer of 2004.

Alpine Club of Canada Cabin at Elk Lakes Provincial Park, BC, Canada. © Murphy Shewchuk

The cabin consists of a kitchen area and living room with tables and a wood burning stove. The sleeping quarters are in a loft above the main floor. The cabin sleeps up to 14 people on covered foam mattresses on bunks. Check with the Alpine Club for reservations and fees.

Return South

If you are driving a motor vehicle, you don't have much choice but to return to Elkford the way you came. If your transportation is "Shanks' mare" or a bicycle, you could continue over Elk Pass and into Alberta and points north or east. As Elk Pass is also the eastern terminal of BC's portion of the Trans Canada Trail, you could meander all the way to St. John's, Newfoundland and the Atlantic coast.

Additional Information

Alpine Club of Canada
201 Indian Flats Rd PO Box 8040 Stn Main
Canmore AB T1W 2T8
Tel: 403-678-3200
Email: info@alpineclubofcanada.ca
Web: http://www.alpineclubofcanada.ca/

Elk Lakes Provincial Park
Web: http://www.env.gov.bc.ca/bcparks/explore/parkpgs/elk_lk/
Elk Valley Bighorn Outfitters
Anna Fontana
Box 275,
Cranbrook, BC V1C 4H8
Tel: 250.426.5789
Email: fontanabighorn@telus.net

Great Divide Trail Association
http://www.greatdividetrail.com/
Recreation Sites and Trails BC
Web: http://www.sitesandtrailsbc.ca/

Autumn Reflections on Second Champion Lake. © Murphy Shewchuk

CHAPTER 12

Highway 3B-Nancy Greene Lake to Salmo: Snow, Gold and Colourful Communities

STATISTICS

For map, see page 164.

Distance: 81 km: Highway 3 at Nancy Greene Lake to Salmo.

Travel Time: One to two hours.

Condition: Paved highway and city streets.

Season: Year around.

Elev. Descent: 870 metres: Nancy Greene Lake to Trail.

Map: British Columbia Highway Map.

Backroad Mapbook: Kootenay Rockies BC.

Communities: Rossland, Warfield, Trail, Montrose & Fruitvale.

If you are heading east in a hurry, stay on Highway 3 east of Nancy Greene Lake junction. However, if you have time to spare, and a penchant for exploring old cities and towns, then consider taking Highway 3B south of Nancy Greene Lake and exploring a few of the Kootenay's oldest communities.

Red Mountain Ski Area

While the communities along Highway 3B are among the oldest in the Kootenays and in British Columbia, the Red Mountain ski area, 25 km south of the junction, can also share that claim to fame.

The extensive mineralization of the Rossland area was first discovered in the 1880s but it wasn't until 1890 that gold was discovered on the south slopes of an extinct volcano called "Red Mountain." These discoveries prompted a full scale rush into the area making the name "Rossland" synonymous with "bonanza." According to historian N.L. "Bill" Barlee, "between 1901 and 1916, fifty percent of the entire gold production of the

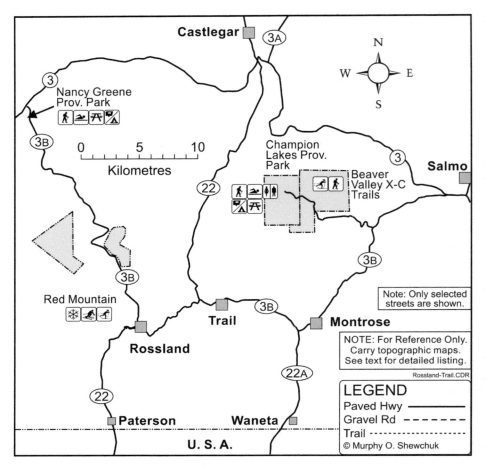

province came from the depths of the prolific mines of Red Mountain."

Gold seekers from around the area flocked to the area pushing the population of Rossland from a few hundred to over 7,000 making it the fourth largest city in British Columbia.

Among the miners seeking their fortune was a large contingency of Scandinavians who soon organized the Rossland Ski Club and held Canada's first recorded downhill ski race on February 15th, 1897. Olaus Jeldness, a Norwegian mining engineer and an avid skier, organized and won the first race. Jeldness supported future skiers by donating the Jeldness Trophy, now on display at the Rossland Museum and Discovery Centre.

While Red Mountain is famous for Olaus Jeldness, for many skiers it is probably better known as the training ground for Nancy Greene. Although born in Ottawa during World War II, her parents moved to Rossland after the war and she was skiing by the age of three. The slopes of Red Mountain

Downtown Rossland. © Murphy Shewchuk

must have been a good training ground for she won her first trophy in the Canadian Junior Championships in 1958.

In the following years Nancy Greene raced all over North America, Europe and South America, winning dozens of championship titles including her first Olympic Gold Medal in the giant slalom in 1968. Her racing feats and ski history would take pages, but recent;y-retired Senator Nancy Greene Raine and her husband Al Raine now live at Sun Peaks Resort near Kamloops.

Red Mountain has changed a lot since Olaus Jeldness started skiing there. For those interested in details, the Resort covers 1,700 hectares (4,200 acres) with vertical drop of 890 metres (2,919 feet). With 110 runs, seven lifts and an average snowfall of 760 cm (300 inches) there should be enough to keep you occupied. If you want more information on conditions or lodging, check out their website at http://www.redresort.com/ .

Le Roi Mine and Rossland Museum

A few minutes south of the main entrance to the Red Mountain Ski Area is the junction with Highway 22 south to the US boundary at Paterson. Also at the junction is the Rossland Museum & Discovery Centre. One of the main exhibits is the Le Roi mine where underground tours were offered until 2009

Father Pat Memorial in Downtown Rossland. © Murphy Shewchuk

when they were discontinued for safety reasons. The museum is normally open in the afternoon Wednesday to Saturday with extended hours during the summer months. Visit their website at http://www.rosslandmuseum.ca/ for up-to-date information.

Much of the Kootenay history centres around mining and the fortunes made and lost in these precarious and often dangerous ventures. The Le Roi mine is no exception. The first claims were staked in the area in 1887. Claims that included the Le Roi were staked in the summer of 1890. One story suggests that the Le Roi claim was given to mining recorder Col. Topping in lieu of a $12.50 mining fee. The Le Roi went on to produce almost $30 million during its lifetime.

Rossland Lions Community Campground
If you are looking for a place to camp, the Rossland Lions Community Campground, a few minutes south of the junction, is Rossland's only campground. It has 18 RV sites, many equipped with power, water and sewer. Add clean, spacious washroom facilities and a nearby ball park and several cycling trails and you will understand why it has been one of our favourite stops in the area. More information is available at http://www.rosslandlionscampground.com/ .

Rossland
Another km east of the junction and you are in the heart of downtown Rossland. As previously noted, its history was intertwined with the mines of the region, but in recent years the focus has shifted to tourism. With numerous old railway beds, mining trails and whiskey running routes, Rossland adds mountain biking to its repertoire. If you are looking for something a bit more challenging than skiing or biking, you could try ridge running. On the other hand, golfing can be challenging enough on the mountainside fairways.

The downtown has proven to be irresistible on our trips through the area. Restaurants, boutiques and bike shops have all parted us from our cash. But it must have been an amicable parting, because we keep going back.

Add the numerous photo-ops that the stately old buildings offer; the opportunity to taste-test the output from the local Rossland Beer Company or the nearby Columbia Gardens Vineyard and Winery and you could be around for a lot more than a day.

Warfield
Highway 3B from Nancy Greene Lake to Trail is no place for big rigs with weak brakes. And the Rossland hill downhill run to Warfield is no exception.

The village history is also closely linked to the mining and smelting in the region. The Consolidated Mining & Smelting Company (CM&S)

Trans Canada Trail marker in Trail, BC.
© Murphy Shewchuk

has been a mainstay of the community since the 1930s. Here, too, the unique architecture offers photographic opportunities.

If you are looking for services there is a hotel and a gas station on Schofield Highway (3B).

Trail

It is another five km down the hill to the Columbia River and the heart of the City of Trail. With a population of roughly 9,000 it is smaller than Nelson, but on a par with Castlegar. Like many of the Kootenay communities, its history goes back to the 1890s and the discovery of rich mineral deposits in the region. In the case of Trail, the rich deposits near Rossland prompted the Le Roi Mining & Smelting Company to enlist the aid of American promoter Fredrick Augustus Heinze. Heinze built the first smelter at Trail (Canadian Smelting Works) and also obtained railway charters.

In 1898, Heinze sold his interests to the British Columbia Southern Railway, a Canadian Pacific Railway (CPR) subsidiary. The smelter company later became known as Consolidated Mining and Smelting Company of Canada, Limited, which was renamed Cominco Ltd. in 1966. Over the next few decades CM&S expanded operations including acquiring the Sullivan Mine at Kimberley. Teck became involved with Cominco in 1986. Teck Cominco changed its name to Teck Resources Ltd. in 2009.

If you are looking for services or lodging, Trail offers the widest selection along Highway 3B. Mixed in with early 1900s architecture are more modern facilities. Worth visiting are the Trail Museum and the Sports Hall of Memories located at the Trail Memorial Centre at 1051 Victoria Street.

While Red Mountain had its skiers, Trail had the Smoke Eaters junior and senior hockey teams. The teams were formed in the 1920s and won

Columbia River south of Trail. BC. © Murphy Shewchuk

Allan Cup and World Championships during their illustrious history. The Smoke Eaters continue today as a Junior A team.

Montrose and Fruitvale

After crossing the Columbia River at Trail, Highway 3B continues eastward along the north bank of the river before climbing out of the valley on the way to the Village of Montrose. The community was initially established as a housing community in the Beaver Valley.

Fruitvale, another five km to the east, started off in 1907 as a land promotion with 10 acre fruit ranches. The rich Beaver Valley soil attracted some 200 families and the community grew with a sawmill, blacksmith's shop, stores and a school. However, somewhat like the history of Walhachin, west of Kamloops, the climate wasn't cooperative and the orchard growth slowed. The community didn't die, but instead adapted to the challenge and has continued to serve the residents of the area as a bedroom community of approximately 2,000 people.

Champion Lakes Park

Six km northeast of Fruitvale is the junction to Champion Lakes Provincial Park. Located 12 km northwest of the highway, it is open from mid-May to

Nancy Greene Lake. © Murphy Shewchuk

October 1st. The 1452 hectare park has three lakes, multi-use trails and 95 campsites plus a day-use area. There are boat launch areas at the lakes with limited parking. BC Parks suggests that trailers or other equipment not be left overnight at the parking areas. Power boats are not allowed on any of the lakes.

The campground is a series of loops on the benchland between Second and Third Champion Lake. The road ends near the north end of the Second Lake. On a late-September trip to the park we camped at the north end of the campground overlooking the second lake. While the park is busy during the summer months, we had most of it to ourselves. The trails through the old growth forest provided photo opportunities for the autumn colour as well as a raucous Steller's jay. There are trails around Second Lake as well as along the east shore of First Champion Lake.

If you are interested in cross-country skiing, The Beaver Valley XC Ski Club maintains approximately 5 km of set trails within the park throughout the winter months. These trails connect with a further 10 km of trails outside of the park.

According to BC Parks, "In the early 1900s, the area belonged to The Columbia and Western Railway but reverted to the crown in 1919. During the 30s and 40s the local rod and gun club stocked the lakes and improved trails to allow access for recreational purposes. The park was established in 1955 and the lakes and creek are named for James W. Champion, an early settler and orchardist of the area. Champion Lakes Park lies in the Ktunaxa/Kinbasket, Okanagan and Sinixt first nation traditional territories."

Highway 3 Junction

Highway 3B ends at the junction with Highway 3, eight km east of Champion Park Road. It is decision time. You can go north and west to Castlegar or continue another 10 km east to Salmo where there are more amenities and a backroad (Highway 6) to Ymir and Nelson.

The 48-km Nelson Salmo Great Northern Trail follows an abandoned railway grade along much of the Highway 6 route. The trail is rough in places and subject to closure due to grizzly bear activity. There is more information on the Trails BC website at http://www.trailsbc.ca/tct/west-kootenay/spur-salmo .

See the Highway 3 chapters for more information on the remainder of the route to Alberta.

Downton Nelson. © Murphy Shewchuk

CHAPTER 13

Highway–3A–Castlegar-Nelson-Creston

STATISTICS

For map, see page 164.

Distance: 165 km: Highway 3 at Castlegar to Creston via Balfour.

Travel Time: Three to four hours plus Kootenay Lake Ferry.

Condition: Paved highway and city streets.

Season: Year around.

Elev. Gain: 135 metres.

Map: British Columbia Highway Map.

Backroad Mapbook: Kootenay Rockies BC.

Communities: Castlegar, Nelson, Balfour, Crawford Bay, Gray Creek & Creston.

If you are looking for a scenic drive that includes century-old cities, alpine trails, a free ferry and plenty of camping and photo opportunities, consider take Highway 3A from Castlegar to Creston via Nelson and the Kootenay Lake ferry. It will add at least 40 km and two hours to your trip PLUS whatever side trips you make. If you are easily distracted allow at least a day or two to make the trip.

Castlegar

Castlegar is the second largest city along Highway 3 in the Kootenays. It is also a good place to learn more about the Doukhobor people who settled here in the early 1900s. The Doukhobor Discovery Centre a few minutes north of the Highway 3A junction with Highway 3 could be a good place to start off your Kootenay heritage tour. The centre is a reconstruction of a typical Doukhobor village, as lived in 1908-1939, showing all of the major buildings, tools, handicrafts, and implements used at that time. Open seasonally from May 1st to September 30th.

I have touched on other aspects of the city in the *Crowsnest Highway 3:*

Part 2 chapter as well as the "Columbia & Western Railway Trail" chapter. While it is easily bypassed on Highway 3 or 3A, it is well worth a tour through the commercial district and the old downtown core.

Kootenay River

Highway 3A crosses the Kootenay River about three km north of the junction and stays on the north side for most of the way to Nelson. Keep a close eye on the river and you may catch a glimpse of the West Kootenay Power hydroelectric dams that harnessed the river for well over a century. The first of these, the Lower Bonnington Dam, was built in 1897 and upgraded in 1924 and 1964. The Upper Bonnington Dam was originally built in 1907 and also upgraded a couple more times. The Cora Linn Dam, about 15 km downstream from Nelson, was initially built in 1932 to increase storage capacity and generation.

The dams were initially built to supply electric power to the mines at Rossland and the Trail smelter. They also served the local communities as well as the Sullivan Mine at Kimberley.

BC Hydro also got into the local hydroelectric game with the Kootenay Canal Project. Completed in 1976, the canal is capable of generating 583 megawatts by diverting water from the Cora Linn reservoir and putting it through four turbines before discharging it back into the Kootenay River. In a massive case of reuse and recycle, this extra generation is made possible by the water storage created by the Duncan Dam north of Kootenay Lake (see the Kootenay Highway 31 chapter) and the Libby Dam on the Kootenay River in the USA.

Nelson

Film director Fred Schepisi recognized Nelson's unique heritage when he brought in Steve Martin, Daryl Hannah and the crew for the filming of *Roxanne* in 1986. With the popularity of the movie, the rest of North America quickly became aware of the jewel that Nelsonites had worked long and hard to polish.

Nelson, the "Queen City of the Kootenays," is built on a mountainside in southeastern BC's Selkirk range. And like its street system, Nelson's economy has had more than its fair share of ups and downs.

Nelson's history began with the gold rush of the 1860s, but the prospectors had nearly all left when immensely rich silver-lead-zinc deposits were discovered in the nearby Selkirk Mountains. Nelson's strategic location made it an ideal terminal for rail and sternwheel shipping and the community quickly grew into a major centre.

Downton Nelson. © Murphy Shewchuk

Hugh Nelson

Contrary to many a visitor's first guess, Nelson's namesake was not Lord Nelson of British Admiralty fame, but Hugh Nelson, a Goldrush businessman who played an important role in British Columbia's entrance into Canadian confederation. Nelson was the delegate from Burrard Inlet at the historic 1868 Yale Convention that called for BC's immediate union with Canada.

John "Truth" Houston

A monument on the corner of Vernon and Ward Streets memorializes Nelson's doughty, flamboyant first mayor. John Houston was a figure of controversy, but to many old-timers he was the founding genius of the city. As the forthright editor of the city's first newspaper, the *Nelson Miner* and later, the *Nelson Tribune*, in 1897 he boldly urged the straggling mining camp to incorporate. According to a rival newsman, Colonel R.T. Lowery, Houston galvanized into action a population made up of "mule skinners, packers, trail blazers, remittance men and promoters with a slight trace of tenderfeet."

Houston went on to win the election and held the office in 1897, 1898, 1900 and 1905. In addition to making his mark in Nelson, Houston Lane in Prince George, and the town of Houston in northern BC are named after him.

Heritage Capital

Despite its small size, Nelson is a veritable historical storehouse. More than 350 turn-of-the-century buildings make Nelson second only to Victoria and Vancouver for architectural treasures. Nelson's isolation from the rest of Canada and its nearness to Spokane meant that the early architecture had an American influence more typical of San Francisco, Seattle and Spokane than Upper Canada. A notable exception is the Nelson Court House on Ward Street. This impressive stone structure was designed by Francis Mawson (F.M.) Rattenbury, the architect who is famous for BC's Parliament Buildings and the Empress Hotel in Victoria.

It was this concentration of heritage buildings that impressed Fred Schipisi and the crew of *Roxanne*. And it was the release of the film that drew visitors and reinforced Nelson's determination to become a vibrant, diverse community.

Plan to Stop

Highway 3A follows much of Front Street through downtown Nelson, The Visitor Information Centre is just south of the highway as are many of the architectural treasures. You may be able to pick up a heritage walking tour pamphlet there to help you identify the magnificent buildings.

While you are toting your camera around the downtown, the rest of the family may want to visit Chahko Mika Mall or ride the Nelson Electric Tramway along the waterfront. Streetcar #23 is a fully functional streetcar that was used in Nelson in the first half of the 20th century. It usually operates seven days a week from mid-May to Thanksgiving.

Nelson's Big Orange Bridge

The West Arm Bridge at Nelson was officially opened on November 7th, 1957 by Premier W.A.C. Bennett and Highways Minister P.A. Gaglardi flanked by numerous dignitaries and serenaded by pipers and drummers of the Kootenay Kiltie Band. It replaced a ferry that had long been outstripped by the local and inter-provincial traffic. The bridge is also your only way to continue east on Highway 3A.

Kokanee Creek Provincial Park

Highway 3A follows a winding route along the north shore of Kootenay Lake, flanked on both sides by stately homes and lakeshore cabins. Don't expect to make time along this route.

Kokanee Creek Provincial Park, 20 km northeast of downtown Nelson,

West Arm bridge Nelson. © Murphy Shewchuk

is the first major stop along the way to the Kootenay Lake Ferry slip at Balfour. At 260 hectares, it isn't a big park but what it lacks in size it makes up for in lakeside diversity with over a km of beach and 170 campsites in three vehicle access campgrounds. The campsites are generally in the trees with a variety of trails that access the beach or meander along Kokanee Creek where the spawning land-locked salmon can often be seen from August to October.

Kokanee Glacier Provincial Park Road

Half a km east of the main entrance to Kokanee Creek Park is the entrance to a steep, rough gravel road that could take you 16 km north to Gibson Lake and the start of the many trails in Kokanee Glacier Provincial Park. See the "Kokanee Glacier Provincial Park" chapter for more information.

Balfour Ferry Terminal

It is another dozen km east to the Balfour Ferry Terminal and the Kootenay Lake Ferry. At the time of writing there was talk about moving the terminal to reduce congestion, in the meantime the eight-km, 35-minute trip is considered to be the longest free ferry ride in the world. The MV Osprey

BLUE BELL MINE

The orebody, known to Indians as a source of lead for musket balls, was staked in 1882 by Bob Sproule, later restaked by Tom Hamill. The resulting lawsuit cost Sproule the property, and in revenge he murdered his rival; was convicted and hanged. Development included a smelter and a townsite. This mine has the longest history in the province.

PROVINCE OF
BRITISH COLUMBIA
19 67

Blue Bell Mine stop-of-interest sign in Riondel. © Murphy Shewchuk

Osprey 2000 Ferry. © Murphy Shewchuk

2000 operates year around and the MV Balfour adds extra sailings in the summer months. Sailings are usually from 6:30 am to 10:20 pm with food services available on the MV Osprey 2000. Check current schedules for up-to-date information and BC Highways reports for delays during the busy summer months.

Riondel Road

The east terminal of the Kootenay Lake Ferry is at Kootenay Bay and Riondel Road is a bit over a km northeast of the ferry slip. The mining community that once was home to the famous Bluebell mine is 10 km farther north.

A stop of interest sign in the heart of the community indicates that the Bluebell Mine had a bit of a rocky start. In 1882 an American named Robert Sproule staked four claims at this location, including the Bluebell. When he left to register his claims, an Englishman, Thomas Hammill, re-staked the claims. Sproule lost the resulting dispute and in a fit of rage, shot Hammill. Sproule was convicted and hanged for the murder.

The Bluebell Mine operated from 1895 to 1929 when it shut down. The operation reopened in 1950 and continued to 1972. Since then the community has become a retirement centre. The Riondel Community Campground, located on the shore of Kootenay Lake, is operated by a non-

Tam O'Shanter Creek. © Murphy Shewchuk

profit society during the summer months. More information is available on their website at http://riondelcampground.ca/ .

Pebble Beach Recreation Site

If you are looking for a bit more privacy, there is a small walk-in or boat-in BC Recreation Site at Pebble Beach about five km north of Riondel. Take Riondel North Road to Tam O'Shanter Creek and continue north on Kootenay Lake Forest Service Road.

There is another larger recreation site a further five km north. The Bernard Beaches (Garland Bay South) rec site has road access and 18 campsites.

There is another rec site at Garland Bay with 22 campsites. Both sites are maintained with $12.00 camping fees during the summer months. Check the Recreation Sites and Trails BC website at http://www.sitesandtrailsbc.ca/ for more information on the access road.

Back on Highway 3A

Crawford Bay, another five km southeast is well worth a stop to explore and camp. This is an artisan community and the North Woven Broom Co., located in a historic log barn alongside the highway is hard to resist. Here you can get brooms woven from antique equipment using natural broom corn and handles made from a variety of wood. The ironwork comes from the Kootenay Forge, also here in Crawford Bay. It doesn't take much imagination to visualize a witch riding an untrimmed broom off into the midnight sky.

If you are looking for a place to spend the night, there are RV parks and chalets. The Kokanee Chalets RV Park backs on the woodland with a trail down to a marsh and the bay.

Gray Creek

After passing through the Crawford Bay community, Highway 3A follows the east shore of Crawford Bay and Kootenay Lake southward with the next potential stop and diversion being at Gray Creek.

No tour through the Kootenays is complete without a stop at the Gray Creek Store. In business since 1913, it has pretty well everything you might need to cover your butt, feed your face or build a roof over your head. Their motto "If we don't have it, you don't need it!" fits to a tee.

If you are interested in an 85 km scenic tour that could take you over Gray Creek Pass to Kimberley, the Gray Creek Store is an ideal place to stop for the latest information. If you want our perspective based on a number of trips on this "shortcut" to Kimberley, check out the "Gray Creek Road: Kootenay Lake to Kimberley" chapter.

Cliffside Views

Highway 3A continues south, sometimes dropping down to lake level and sometimes climbing well above the rocky points. If you find yourself being caught up in the southbound ferry traffic, find a spot to pull over and let the "madding" crowds go by. You will find the drive much more relaxing when you aren't blocking the way of those in a hurry.

Lockhart Creek Provincial Park

Located about 15 km south of Gray Creek and 40 km north of Creston, Lockhart Beach Provincial Park is one of the few public campgrounds along the south arm of Kootenay Lake. The 18 first-come, first-served campsites are located in the trees a short walk from the sandy beach. As with most BC Parks, self-sufficiency is the key to enjoyment and survival.

If you are interested in a longer hike, there is a well-maintained trail to the east along the north side of Lockhart Creek. On one autumn trip through the area we were pleasantly surprised to view Kokanee spawning in the creek.

Duck Lake

There are numerous viewpoints and potential stops between Lockhart Creek and Creston, but the last major detour is to explore Duck Lake and the marshes at the south end of Kootenay Lake. This is part of the Creston Valley Wildlife Management Area–see the "Ancient Valley of Ducks" chapter. Watch for Lower Wynndel Road to the west about eight km north of the junction with Highway 3. Follow it south for half a km and look for a tricky turn down the hill to the west. Then take Duck Lake Road west for another km.

After crossing the bridge over the channel, take Channel Road to the right (north) along the west side of the channel. It is about 7.5 km to Duck Lake and the narrow gravel road ends about 2.5 km later.

The road is gated near Duck Lake and the gate may be closed during the sensitive nesting season. Regardless, you could have some excellent opportunities to view and photograph the wildlife that call the rich marsh home.

Creston

With a town population of roughly 5,500 people, the available services seem to outweigh what the town might demand. However, Creston's location in an important agricultural area and on a major highway seems to support the diversity of stores and other facilities. Creston-based Columbia Brewery, home of world-famous Kokanee beer, has been supplying that broader market since 1959. Available throughout British Columbia for decades, Kokanee lager and Kootenay True Ale has recently reached as far east as Newfoundland and Labrador.

Creston's unique landmark is the pair of grain elevators on the western edge of downtown. Dating from the mid-1930s, they are said to have operated until the 1980s.

Creston is also decision time. Do you head east to the Rockies or west over Kootenay Pass to Salmo and Castlegar and complete a circle tour. The decision is yours, but don't forget to stop at the Creston Marsh.

Kokanee Lake in Kokanee Glacier Provincial Park. © Murphy Shewchuk

CHAPTER 14
Kokanee Glacier Provincial Park: Glaciers, Lakes and Wilderness

STATISTICS

For map, see page 186.

Distance: 16 km: Highway 3A to Gibson Lake Parking Area.

Travel Time: Approximately one hour.

Condition: Rough, steep gravel road not suitable for low clearance vehicles.

Season: Closed in winter.

Elev. Gain: 1,020 metres.

Backroad

Mapbook: Kootenay Rockies BC.

Map: British Columbia Highway Map.

Communities: Balfour and Nelson.

Thirty-two Thousand Hectares of Glaciers, Lakes and Wilderness

One of British Columbia's oldest mountain parks is accessible via a 16-km gravel road from Highway 3A, approximately 20 km northeast of downtown Nelson. It will take an all-wheel-drive SUV or truck to get you to the Gibson Lake parking area. (BC Parks strongly recommends against RVs.) But once you are there, you can lace up your hiking boots, shoulder your pack and enjoy the wilderness. The only limitations are the season and your abilities.

The BC Parks Kokanee Glacier Provincial Park website has a host of suggestions to make your drive up safe and your adventures in the park enjoyable. There is not any vehicle camping in the park—you will have to settle with Kokanee Creek Park at the foot of the road to the alpine. However, with 169 campsites, trails along the creek and access to Kootenay Lake beaches, it won't be tough to take. The alpine park does have

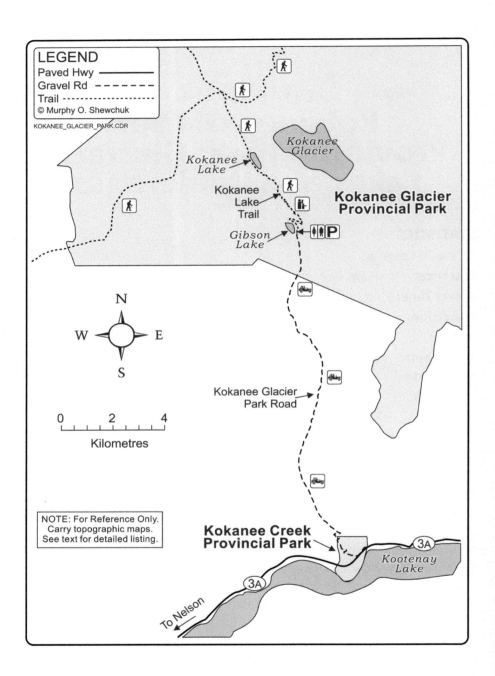

LEGEND
Paved Hwy ——————
Gravel Rd — — — —
Trail ·····················
© Murphy O. Shewchuk

KOKANEE_GLACIER_PARK.CDR

Kokanee
Glacier

Kokanee
Lake

Kokanee
Lake
Trail

**Kokanee Glacier
Provincial Park**

Gibson
Lake

N
W E
S

0   2   4
Kilometres

Kokanee Glacier
Park Road

NOTE: For Reference Only.
Carry topographic maps.
See text for detailed listing.

**Kokanee Creek
Provincial Park**

3A

Kootenay
Lake

3A

To Nelson

Hikers at Kokanee Lake in Kokanee Glacier Provincial Park. © Murphy Shewchuk

wilderness walk-in (or ski-in) campsites and a cabin at Kaslo Lake managed by the Alpine Club of Canada. There are fees for the wilderness campsites and the cabins. It is best to check with the BC Parks website for current details.

Summer Travel

With some of the glacier high points reaching 2,800 metres (9,200 feet) the mountains grab the moisture being carried eastward from the Arrow Lakes and Slocan Lake. The result is obvious—snow and ice in the alpine. And roads that can be impassable from October to July.

We bounced up the road to Gibson Lake and hiked the trail to Kokanee Lake one warm late September Sunday nearly a decade ago. The wildflowers were long past their prime and there was a dusting of snow on the alpine ridges, but the skies were beautifully clear and the fall colours fantastic.

The warm weather had brought out plenty of families to take the last excursion into the mountains before winter closed the road. Babies in backpacks bounced along the 4.5 km trail to Kokanee Lake. It is worth noting that the trail climbs over 412 metres before dropping down to the

Kokanee Lake in Kokanee Glacier Provincial Park. © Murphy Shewchuk

lake. (At two hours for the trip in, I was a little slower than most of the younger crowd—my excuse was I was stopping for photo-ops.)

The trail continues along the west side of Kokanee Lake and north past Keen and Garland Lakes to Kaslo Lake where there is a campsite and cabin.

Kaslo Lake appears to be the hub of a network of trails, some heading east to Kalma Lake where there is another cabin.

Additional Information

BC Parks Kokanee Creek Provincial Park

Web: http://www.env.gov.bc.ca/bcparks/explore/parkpgs/kokanee_crk/

Hikers on Kokanee Lake Trail in Kokanee Glacier Provincial Park. © Murphy Shewchuk

Climbing up Gray Creek Forest Service Road to Gray Creek Pass. © Murphy Shewchuk

CHAPTER 15

Gray Creek Road: Kootenay Lake to Kimberley

STATISTICS

For map, see page 192.

Distance: Approximately 85 km Highway 3A at Gray Creek to Highway 95A at Kimberley/Marysville.

Elev. Gain: Approximately 1,500 metres.

Travel Time: Three to four hours.

Condition: Mostly gravel, some steep and rough sections.

Season: July through October. Best in dry weather-closed in winter.

Topo Maps: Crawford Bay, BC 82 F/10. (1:50,000).

St. Mary Lake, BC 82 F/9.

Cranbrook, BC 82 G/12.

Backroad Mapbook: Kootenay Rockies BC.

Communities: Crawford Bay, Gray Creek, Marysville and Kimberley.

The Gray Creek Forest Service Road is a route of many descriptions.

In simple terms, it is a back-country shortcut from Kootenay Lake, near Crawford Bay, eastward over the Purcell Mountains to Marysville and Kimberley. The road is little more than 85 km long and approximately one quarter of that is paved.

Some compare it to the road from Anahim Lake to Bella Coola. I've travelled both in recent years, and I think the point is debatable. While the Bella Coola road has some frightening cliff-side hairpin turns and some steep grades, I think that Gray Creek Road has equally steep grades and sharp hairpin turns. The only difference, for what it's worth, is that if you miss a turn on the Gray Creek Road, you are more likely to end up in a huckleberry

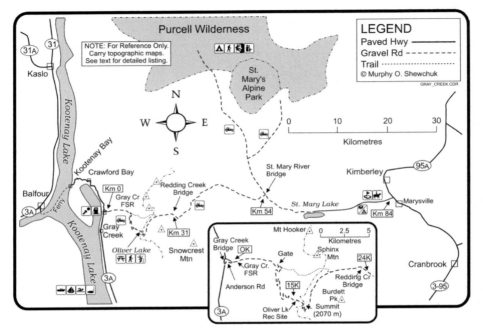

patch or snuggled up to a tree than sailing endlessly through the air. Little consolation for your vehicle, but probably more survivable for you.

Others describe the Gray Creek forest route as a scenic route—a western Canada getaway not to be missed. In fact, it is a recommended route in a German touring guidebook. The route's appeal is that it is a subalpine trip which reaches nearly 2,100 metres above sea level. What's more important is that some consider it to be true wilderness—tourists can travel nearly 80 km without seeing a house.

Something Old, Something New

Gray Creek, according to the Akriggs in *1001 British Columbia Place Names*, was named after John Hamilton Gray (1853-1941), a land surveyor and a son of the Hon. Mr. Justice John Hamilton Gray, one of the Fathers of Canadian Confederation.

While the current road over the ridge recently celebrated its 25th anniversary, Gray Creek Pass had not gone unnoticed prior to the construction in 1989, 1990 and 1991. During the peak of Kootenay mining and railway construction that filled the two decades surrounding the turn of the last century, this pass was considered for a railway route. In the mid-1890s, an extension of the British Columbia Southern Railway was proposed to bring coal from the rich ore bodies of the Crowsnest area to the smelter at

Oliver Lake at Gray Creek Pass. © Murphy Shewchuk

Pilot Bay, on Kootenay Lake. Built to serve the Blue Bell Mine at Galena Bay (now Riondel), the Pilot Bay Smelter was in desperate need of cheap coal and other supplies. The railway link over the Purcell Mountains was never completed and by 1900, the Pilot Bay Smelter had closed, never to re-open.

Powerline Route

The Blue Bell Mine was resurrected several more times before the ore finally ran out in 1971. It was during one of these rich periods in the late 1940s and early 1950s that Gray Creek Pass became the focus of attention.

The series of hydroelectric plants on the Kootenay River between Nelson and Castlegar were generating power for the smelter at Trail, but Kimberley also needed power for a new fertilizer plant. The high voltage power line over the Gray Creek Pass was constructed in 1950-51 by West Kootenay Power and Cominco.

While the prime load was at Kimberley, the line had a major impact on Kootenay Lake and several neighboring communities, including Riondel and Creston. Crossing Kootenay Lake was a monumental task. Three 1 1/4 inch diameter galvanized steel cables, each weighing 17 1/2 tons and 10,656 feet long, were hoisted into place in March, 1952. The span stretched from three towers on the bluff north of Coffee Creek across to a 366 foot tower on the east side of the lake, north of Kootenay Bay. At the time it was constructed, this was the longest water crossing in the world.

The $63 million project allowed the Blue Bell Mine at Riondel to shut down its diesel generators and go into full production. It also prompted the creation of the first road over the 6,100 foot (1,860 metre) Gray Creek Pass. The steep four-wheel-drive powerline road wasn't built for public traffic, but it was not long before lobbying started for a highway between Kootenay Lake and Kimberley. There were several promotional trips over the powerline road in the early 1960s, before the Salmo-Creston section of Highway 3 was opened.

New "Public" Road

Other highways superseded Gray Creek Pass, but the local promoters on both sides of the Purcell Mountains didn't give up. A new route was finally carved over the height-of-land in the late 1989 and 1990 and officially opened on July 1, 1991. It is about 16 km longer and it climbs about 200 metres higher than the right-of-way. Instead of going straight up and over the ridge, the road swings south, climbing slightly more gently to the summit via the south fork of Gray Creek and then descending via Baker Creek to Redding Creek.

Check your brakes

The access from Highway 3A is not well marked. If you are coming into the area from the Balfour-Kootenay Bay ferry, watch for the Gray Creek Store and Gray Creek Bridge about 13 km south of the Kootenay Bay terminal. You can reach the start of Gray Creek Pass Forest Service Road from Oliver Road on the north side of Gray Creek or Anderson Road on the south side of the creek. Anderson Road is probably a little less confusing, but the best suggestion is to check with the staff at the Gray Creek Store, about 300 metres north of the bridge. (This may also be a good location to top up the larder and the fuel tank and check your brake fluid.)

After about 1.2 km and a few switchback turns, you should reach a junction and the signs marking the start of the forest road over the mountain. It is, according to the signs, 88 km to Highway 95A at Marysville.

If you find yourself detouring into St. Mary's Alpine Park, you could easily double that distance before your next fuel stop.

The road to the summit defies description. Not because it is unusually bad, but because there is only so much that can be said about a grinding, first gear climb and dusty hairpin turns. You can let your engine cool off every once in a while by stopping to enjoy the view, the wildflowers or the

Katharine hiking on Oliver Lake Trail, Gray Creek Pass. © Murphy Shewchuk

huckleberries, depending on the season. On our trips we spotted deer and a Steller's Jay on the west side, and a Barred Owl near St. Mary Lake. If you prefer to bull your way through, there is a beautiful spot to stop for a rest or a hike just before the summit.

A Hidden Lake

The Oliver Lake Recreation Site deserves more than just a look. Oliver Lake, hidden in a hollow near 15K on the roadside markers, is named after George Oliver, a trapper who came to the Gray Creek area about 1906. He lived into his 90s, and many of his descendants are said to still live in the Gray Creek area.

Even if you are easily distracted by huckleberries, it's less than a five minute walk to the lake. If you are looking for that perfect spot to photograph the morning mist or capture reflections of the golden yellow subalpine larch, there is a well-built trail around the lake. It shouldn't take you more than twenty minutes to walk around this tarn—pack your camera and listen for the call of the pikas.

The camping area is basically an extra wide section of the road with a couple of tables and firepits, and an outhouse. There are no services and no charges–if you pack it in, you pack it out.

Although the weather and our schedule didn't permit any serious hiking on our most recent mid-September trip, there are hiking trails along the ridge that are definitely on our list for the next tour of Gray Creek Pass.

Steep Grades

The 16K marker coincides with the summit. One source said that several Greyhound buses from both sides met at this point to celebrate the official opening of the road. I'm not sure how much better the road was in 1991, but I certainly wouldn't recommend it for anything bigger than a truck and camper.

I checked my GPS altimeter—it read 2,066 metres (about 6,780 feet). Then I read the ominous yellow sign. "Steep grades to 14% over next 14 km.

Use lower gears. Excessive use of brakes may result in brake failure."

I soon discovered that, given the editorial opportunity, I would quickly change the word "lower" to "lowest". Semantics, maybe, but in this case it could mean survival.

Tempting Side Trips

Aside from the steep grade, loose fill and the occasional washout, the Gray Creek FS Road descent to Redding Creek should be uneventful.

North American Pika (Ochotona Princeps) in rock slide at Gray Creek Pass, British Columbia, Canada. © Murphy Shewchuk

(A relative recently made the trip and had to cut a windfall lying across the road. He was happy that he carried a chain saw.) The road begins to level off about 10 km from the summit and then it follows Redding Creek to the St. Mary River. Keep left at the junction with Redding Creek FS Road at the 24K marker. Turn right at the junction after crossing the St. Mary River (at the 40K marker or about 37 km from the summit). A left turn can take you up the St. Mary's River and into the Purcell Wilderness or St. Mary's Alpine Park.

The Purcell Wilderness Conservancy Park encompasses 202,709 hectares of rugged backcountry including six large drainages flowing east to the Columbia River system and three flowing west to Kootenay Lake; all of which rise in the glaciated backbone of the Purcell Mountain Range. BC Parks advises that visitors to the Purcells should be experienced, self-sufficient wilderness travellers capable of interpreting topographical maps and route-finding. Note that the use of vehicles, ATV's, snowmobiles, bicycles and helicopters to access the Park are prohibited.

St. Mary's Alpine Provincial Park is a 9,146-hectare wilderness paradise for the experienced backcountry traveller. It is also a non-motorized area except for the Forest Service and access roads. Visit the BC Parks website for detailed access and usage information.

If exploring the Purcell high country interests you, get Janice Strong's book, *Mountain Footsteps: Hikes in the East Kootenay of Southwestern British Columbia*, before you head for these hills. Suitable detailed maps, a compass (in case the GPS batteries go flat), alpine wilderness hiking equipment; and plenty of "bush sense" are also essential.

Civilization

It's a good gravel road for a dozen km to St. Mary Lake and then it's pavement the rest of the way to Highway 95A between Kimberley and Marysville. If you are looking for outdoor recreation a little less strenuous than the Purcell Wilderness, Kimberley Nature Park and the Alki Creek Hiking Trail is located north of St. Mary Lake.

If you are looking for a place to camp before heading into Kimberley (or after you've "done" the Platzl), consider Kimberly Riverside Campground, about 14 km east of St. Mary Lake and three km west of Highway 95A. Once you reach Highway 95A, it is about 5.5 km north to the Platzl in Kimberley or a km south to Marysville.

⁓

Additional Information
Kootenay Lake Chamber of Commerce
PO Box 120
Crawford Bay, BC V0B 1E0
Tel: 250-227-9267 (summer only) or 250-227-9315 (year-round)
Fax: 250-227-9441
Email: info@kootenaylake.bc.ca
BC Kootenay Rockies Tourism
1905 Warren Avenue,
Kimberley, BC V1A 2Y5
Tel: (250) 427-4838
Fax: (250) 427-3344
Email: info@kootenayrockies.com Web: www.kootenayrockies.com
Mountain Footsteps
Hikes in the East Kootenay of Southwestern British Columbia by Janice Strong
ISBN 9781926855295
Published by Rocky Mountain Books, Calgary, AB

GPS References for major points of interest

Ref: WGS 84 - Lat/Lon hddd.ddddd

Wpt	Km	Description	Latitude	Longitude	Elev.
W01	0.0	Hwy 3A & Anderson Road	N49.62061	W116.78740	554 m
W02	1.2	Gray Creek Pass FS Road	N49.62265	W116.77621	661 m
W03	6.7	Gate & Powerline Road	N49.61974	W116.71211	1194 m
W04	16.8	Oliver Lake Rec Site	N49.58499	W116.68498	1996 m
W05	17.7	Height of land	N49.58105	W116.67584	2066 m
W06	23.8	Jct. from right, keep straight	N49.60729	W116.65093	1734 m
W07	30.2	Jct. & red buildings: go left.	N49.60820	W116.57683	1354 m
W08	30.7	Cross Redding Creek	N49.61016	W116.57259	1320 m
W09	34.9	Cross Redding Creek	N49.63743	W116.53999	1264 m
W10	53.6	Cross St Mary's River	N49.65187	W116.32910	1007 m
W11	53.7	Jct. St. Mary's-Redding FSR	N49.65299	W116.32832	987 m
W12	66.5	Pavement & St. Mary Lake	N49.61436	W116.18010	975 m
W13	80.6	Campground	N49.63520	W115.99740	975 m
W14	83.5	Hwy 95A	N49.64089	W115.96771	966 m

Lost Lake near the summit of Monashee Pass on Highway 6. © Murphy Shewchuk

CHAPTER 16

Highway 6: Vernon to Nakusp Motorcycles and Mountain Passes

STATISTICS

For map, see page 164.

Distance: 195 km: Vernon to Nakusp

Travel Time: Three to four hours.

Elev. Change: 850 metres.

Condition: Paved two-lane mountain highway with lots of turns.

Season: Maintained year around.

Monashee Pass could get lots of snow in winter.

Map: British Columbia Highway Map.

Backroads Mapbook: Thompson Okanagan and Kootenay Rockies, BC.

Communities: Vernon, Lumby, Cherryville, Fauquier, Burton & Nakusp.

Highway 6 crosses at least two mountain passes and parallels two major lakes and several major rivers on its 407-km run from Vernon in the Okanagan Valley to Nelway on the Canada-USA boundary, south of Salmo. It is a twisting two-lane highway with enough ups and downs to test your brakes and driving ability, particularly if you are piloting a big motorhome or pulling a large travel trailer.

Motorcyclist's Favourite

It is these same characteristics that make this road a favourite Kootenay-Columbia route for motorcycle travellers. Reviewers on the BestBikingRoads.com website give sections of it five stars. "…Hwy 6 has just about everything-big sweepers, some tight twisties, a mental sinuous section near Needles, broad valleys, big mountains and forests. The Needles-Fauquier ferry across Lake Arrow is free."

Attractions Abound

We don't drive a big motorhome or a motorcycle. Our truck camper is our home on the road and it has served us well as we have meandered our way along portions of Highway 6 on numerous occasions.

In this chapter I will cover Highway 6 from Vernon to Nakusp, one of our favourite highways across the province. I won't attempt to touch on everything there is to see along the route. This would take the whole book and would soon be out-of-date. Instead, I will cover the points of interest that could interest you if you aren't in a hurry and enjoy back-country exploring without a deadline.

Vernon Starting Point

The west end of Highway 6 joins Highway 97 on the south side of Vernon, the north Okanagan's largest community. There are plenty of services to fill your needs before you hit the road. In addition to various hotels, motels and RV parks, there is a provincial park nearby on Okanagan Lake. Ellison Provincial Park has 71 campsites, a beach and enough trails around the rocky headland to keep you fit.

Heading East

The four-lane section of Highway 6 soon runs out as it passes through the Coldstream commercial area and begins a relatively straight run through Lavington and Lumby. If you had a late start, the Lumby Lions Campground has quiet serviced campsites along Duteau Creek and Bessette Creek, a few blocks north of downtown. We spent a mid-August morning there serenaded by song birds and the muffled sounds of the creek—after a lightning storm rocked the campground and cut off the power.

If you have plenty of time on your hands, you could head north on Shuswap Avenue and take Lumby-Mabel Lake Road for 38 km to Mabel Lake Provincial Park. If you are really serious about backroads, you could continue another 75 km north along the east side of Mabel Lake, past Wap Lake to Three Valley Gap on the Trans-Canada Highway.

Winding Through Farmland

Highway 6 begins a steady climb east of Lumby before dropping down to the Shuswap River. With a few sharp turns and steep sections, this is a bit of a taste of the road to come.

Motorcyclists at McIntyre Lake near the summit of Monashee Pass on Highway 6.
© Murphy Shewchuk

There is a BC Hydro picnic area near the Shuswap River at the bottom of the hill. The trees provide shade and there is access to the river.

Monashee Provincial Park

Frank's General Store (25 km east of Lumby), at the junction of Highway 6 and Sugar Lake Road near Cherryville, is your last chance to stock up on fuel and supplies before heading to the hills.

Sugar Lake Road is also another possibility to head north into the mountains. It is about 16 km north to Sugar Lake and another 20 km farther north to Monashee Provincial Park. This is basically an undeveloped mountain wilderness park without any vehicle camping facilities. There is a trail to Spectrum Falls and a six km trail that can take you to Spectrum Lake.

If you aren't up to wilderness camping or hiking, there is a small BC Recreation Site on Greenbush Lake, approximately 75 km north of Highway 6. Note that this is an active forest road and may be rough or impassable at times.

The Climb Begins

Frank's General Store also marks the start of the 750 metre climb southeast to Monashee Pass. For the naturalist in the crowd, this marks the obvious transition zone from the arid Okanagan to the interior rainforest slopes of the Monashee Mountains. For the road warrior this is also the start the "interesting" route with numerous hairpin turns and 30 km-per-hour corners. Despite the grade and twists, this is also a route for trucks carrying wood chips to Castlegar, so use caution when passing.

Route 6 Campground and Gold Panner Café and RV Park, 35 km east of Lumby, offer respite for a tired or hungry traveller.

McIntyre Lake

The marshes near McIntyre Lake mark the actual pass even though the highway climbs another 50 metres in elevation before beginning its winding descent to Lower Arrow Lake. Kettle River FS Road, five km south of the lake, marks another possible diversion. This gravel Forest Service road could take you 113 km south to Westbridge on Highway 33 and another 13 km south to Highway 3 at Rock Creek. There is a beautiful waterfall and several small BC recreation sites along the way. Check out the "Up the Kettle River without a Paddle" chapter in this book.

Lost Lake Rest Area

Highway 6 swings north and then east as it climbs to the 1,250 metre highway summit. There is a small lake and rest area south of the highway near the summit. A gravel road to the north leads another couple of km to Monashee-Kettle recreation site along the Kettle River. There is also a resort at Keefer Lake and a small rec site at Holmes Lake, 26 km to the north east.

The highway soon enters the Central Kootenay Regional District on a winding descent to the Inonoaklin Creek valley. With a drop of 670 metres and numerous 30 and 40 kph turns in the 40 km run to Edgewood Road, it could test your driving skills.

Edgewood

Inonoaklin Valley Road (a.k.a. Edgewood Road) heads south to the small community of Edgwood. The community was one of many displaced when the Hugh Keenleyside Dam (on High Arrow Dam) raised the level of Lower Arrow Lake in 1968. This flood control dam is part of the Columbia River Treaty with the United States.

With the raising of the lake level, Edgewood replaced Killarney, a few km

McIntyre Lake near the summit of Monashee Pass on Highway 6. © Murphy Shewchuk

to the south. The lakeside Inonoaklin Park at Edgewood is a pleasant place for a lunch stop. One of the roads down to the lake is supported by rock walls that were built by Ukrainian Canadians detained here during World War I.

Whatshan River and Whatshan Road

Highway 6 swings north for four km before descending to the Whatshan River Bridge. Whatshan Forest Service Road, just across the river, heads north to Whatshan Lake with a couple of recreation sites on the east side of the lake, and a retreat and rec site on the lake's southwest side of the lake. For the fisher, there are reports of up to 1.5 kg Rainbow Trout as well as Bull Trout and Kokanee.

Whatshan Lake is a 30-km-long BC Hydro reservoir supplying water to a 54 megawatt hydroelectric powerhouse on the west shore of Lower Arrow Lake. The 12 metre (39 foot) concrete dam was built in the early 1950s. The head gates of the 3.4-km-long tunnel are visible from the forest service road along the east shore of Whatshan Lake.

Needles/Fauquier Cable Ferry

The three-km descent to the ferry slip at Needles may also test your brakes. The free ferry runs on a half hour schedule from 5:00 am to 10:00

pm. It can carry up to 30 vehicles and may be busy during the height of the tourist season.

Fauquier has most of the services needed by Highway 6 travellers. If you are heading west, this could be a good spot to stock up on fuel and supplies.

Mountainside Road

Most of the road north to Nakusp winds along the mountainside high above Arrow Lake. The views are excellent where it is safe to pull over and enjoy them.

The road drops down to lake level at the Cariboo Creek causeway at Burton, 22 km north of the ferry. This is also one of the many communities displaced by the Keenleyside Dam. Burton's history goes back to the 1890s when it was a steamboat stop for a gold discovery in Cariboo Creek. The old Townsite was moved east and rebuilt above the high water mark.

The lakeshore campground at Burton Historical Park (at the end of Lakeview Park Road) is one of our favourite stops on any tour through the area. It has 37 sites and parking for a picnic or a walk down the old road to the lake.

At last visit the campground was undergoing renovations, so those numbers may change. For the fishers, there is also a boat launch and dock. Rumours are that the lake contains Dolly Varden (Bull Trout), Kokanee (land-locked salmon), Rainbow Trout, Gerrard Trout, White Fish, and fresh-water Ling Cod.

Arrow Park Ferry

The next major diversion is Arrow Park Ferry, 13 km north of Burton. This is another of BC's numerous inland cable ferries. It runs "on demand" from 5:00 am to 9:20 pm.

The "cable" reference means the ferry is tethered to an underwater cable that stretches across the lake, preventing the boat from drifting downstream in the case of a mishap.

If you haven't had enough backroads exploring, you could take the ferry across to the west side of Lower Arrow Lake and follow the gravel forest roads south to Whatshan Lake and Highway 6, or north to Highway 23 at Shelter Bay. We did the route from Highway 6 via Whatshan Lake to Shelter Bay a few years ago and my wife was not impressed with some of the narrow sections.

McDonald Creek Provincial Park

While Burton Historical Park might appear to be a bit rustic, the same can't

Lower Arrow Lake from from Needles-Fauquier Ferry. Arrow Lake is on British Columbia's Columbia River in the Kootenay District. © Murphy Shewchuk

be said for busy McDonald Creek Provincial Park, 10 km north of Arrow Park Ferry road. It is open May 1 to September 30. With 73 campsites—all reservable—it may be wise to plan ahead during the busy summer season.

Nakusp

With a population of about 1,600, Nakusp is the largest community on the Arrow Lakes. First Nations history in the area dates back 3,000 to 5,000 years. Fur traders first visited the region in 1811 and settlers arrived in the early 1890s.

Nakusp was initially a steamboat town on the route from Revelstoke to Castlegar with supplies to service the miners of the Silvery Slocan. The Nakusp & Slocan Railway was built to the silver mines at Sandon in 1895. The section from Nakusp to Rosebery operated for nearly a century before the last train run in March, 1989. The N&S Railway grade from Rosebery to Three Forks (near Sandon) is now the 13-km-long Galena Trail. There is more information on the Trails BC website at http://www.trailsbc.ca/ as well as the Bike Pirate website at http://www.bikepirate.com/galena/ .

The Keenleyside Dam also prompted changes to the Nakusp waterfront. Its walkway is a good way to catch a glimpse of what remains of the pre-dam community, while also enjoying the gardens.

Today the busy downtown core is well worth a stop before heading north to Revelstoke or south to New Denver. The Nakusp & District Museum is open May to September and has lots of information and artifacts pertaining to the First Nations and European settlers.

The shops and restaurants are hard to resist. If you need fuel, there is a service station at the junction of Highway 6 and 23 at the north end of town. Nakusp Hotsprings, 14 km to the northeast is a year-around playground with a hot pool, chalets and a campground.

Displays in Nakusp Museum. © Murphy Shewchuk

Additional Information:

Nakusp Hot Springs
8500 Hot Springs Road PO Box 280
Nakusp BC V0G 1R0
Ph: 250-265-4528
Toll Free: 1-866-999-4528
Web: http://www.nakusphotsprings.com/
Needles/Fauquier Cable Ferry Schedule
Western Pacific Marine
Web: http://arrowbridge.ca/ferry.php

Slocan Lake from Highway 6 viewpoint with Valhalla Park in background. © Murphy Shewchuk

CHAPTER 17

Highway 6: Nakusp to South Slocan (Hwy 3A) Mountains, Lakes and Silver Cities

STATISTICS

For map, see page 164.

Distance: 125 km: Nakusp to South Slocan.

Travel Time: Two to three hours.

Elev. Change: 325 metres.

Condition: Paved two-lane mountain highway with lots of narrow sections and turns.

Season: Maintained year around.

Summit Lake area could get lots of snow in winter.

Map: British Columbia Highway Map.

Backroads Mapbook: Kootenay Rockies, BC.

Communities: Nakusp, Hills, New Denver, Silverton, Slocan and South Slocan.

Nakusp & Slocan Railway

The Nakusp & Slocan Railway, constructed in 1894, connected to the waterfront on Upper Arrow Lake on either side of Kuskanax Creek, then looped south to gradually gain altitude before climbing southeast above Box Lake. It continued to climb and remnants can be seen along the east shore of Summit Lake. Just past the east end of Summit Lake the rails began their southeast descent to Slocan Lake following Bonanza Creek. The route followed the east shore of Slocan Lake south to Rosebery where there was another steamboat dock. It then continued south along the lake to about three km from New Denver before it began the steep climb up Carpenter Creek to Three Forks and on to Sandon.

Galena Trail

The Galena Trail follows much the same route as the N&S Railway from Rosebery to New Denver and Three Forks. It can be accessed at Rosebery and in New Denver on Denver Siding Road. The upper end is accessible from a wide section of Sandon Road just off Highway 31A. The North Slocan Trails Society is involved with the maintenance of the trail and several others in the area. You can find out more on their website at https://slocantrails.wordpress.com/ or Facebook page at https://www.facebook.com/NorthSlocanTrailsSocietyNewDenverBC/. Trails BC also has information on a wide variety of trails in the province.

Highway 6

The highway follows much the same route as the railway to the east end of Summit Lake before climbing up above the Bonanza Creek valley. There is a private campground at the northwest end of the lake and a BC Provincial Park less than a km farther along. If you are just interested in getting off the highway there is a very pretty lakeshore rest area another km farther along. Summit Lake Ski and Snowboard Area, near the east end of the lake, has most everything you could want except giant hotels and exorbitant prices. Note that they accept cash only. Visit http://skisummitlake.com/ for all the details.

Hills

While there are definitely hills in the area, apparently the name comes from two brothers named Hill who set up a sawmill during the 1920s. Several Doukhobor families established farms and a community here in 1929-1934. A one-room school followed. When the road to New Denver opened the students went there and the Hills school became a community hall.

The famous Hills Garlic Festival was founded in 1993. A decade later, it moved to Centennial Park in New Denver. The reason, people said, was because the Hills community didn't have a fire department to deal with any spark from the increasing crowds.

New Denver

I've covered New Denver in the Highway 31A chapter, but I will add a few more bits of its colourful history here. According to Elsie G. Turnbull in *Ghost Towns and Drowned Towns of West Kootenay*, "The community owed much of its prosperity to the Bosun Mine, 3 miles (5 km) down the lakeshore. Here on a ranch owned by a young Englishman, Joseph

New Denver

SILVERY SLOCAN HERITAGE TOUR

Silver outcroppings on Kootenay Lake were noted in 1844 by the Hudson's Bay Company, however prospecting did not begin until 1882. Rapid development of mines and the towns that supported them quickly followed. We invite you to discover the diversity of our celebrated mining history by following the Silvery Slocan Heritage Tour.

By April 1892, just 7 months after the discovery of high-grade silver near Sandon, 500 prospectors were camped at present day New Denver. Hotels stores, bars, restaurants, churches and laundries were quickly erected. Soon after, New Denver became the governmental and residential centre serving the mining district. Sternwheelers, boats and paths connected the community with the rest of the Kootenays until 1894, when the Canadian Pacific Railway began construction of the Nakusp and Slocan branch line to Sandon. With the decline in production of the Slocan area mines, the population of the town similarly decreased. In 1942, New Denver became the West Kootenay administrative centre of the British Columbia Security Commission in charge of relocating people of Japanese descent from the West Coast. Almost two thousand Nikkei lived in small two-family houses built in the New Denver area during the war. Since the 'Fifties, mining and forestry have remained dominant industries.

NEW DENVER MUSEUM originally built as a bank in 1897

Silvery Slocan Sign at New Denver Centennial Park. © Murphy Shewchuk

C. Harris, a prospector discovered rich ore. Several months' work paid for a road, wharf, and blacksmith shop, as well as providing funds for a waterworks system in New Denver and the Bosun Opera House." Elsie Turnbull's book is full of stories of the communities and characters of the region. Fortunately, unlike many books published on the Silvery Slocan, it was still in print at the time of writing.

The main New Denver drag is 6th Avenue, which heads east to the lakeshore from the junction of Highway 6 and 31A. This comprises the "business district," with other important businesses such as the BC Liquor Store and the Post Office on Josephine Street.

If you continue south across Carpenter Creek on Highway 6 (a.k.a.

Union Street) the next major diversion is 3rd Avenue, particularly if you are looking for a campground or public beach. Centennial Park can be a busy place especially during the summer months.

The Nikkei Internment Memorial Centre, described as a powerful reminder of the forced removal of the Japanese Canadian population from the West Coast during the Second World War, is located at 306 Josephine Street, just south of 3rd Avenue. It is well worth a visit.

Valhalla Provincial Park

Directly across Slocan Lake is Valhalla Provincial Park. The 50,060 hectare park extends along most of the lake from just west of New Denver to Slocan City. In addition to a mountain wilderness, there are numerous beach water-access campsites including a two-km paddle from the New Denver campground. When we last camped at New Denver, our campground neighbors were gone for few days when they paddled their kayaks across the lake.

Silverton

This community, a few minutes south of New Denver, also owes its start to the Silvery Slocan mining boom. The nearby mines supplied the village with prospectors and while the town supplied the services: hotels, general stores, a druggist and a newspaper where among the most notable. Add a wharf to load the rich galena ore onto sternwheel steamers and everything ran full steam ahead. The mining era waned with the end of World War One, and when the Great Depression was over, Silverton recovered as a new community. Today Silverton Building Supplies is an important stop, particularly if you are looking for propane for your RV.

Across the highway, the artifacts of the bygone mining boom can give you a glimpse of the hardware used to extract the millions of dollars in silver ore from the mountainside.

If you are looking for a spot to camp, Silverton has two campgrounds: a small one at Lakeside and another 20-unit site at Creekside. Rates are reasonable and they have well-equipped washroom facilities. There is also a boat launch located at the foot of Leadville Street and parking is available for boat trailers and vehicles.

Slocan Lakeshore Drive

If you are interested a somewhat more unusual camping experience, Bannock Point Recreation Site, approximately 4.5 km south of Silverton, has 10 walk-in campsites spread out along the treed and rocky shores of Slocan

Museum at New Denver. © Murphy Shewchuk

Lake. If you have a boat, you can access the campground via the lake about 4.0 km south of Silverton.

Highway 6 winds south high above the lake. This no road for speeding or indiscriminate passing as you could meet a chip truck.

The Cape Horn Bluffs along the highway, approximately five km north of the foot of the lake, were a major challenge to drivers when we first meandered through the area a few decades ago. However major work in the 1990s opened up a new section of two-lane highway to bypass the narrow section sandwiched between the lake and the cliffs. If you can find a safe point to park, the view up the lake from the north end of the bluffs is spectacular.

Slocan Bluffs

If you are interested in an entirely different view: one with a cliff-hugging perspective, the Slocan Bluffs could be for you. Peak Freaks lists it as one of the most popular climbing areas in the Kootenays. The location is along the old highway with access from the corner of Slocan Street and Delany Avenue in Slocan.

Slocan City

Take Giffin Avenue northwest into Slocan (a.k.a. Slocan City) and your next opportunity to camp is about 100 metres down the hill and to your right. Springer Creek RV Park & Campground is another 100 metres off Giffin Avenue. It has a variety of camping options and a trail that leads up to a waterfall. It can be a quiet place to camp except on the mid-July Slocan Unity Music Festival weekend. The family-oriented festival takes place down on the beach at the foot of the lake with a broad

Valhalla Pure Store at New Denver. © Murphy Shewchuk

selection of international and local musicians.

If you are looking for grub or groceries, Slocan has a variety of choices. The ladies at the Harold St. Café will be happy to serve you breakfast and, if business is slow, bring you up-to-date on the latest news.

Slocan Valley Rail Trail

The route was established in the 1890s as the Columbia and Kootenay Railway, built to carry machinery, supplies and the rich galena ore to and from the CPR mainline at Revelstoke, and connecting with steamers and barges on the Arrow Lakes. Low water and winter ice made the Arrow Lakes unpredictable and then railway was extended to Slocan Lake in 1897. Paddlewheel steamers could the ply the lake to Rosebery and the Nakusp &

Slocan Railway, also a CPR subsidiary, could take the traffic to Nakusp on Upper Arrow Lake.

The line operated for nearly a century before being abandoned and turned over to the Trans Canada Trail Foundation, which in turn transferred ownership to Tourism British Columbia. Several years later Tourism BC turned over ownership to the provincial government and the trail is now the responsibility of the Ministry of Forests, Lands and Natural Resource Operations. The Slocan Valley Rail Trail Society took over stewardship of the right-of-way in 1994 and has worked hard since to develop a non-motorized, family-oriented year-around recreational trail.

The 45-km-long route follows the Slocan River from Slocan to South Slocan with trailheads and amenities at several communities along the way. Details and maps are available on the Slocan Valley Rail Trail Society website at www.slocanvalleyrailtrail.ca/ .

Lemon Creek & Points South

The Lemon Creek Lodge, about eight km south of Slocan is the next of many opportunities to access services along the busy corridor to South Slocan, whether you are driving Highway 6 or cycling or skiing the rail trail. I won't attempt to cover what's available, but check out Appledale, Winlaw, Lebahdo, Passmore, Slocan Park, and Crescent Valley on your way south to the junction with Highway 3A just south of South Slocan.

Your options are many. You can take Highway 3A/6 north to Nelson and then continue south on Highway 6 through Ymir to Highway 3 at Salmo. Then you could continue south to Nelway on the US Boundary or east to Creston. At Nelson you could also continue east on 3A to the junction with Highway 31 with an option to explore Kokanee Glacier Park along the way. Meanwhile back at South Slocan, you can Take Highway 3A south to Castlegar where more options abound.

Additional Information
Slocan Valley Rail Trail Society
Phone: 1-888-683-SVRT (7878)
E-Mail: slocanvalleyrailtrail@yahoo.ca
Web: www.slocanvalleyrailtrail.ca

SS *Moyie* Sternwheel steam boat at Kaslo Visitor Info Centre. © Murphy Shewchuk

CHAPTER 18

Highway 31A New Denver to Kaslo: Silver Mines and Rushing Rivers

STATISTICS

For map, see page 270

Distance: 46 km: New Denver to Kaslo.

                6 km: Hwy 31A to Sandon.

Elev. Change: 520 metres.

Travel Time: One to two hours, plus detours.

Condition: Hwy 31A is paved. Sandon Road is gravel.

Season: Maintained year around. Use caution in winter.

Map: British Columbia Highway Map.

Backroads Mapbook: Kootenay Rockies BC.

Communities: New Denver, Sandon and Kaslo.

If you are interested in a slow tour through some of the Kootenay's most picturesque and richest backcountry, Highway 31A between New Denver and Kaslo could fit the bill without adding too many bruises to your chariot. While the 46-km trip could take you under an hour if you are travelling light and ignore everything but the road, you could, alternatively make a day of it and still run out of time.

New Denver

Located on the shores of Slocan Lake, many of the homes at New Denver reflect another part of British Columbia's history, one which has received political and literary prominence in recent years. The oldest and sometimes grandest buildings reflect life when silver was king and New Denver was an important paddle wheel steamer stop on Slocan Lake.

To complicate the research of the Silvery Slocan, the village had a couple of names before New Denver stuck. According to Greg Nesteroff of the *Nelson Star*, one December, 1891, news story referred to the community at the foot of Carpenter Creek as Slocan City. It wasn't long before it was renamed Eldorado and Slocan City became the name for the community farther south at the foot of Slocan Lake. Eldorado did not last very long. By July, 1892 it appears that the name was officially changed to New Denver. If you are confused, you certainly aren't the first.

Historic 6th Avenue

Take a stroll down 6th Avenue. The first building on your right (north side of the avenue) is the new Valhalla Pure Outfitters store. It replaced their original store located down by the lake front on the corner of Eldorado Avenue and 6th Avenue. The original store opened on Canada Day, 1990. I have a feeling that my wife and I stopped there in the first years it was open. We've also stopped at the new New Denver store to replenish our clothing and gear. As Valhalla Pure specializes in summer outdoor clothing and equipment, they are usually closed from late October until early May.

Across the avenue and down a bit is St. Anthony's Roman Catholic Church, established in 1897. Now referred to as St. Anthony's Mission, it is served by a pastor residing in Castlegar. Back on the north side and a couple of blocks down is the Silvery Slocan Museum located in the century-old former Bank of Montreal Building. It is open from the May long weekend through to Labour Day.

All these references to "Slocan" made me search my bookshelves for my *1001 British Columbia Place Names* book. The Akrigg's answer is that the name goes back to 1859 when members of the Palliser expedition passed the mouth of the "Schlocan" or "Sloghan" river. They suggest that the name could have come from a Shuswap Indian words meaning "frogs" or possibly "catch salmon".

Camping and Nikkei Heritage

Across Carpenter Creek on the south side of New Denver is Centennial Park with a campground, sports field, swimming beach and boat launch. The campground can be a busy place in summer, particularly during the Hills Garlic Festival. On the south side of the park is the Japanese-style Kohan Garden.

A couple of blocks east, at 306 Josephine Street, is the Nikkei Internment Memorial Centre, a National Historic Site commemorating the Japanese Canadians that were housed here during World War II.

Slocan Lake at New Denver, BC, Canada. © Murphy Shewchuk

Sandon

Highway 31A climbs quickly out of downtown New Denver, following the north side of Carpenter Creek. Eight km east it passes Sandon Road, another potential diversion. A few hundred metres southeast on Sandon Road is a wide parking area and a trail heading down to Carpenter Creek and the Galena Trail Three Forks trailhead. If you are into mountain cycling or hiking, you could take the trail down to New Denver and north along Slocan Lake to Rosebery.

Sandon, six km south on Sandon Road, was known continent wide in 1898, as the capital of the Silvery Slocan region. It was a complete mining town with everything a man could want including 23 hotels and saloons. Two railroads; the Kaslo and Slocan Railway, and the Nakusp and Slocan Railway vied for the miner's trade.

The entire city of Sandon burned to the ground on May 3, 1900, but was quickly rebuilt. By the 1950s the ore was exhausted and in 1955, Carpenter Creek, in a wild rampage, scattered most of the town down the canyon. In the summer months, you can tour through the Sandon museum and read about its colourful past in the old newspapers displayed on the wall. See the "Sandon and Idaho Peak" chapter for more information.

Heading for the Summit

Highway 31A continues its sinuous climb to the northeast up Seaton Creek. It passes several marshes, complete with beaver dams, before reaching Bear Lake on the left (north) and the rather inconspicuous pass. At an elevation of 1,085 metres, this is the high point on Highway 31A. Bear Lake is the headwaters of the Kaslo River and can be a favourite for fishers as well as Fish Lake, half a km farther east.

Fish Lake can also be a favourite for western toads and hungry moose in mid-August. There is a small pullout two thirds of the way along the lake and a rest area at the east end.

Retallack

The red buildings of Retallack have stood for decades as ghosts alongside the highway about five km east of Fish Lake.

N.L. "Bill" Barlee, in *Gold Creeks and Ghost Towns*, suggests that sometime after the big discoveries at Sandon, a prospector named Kamplan who had staked an iron stain, showed and succeeded in selling it to J. Eaton for $200. Eaton sunk a pick into the outcrop which proved to be almost solid galena. Eaton contented himself with taking out almost a million dollars in ore and a new camp was born.

According to Don Blake, in *Valley of the Ghosts*, that mining camp started off as *Bell's Camp* after the brothers who set it up and controlled much of the commerce. When the K&S Railway came through in 1895 the name was changed to *Whitewater* and later to *Retallack* after Mr. John Ley Retallack, a Notary Public and mining promoter.

While there are still valuable minerals in "them thar hills", a new kind of prosperity is coming out of what the early miners would have called dangerous and backbreaking terrain. The Retallack Lodge located on a city block of the old townsite started off as a dream of local miners in the 1990s. It took half a dozen years to get through the red tape, but by the late 1990s, Retallack Resort & Alpine Adventures was established, a lodge was built and a catskiing operation underway. The company has since evolved into one of the world's largest heli-biking and backcountry mountain biking operations, adding to their snowcat-accessed powder skiing. Much more information is available on their website at http:// www.retallack.com/ .

Kaslo River. © Murphy Shewchuk

Kaslo River Valley

If you aren't into organized mountain-biking, there are hundreds of km of old railway grades, wagon roads and mule trails in the Kaslo River valley and the surrounding mountains. The Kootenay Rockies Backroad Mapbook presents an overview and more detailed information is often available online or in pamphlets available at local information centres.

The Kaslo Trailblazers are one of the groups that are active in trail development and maintenance in the Silvery Slocan. Their website (http://www.kaslotrailblazers.org/) details some of their projects, including publishing trail maps available in Kaslo and Nelson.

The afore-mentioned *Gold Creeks and Ghost Towns* and *Valley of the Ghosts* books are valuable historical resources. They both appear to be out of print, but *Gold Creeks and Ghost Towns* is listed on www.amazon.ca .

The Last of the Kootenay Sternwheelers

Kaslo lies on the shores of Kootenay Lake, or more correctly extends from the lakeshore up the Kaslo River Valley, making it a bit of a challenge if you do your exploring on foot or via wheelchair. It is at the junction of Highway 31A and Highway 31. If you are coming down the hill from New Denver, pay close attention to the street signs or you could end up a bit confused.

At Kaslo, stop to look at the reminders of the 1890s when Kootenay mining was at its peak. Although it wasn't a mining town, Kaslo was the eastern gateway to the "Silvery Slocan". It served as the centre of commerce for the area and the terminus of the narrow gauge Kaslo & Slocan Railway, a Lilliputian challenge to the formidable Canadian Pacific Railway.

While at Kaslo, tour the museum ship, SS Moyie, the last of the sternwheelers that once plied Kootenay Lake. The SS Moyie was prefabricated in sections in Toronto, Ontario, and was originally intended for the Stikine River as part of the route to the Klondike gold fields. But the draw of Klondike gold lost to Kootenay silver and the Moyie was launched in Nelson on October 22, 1898. She hauled passengers and freight for three generations before her last run on April 27, 1957. When the SS Moyie was retired, Kaslo launched a successful campaign to acquire the stately vessel. In 1978, the SS Moyie was designated a Historic Site and now the Moyie is open to tourists from mid-April to mid-October.

Visit Front Street

Front Street starts at Lighthouse beach and runs up the hill past the S.S. Moyie to Kaslo's main shopping block. The Landmark Bakery and Coffee House is one of the places that is difficult to walk by without gaining a few calories. Across the street is Buddy's Pizzeria and Home Hardware, just in case you need something for your camper or RV. Add the Bluebell Bistro and Rosewood Café and most of your needs should be satisfied. There is a gas station on Hwy 31 (a.k.a. 4th Street) and a sports shop a little farther south.

Kaslo Jazz Etc. Festival

Kaslo Bay Park is home to the local summer music festival with a floating stage on the lakeshore. The 2017 celebration is scheduled for August 4–6. Check out http://kaslojazzfest.com/ for the latest information.

The Langham Cultural Centre, at 447 A Avenue, has a much more laid back year-around program. The beautiful building started off as the Langham Hotel in 1896. When the Silvery Slocan waned, the hotel passed through half a dozen incarnations before being resurrected by the Langham Cultural Society in 1974. Today, it provides space for a variety of cultural activities as well as home for a small Japanese Canadian Museum. The detailed story can be found at http://thelangham.ca/ .

South or North

If you aren't planning to stay or backtrack, you have two options. Both involve Highway 31, covered in a separate chapter, and many scenic views of Kootenay Lake.

‿✺‿

Additional Information
Kaslo Trailblazers Society
P.O. Box 1024
Kaslo, BC, V0G 1M0
Email: kaslotrailblazers@gmail.com
Web: http://www.kaslotrailblazers.org/

Trail to Forest Fire Lookout on Idaho Peak. © Murphy Shewchuk

CHAPTER 19

Sandon and Idaho Peak: Silver Mines and Mountain Tops

STATISTICS

For map, see page 228.

Distance: 8.3 km: Hwy 31A New Denver to Sandon Road

38.5 km: Hwy 31A Kaslo to Sandon Road

6 km: Sandon Road—Hwy 31A to Sandon.

Condition: Hwy 31A is paved.

Sandon Road is gravel.

Season: Maintained year around. Use caution in winter.

Backroads Mapbook: Kootenay Rockies BC.

Communities: New Denver, Sandon and Kaslo.

If you are looking for backroads and hiking trails with a little bit of challenge, the Sandon area in the heart of the West Kootenay could satisfy both counts. Add colourful history, spectacular views and alpine meadows, and a visit to the area could definitely make your day.

The Heart of the Silvery Slocan

As noted in Chapter 18, Sandon became known continent wide in 1898 as the capital of the Silvery Slocan region. It was a complete mining town with everything a man could want including 23 hotels and saloons. Two railroads; the Kaslo and Slocan Railway, and the Nakusp and Slocan Railway vied for the miner's trade.

The entire city of Sandon burned to the ground on May 3, 1900, but was quickly rebuilt. By the 1950s the ore was exhausted and in 1955, Carpenter Creek, in a wild rampage, scattered most of the town down the canyon.

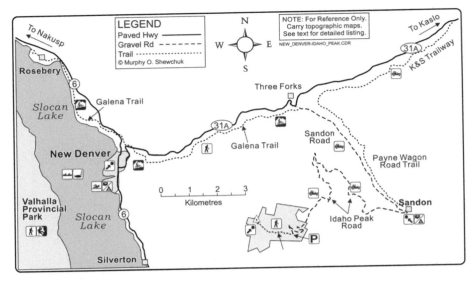

History filled with Intrigue

The late N.L. (Bill) Barlee, in "Gold Creeks and Ghost Towns" describes the intrigue surrounding the first claim staked in the Sandon area: "Some towns cast a lingering spell and down their streets history still walks-it does in Sandon.

"When they speak of ghost towns the name of Sandon always comes to the fore. It had that special and perhaps intangible air that only a few towns possess. It had it all-great mines, iron men, triumphs, disasters and that unique quality sometimes called colour.

"Even its beginning had style. In the fall of 1891, two prospectors, Eli Carpenter and John Seaton, returning to Ainsworth after an uneventful prospecting trip north of Slocan Lake took a shortcut through a previously unmapped mountainous region east of the lake. And fate was looking over their shoulders for as they struggled to the top of an unnamed 7,100 foot mountain they accidently stumbled across an outcrop of ore-silver ore that looked so rich that they excitedly broke off some samples and hastily beat their way back to Ainsworth. Once there, Carpenter took the samples to be assayed while his unsuspecting partner waited anxiously. Several days passed before the greatly anticipated assay reports were given to Seaton and he was dumbfounded when he read them: the assays indicated that the rich looking ore was virtually worthless. Dismayed, Seaton made his way to a saloon nearby to contemplate his poor fortune, unaware that the crafty Carpenter had switched ore samples on him.

"As the despondent prospector sat drinking to his ill-luck, he was

Silversmith Hydro-Electric Station Sign, Sandon, BC. © Murphy Shewchuk

approached by the proprietor who cautiously advised him that Carpenter had been overheard making plans with John Sandon and others for a return trip to the mountain. Outraged, the resolute Seaton acted quickly and had soon gathered together four Irishmen; Hennessey, Hennessey, McGuigan and Flint. The men swore a partnership and called themselves the Noble Five.

"Although Carpenter had already left, the five prospectors set off up the west side of Kootenay Lake. At the Kaslo River they turned west once more. Struggling up through the tangled undergrowth in that draw they found the mountain and located their claims; and the claim which became the most celebrated of that rich group was named-the Noble Five."

Another less intriguing story centres on the famous "Big Boulder". It seems that about a year after Carpenter and Seaton made their discovery, J.W. Cockle found an almost solid galena boulder that weighed in at 125 tons. Cockle staked the immediate area and sold the boulder for $2,000 to help finance his big dreams. It yielded $20,000 in silver to the purchaser. To add to Cockle's dismay, it turned out that the boulder had rolled down the mountain off the North Star property and Cockle's claims were worthless.

Steam Railway Locomotive, Sandon, BC. © Murphy Shewchuk

Klondike Silver Corp.

As you approach Sandon, you may notice mine buildings across Carpenter Creek. These are part of the Klondike Silver Corp. operations which, in August, 2016, appeared fairly quiet. According to their online report: "The Slocan Mining District has produced more than 24 million ounces of silver since the first discoveries in the late 1800s transformed this scenic wilderness into the silver-mining center of Western Canada. Klondike Silver is the dominant land-holder of the camp. Along with the 100-tonne-per-day permitted flotation mill in historic Sandon, the Company owns the past-producing Silvana, Wonderful and Hinckley Mines, seven other dormant mines and extensive exploration properties."

Steam Locomotive #6947

The next Sandon artifact you will see is a 1908 steam locomotive along with a tender and a few other pieces of rolling stock. It was not there on my earlier intial visit to Sandon, so it came as a bit of a surprise when I visited in the late 1990s. The locomotive is owned by Wrightway Charter Co. Ltd. and is believed to have served Sandon during the 1920s. For the railway buff, the convoluted history and technical specs are available on the Sandon website at www.sandonbc.ca. (Note the ".ca" not ".com".) If you are primarily

Silversmith Hydro-Electric Station Alternator, Sandon, BC. © Murphy Shewchuk

interested in a photo-op, it is available year around with more information at the Prospector's Pick gift shop in Sandon.

An interesting bit of history is that two quiet different railroads vied for the lucrative galena ore. The Kaslo and Slocan Railway was a narrow gauge line (3 foot–914 mm) that wound its way up the Kaslo River from Kootenay Lake. There were steep sections–over 3.3 percent, tight curved and mountain hillsides stripped of timber by forest fires. A large portion of the 53-km line is now under the blacktop of Highway 31A. Some of the remainder has been resurrected as recreation trails.

The Nakusp and Slocan Railway was a standard gauge line (4 foot 8 1/2 inches–1,435 mm) that ran from a steamboat slip on Arrow Lake at Nakusp, up south along the present route of Highway 6 past Summit Lake to Slocan Lake at Hills and then along to another steamboat slip at Rosebery (named after Archibald Philip Primrose, 5th Earl of Rosebery). It then continued to New Denver before making the steep climb up Carpenter Creek to Three Forks and then on to Sandon. By 1895 the two rail lines were hauling ore out of the Silvery Slocan. By the 1970s, Sandon was without a rail line from either direction. The Three Forks to Rosebery section of the N&S Railway is part of the historic Galena recreation trail.

THE SLOCAN MINES

Silver was the key that opened the Slocan. Discovery in 1891 of the rich outcrops of the "Slocan Star" and "Payne" touched off the wildest lode excitement in our history. The silver-lead ore was easily and cheaply mined, speeding development, and the area boomed. Roads, towns and railways remain, linking the present with an era when silver was king.

PROVINCE OF
BRITISH COLUMBIA
19 69

Slocan Mines Sign, Sandon, BC. © Murphy Shewchuk

Brill Buses

Something else that is a bit of a jolt is the line of Brill Buses on the river side of Slocan Star Street. In this case there isn't a historical connection except that the owner of the buses has property in Sandon.

The Prospector's Pick

No visit to Sandon is quite complete without a stop for an ice cream cone, and the only place that has ice cream is The Prospector's Pick. It is also the source of local books, visitor information and camping information. The store is open 10:00 AM-5:00 PM, 7 days a week, from the May holiday weekend until Thanksgiving.

Sandon Museum

In the summer months, you can tour through the Sandon Museum located in the old Mercantile Building and read about Sandon's colourful past in the old newspapers that are displayed on the wall. To complement the "writing on the wall", the Museum sells the *"Sandon Paystreak"* newspaper for $2.00. Currently published by the Valley Voice in New Denver, it is full of information on the history of Sandon and the surrounding mines. The story of the *Sandon Paystreak* dates back to September 1896 and is as colourful as the mines and characters described on its pages.

While the museum doesn't have the 125 ton galena boulder for you to ogle, it does have a sizable galena rock to get the feel of what lead-silver sulphide ore is like. Be generous with your donation to the Sandon Museum "kitty", like most community museums, it is operating on a very short, very frayed shoestring.

Silversmith Hydro Electric Station

It is really difficult to visualize a city cramped into the valley at Sandon, yet in the 1890s, Sandon had all the modern conveniences: theatres, stores, 29 hotels, 28 saloons, factories and mills–and, I suspect, a red light district. However the "light" didn't come from a candle or lantern.

The sometimes wild Carpenter Creek and the host of other creeks that tumbled down off the surrounding mountains were harnessed to drive eight different hydroelectric systems–all driven by Pelton wheel turbines. (An example of a Pelton wheel is in the open-air display in downtown Silverton.) The 1897 Silversmith (Slocan Star) generating station is the only hydro plant to survive the booms and busts of over a century. It started off as a DC generator and was converted to alternating current (AC) in 1916 with a

Forest Fire Lookout on Idaho Peak. © Murphy Shewchuk

10-year-old second-hand plant. The Pelton wheel also drove an industrial compressor to provide air for the underground mines.

The station has seen a few renovations since and, when I visited in 2016, Silversmith Power & Light Corp. was replacing the last of the aging wood stave pipes AND delivering green energy to the BC Hydro grid. In the process it has become Canada's oldest continuously operating hydroelectric plant. Unlike many other such plants around the world, it invites visitors to tour the operation in the summer months—donations gratefully accepted.

Idaho Peak Road Length: 11 km
Elevation Gain: 1,040 metres

First off, this is no road for motorhomes, truck campers or anything much bigger or taller than a pickup truck. The switchback turns could prove impossible for long vehicles and the overhanging trees will take chunks off the roof of your camper. The best vehicle is probably an all-wheel-drive SUV with good tires. Because the road climbs to over 2,120 metres (6,950 feet) the season is likely to be limited to mid-July to the end of September.

Add to that the fact that much of the gravel road after the initial two km is one lane with a cut bank on the uphill side and steep drops on the downhill side. To compound things even more, some of the drivers you could meet on the road won't want to give you much room to get by.

If you are driving a big RV or are unsure of your courage or abilities to drive a narrow mountain road there is another option. John Matthews, a professional driver, operates the Idaho Peak Shuttle during the summer months with potential pickups in Silverton, New Denver and Sandon. He has normal pick-up times in New Denver of 9:00 am, 1:00 pm and, for those interested in evening photography, 5:00 pm. This gives you about 2.5 hours to hike to the lookout and back. If you want to make a day of it, I suspect you can arrange to go up on the morning trip and come back down on the mid-afternoon trip. Regardless of your choice it is advisable to book in advance via the website at http://idahopeakshuttle.ca/ .

If you are curious about the name, according to Canada Department of Mines reports, development of the Idaho claim began in 1892. The ore was rich and in 1894 it produced 275 tons of ore averaging 185 ounces of silver and 69 percent lead.

Idaho Peak Trail Length: 1.6 km
Elevation Gain: 160 metres

The trail from the main parking lot starts at over 2,120 metres (6,950 feet) and climbs to 2,285 metres (7,496 feet), according to my trusty GPS. Along the way it skirts a knoll and then follows a hog's back ridge with little reassuring room for those with a bad case of acrophobia.

I took advantage of John Matthews' shuttle service on a recent mid-August morning leaving my camper in New Denver, and did the hike to the top. While it wasn't exactly "lonely at the top" as some vehicle commercials suggest, there was a cool breeze and most of the wildflowers on the south facing slopes were past their prime. The meadows to the north were still in beautiful colour.

Trail to Forest Fire Lookout on Idaho Peak. © Murphy Shewchuk

The trail is rough in places and shows signs of erosion from spring runoff. This is no place for flip-flops or casual shorts and spaghetti tops. The wind can blow in on short order and bring with it cold alpine mist—a recipe for hypothermia if you aren't equipped for the worst.

Idaho Park is, however, an excellent place for a good camera and fresh batteries. The view to the west is Slocan Lake and the Valhalla Wilderness area. To the north is the Coal Range. To the southeast are Kokanee Glacier and more mountains reaching over 2,600 metres.

Although we didn't see a lot of wildlife, a friend reported seeing a grizzly in the area a couple of weeks later.

According to Sites & Trails BC, "There are two trails to Idaho Lookout. Both meet on the ridge for the last leg of the hike up to the summit. They are the same length, but one is less travelled. If you would like to take the less travelled trail to the lookout, park at the Alamo parking area." On the day we made the trip, the small main parking lot was packed by noon and John Matthews was suggesting to anyone we met on our way down that they consider the Alamo parking area.

If you still haven't had enough of exploring the area, you could camp at Sandon or take advantage of a variety of attractions and facilities at New Denver or Kaslo.

Additional Information
Idaho Peak Shuttle
306-Fourth St. Silverton, BC V0G 2B0
Cell (250) 505-4368
Sandon Historical Society
PO Box 137,
New Denver, BC V0G 1S0
Phone: (250) 358-7920
Email: sandonmuseum@netidea.com
The Prospector's Pick
PO Box 308,
New Denver, BC V0G 1S0
Phone: (250) 358-2140
Email: sandon.bc.canada@gmail.com
Web: http://www.sandonbc.ca/index.html

Lardeau River, north of Lardeau, BC. © Murphy Shewchuk

CHAPTER 20

Kootenay Highway 31: Giant Lakes, Fighting Trout, Hotsprings and Silver

STATISTICS

For map, see page 240.

Distance: 177 km–Balfour–Trout Lake–Galena Bay.

Travel Time: One day, with stops.

Elev. Gain: Approximately 200 metres.

Condition: Mostly paved (80 km gravel with rough sections).

Season: Best in dry weather.

Trout Lake section may be closed in winter.

Backroad Mapbook: Kootenay Rockies BC

Communities: Nelson, Kaslo, Nakusp and Revelstoke.

The history of British Columbia's Kootenay region is truly fascinating. Ever since David Thompson began his three-year-long exploration of the Columbia River system early in 1808, travellers have marveled at the rugged beauty and riches of the Kootenays. Stories of the riches of the fur trade were supplanted in 1864 by the cry of "GOLD" in Wild Horse Creek. When the gold rush subsided, interest in the region waned until it was rekindled by the discovery of rich galena (lead-zinc-silver ore) outcroppings of the Riondel area in 1882. Four years later, the Hall brothers established the rich Silver King Mine on Toad Mountain near the present site of Nelson and before the end of the 1880s; stern wheel steamboats were plying the waterways of the Kootenays.

Railway Battle

Railroads followed the steamboats and a battle raged between the northwest's two railway giants for control of the lucrative traffic to "The Silvery Slocan." William Van Horne and Thomas Shaughnessy of the

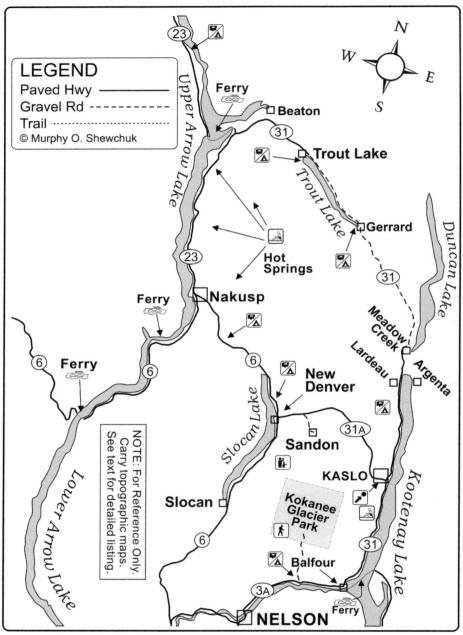

Canadian Pacific Railway pitted their resources against James J. Hill's Great Northern Railway. The result was a two-decade-long boom in mining and railroad building unequalled elsewhere in the country.

The colourful stories of the communities along Highway 31 turn up in a variety of local histories. They include James W. Cockle's 120-ton lead-silver boulder that he sold for $2,000 cash; Seaton and Carpenter's race to stake a claim to a rich deposit near Ainsworth and too many others to mention here. Different versions of the same tales add to the interest and sometimes create a bit of confusion, particularly when the stories disagree. But, the fun is in the finding, as every backroads explorer knows.

Balfour Ferry Starting Point

One of the most difficult decisions to make in exploring the Kootenay region—and writing about it—is establishing a starting point. Where should the km references begin on a trip that may include paved highway, gravel roads and numerous opportunities to detour?

In the case of Highway 31 between Kootenay Lake and Upper Arrow Lake, the decision was easy: Include the whole highway with the Balfour slip of the Kootenay Lake Ferry as the starting point. Backroads explorers travelling via Nelson or Creston pass through Balfour while those coming over the mountain from Nakusp to Kaslo can either deduct 35 km from the references or take a half hour detour south to Balfour and gain the advantage of seeing this section of scenic Kootenay Lake in both directions.

Selkirk Mountains

From the foot of the Balfour ferry slip, Highway 31 winds northeast then north along the base of the Selkirk Mountains. High above to the west are the alpine trails and wilderness of Kokanee Glacier Park, while across Kootenay Lake rise the snow-capped peaks of the Purcell Mountains. Coffee Creek, at Km 10.4, marks the start of one of the many access roads or trails into Kokanee Glacier Park where the abandoned galena mines still serve as reminders of the rich period that opened the country.

Hotsprings

Ainsworth Hot Springs, at Km 15, is also a reminder of that colourful past. Named after John C. Ainsworth, one of the earliest prospectors in the region, the hotsprings are said to have been discovered by natives around 1800, long after wildlife had learned of the healing abilities of the high mineral content odorless water. At the peak of the mining boom, six hotels were built to take advantage of the hot springs.

Today the Ainsworth Hot Springs Resort offers a 41-room hotel, restaurant, hot pools and a cave with mineral water at 42°C / 108°F that is well worth exploring.

Cody Caves

The drive north of Ainsworth passes picturesque mine buildings, remnants of the old Western Mines mill and a side road up to the Cody Caves. The 10-km-long rough summer road leads to the cave entrance. The fragile caves are protected as part of Cody Caves Provincial Park. A tour company offers a variety of guided tours. Check their website for details.

A minute or two beyond the Cody Caves junction is the Woodbury Resort and Marina and another trail to Kokanee Glacier Park. If you are looking for a cabin, a place to camp or a fishing adventure, the "Jones Boys" offer plenty of choice.

Mirror Lake

Highway 31 climbs well above Kootenay Lake, offering some excellent views, especially to the north, before it swings inland near Mirror Lake. There is a campground on the private lake that provides safe swimming, canoeing or kayaking, particularly when whitecaps roll down Kootenay Lake.

Kaslo

Kaslo, at Km 35, was once the fifth largest city in British Columbia. Now, with a population of 1,000, its prominence in the province has diminished somewhat, but still it remains the largest community along Highway 31 and it deserves a day to visit the historic S.S. *Moyie*, a sternwheeler converted to a museum; the Langham Cultural Centre and the downtown shops.

Kaslo is also the junction of Highway 31 and 31A. Highway 31A leads to still another entrance to Kokanee Glacier Park, historic Sandon and New Denver, on Slocan Lake. North of Kaslo, Highway 31 climbs quickly to the top of a bluff overlooking Kootenay Lake before it begins a roller coaster journey along the still-paved highway toward the head of the lake. The lovely bays and cultivated benches are inviting and they, too, carry tales of storm ravaged boatmen and a local cherry industry that died suddenly, ravaged by disease.

Lost Ledge Creek

Many of the sheltered beaches along Kootenay Lake are too far from the highway and too difficult to reach for recreational comfort. But the beach at Lost Ledge Creek is different, and the BC Parks campground here (Km 58) offers an opportunity to dip into the booty from the bakery raid or a welcome respite from a day of travelling.

Wheelhouse of SS *Moyie* at Kaslo BC. © Murphy Shewchuk

Lardeau

Five km later, at Km 65, the traveller rounds a bend and the community of Lardeau and the remnants of a railway beachhead come into view. Lardeau, near the head of Kootenay Lake, is little more than a dot on most maps (on some maps it is not shown at all), but at the turn of the century the Lardeau region was the scene of considerable inter-company railway rivalry.

In 1898 James J. Hill's United States-based Great Northern Railway announced that it would build a line north from its terminus at Kuskanook, along the east side of Kootenay Lake, to the mineral-rich Trout Lake area in the Lardeau Valley. The Canadian Pacific Railway company countered with a proposed extension from its spur connection between Revelstoke on the mainline and Arrowhead (then the head of Upper Arrow Lake) through the Trout Lake area to Kootenay Lake. Indeed, Canadian Pacific Railway maps of the period show such a proposed extension.

The Great Northern obtained a charter for the Kaslo and Lardo-Duncan Railway and in 1901 both companies began constructing parallel lines north from the upper end of Kootenay Lake. The Canadian Pacific was able to delay Great Northern construction over a legal matter long enough for the short-lived nature of the mining boom to become apparent and the American railway abandoned the project before steel rails were ever laid.

Only the Canadian Pacific's Arrowhead and Kootenay Railway was completed and only from Lardeau to Gerrard, at the foot of Trout Lake. The extension to Arrowhead was never constructed. Like many other lines built in the region, this railway was entirely dependent on steamboat connections

Duncan Dam, north of Lardeau, BC, Canada. © Murphy Shewchuk

for both ends of its service. When mining waned, the railway remained in service until 1942 when economics forced its abandonment.

Duncan Dam and Duncan Lake

North of Kootenay Lake, Highway 31 passes through the rich Meadow Creek farmland. A 2.5 km side road leads northeast to the Duncan Dam viewpoint at Km 78. Duncan Dam, completed in 1967, was the first of the three dams built as part of the Columbia River Treaty. It created a 45-km-long reservoir which provides flood protection and storage for the hydro-electric power plants farther downstream. Access to the lake is via Howser Station Road, near Km 85.

Lardeau River

While the "highway" designation remains, the pavement runs out as you continue up the Lardeau River Valley. The wide, easy grade is a reminder of the railway tracks that once carried freight to the rich silver mines of the Lardeau. Rapids and log jams make the river uninviting for canoeing or kayaking, but a brown bear and a blue heron both appeared to enjoy the fishing. Wide pull-offs and beaches near Km 91 and Km 96 show signs of occasional use by human fishers. The road crosses over

Duncan Dam Spillway, north of Lardeau, BC, Canada. © Murphy Shewchuk

to the southwest side of the river near Km 97, just below a spectacular canyon.

Gerrard Rainbow Trout

The upper reaches of the Lardeau River are protected as part of 79,000 hectare Goat Range Provincial Park, the only natural spawning site of the "Gerrard" rainbow trout.

Highway 31 crosses over to the north side of the Lardeau River at the foot of Trout Lake (Km 118). There is a viewing platform and information signs just downstream from the bridge on the north side of the river. There is also a turnoff to Craig Creek Forest Service Road on the south side of the bridge—and a rudimentary campground a hundred metres up the road. Over the decades that we have visited the area, the campground has changed from a typical Forest Service recreation site to a BC Parks campground; it now seems to have reverted to user-maintained status of indeterminate ownership. Bring your own toilet paper and pack out your garbage.

A few pilings in the lake and an overgrown foundation are all that remain of the community of Gerrard. Selkirk City was the name used on the early maps to describe Gerrard, but now few maps acknowledge that a

Mount Wilkie Glacier and Trout Lake from Highway 31, north of Lardeau. © Murphy Shewchuk

community ever existed here at the northern terminus of the Arrowhead and Kootenay Railway. Most backroads explorers would easily miss the significance of the location were it not for a bronze plaque on a stone monument "Dedicated to the pioneering spirit of the residents of Gerrard and to the memory of Esther Brandon and her three sons..."

High above Trout Lake

Highway 31 soon reflects the fact that it no longer follows the railway bed as the road begins an undulating, winding climb to the benches high above Trout Lake. Snow-capped mountains thrust their jagged peaks into the sky to the southwest, but the wise traveller will pull well off the roadway to enjoy the view.

Logging takes place near the road along this section and the ever-present chance of meeting a logging truck on the next bend means caution must be used. Despite many narrow places, the road is still passable for most vehicles although you might not want to pull a holiday trailer over this road in wet weather. The boundary between the Kootenay Lake and Arrow forest districts is near Km 133 so the narrowest section of the road should have the lightest traffic.

East end of Trout Lake at Gerrard, north of Lardeau, BC. © Murphy Shewchuk

Trout Lake City

A short stretch of pavement begins at Km 144.0 on the outskirts of the community of Trout Lake. The highway bypasses the settlement that was once the focal point of the upper Lardeau.

It was called "Trout Lake City" in the 1890s, writes N.L. "Bill" Barlee in *West Kootenay-Ghost Town Country* and it was in the heart of the Lardeau, one of the most heralded mineral belts in British Columbia. Surrounded by active mineral camps, Trout Lake's many commercial enterprises catered to a rapidly growing population. The Windsor Hotel, 200 metres from the lake, was built in 1896 during the peak of activity and was still in use in early 2017. When the rush subsided, the outlying communities disappeared while Trout Lake managed to cling to life.

Lakeshore Camping

If you are looking for a place to camp, there is a community campground at the head of Trout Lake. You may have to do a bit of exploring to find it, but if you head south through the community, look for Lardeau Street and follow that to the lakeshore. Because of the marshland surrounding the beach, the

Beaton on Upper Arrow Lake south of Revelstoke, BC. © Murphy Shewchuk

toilet is located well away from the campground. This shouldn't be a problem for self-contained campers, but if you don't have your own facilities, plan ahead. As an extra note, there is charge of $10.00 per night, so bring cash.

A signpost at Km 145 (Km 20 from the west) marks a side road to Ferguson, once a booming silver and gold mining centre, now little more than a ghost town.

Beaton

Beyond the junction the highway continues past Staubert Lake (with a picnic site and boat launch) through pure stands of cedar and upland swamps to another junction to Beaton at Km 158. It is about 5.5 km northwest to Beaton and access to the northeast arm of Upper Arrow Lake.

Back at the junction, Highway 31 swings west and soon becomes pavement again as it begins the long descent to Upper Arrow Lake.

Straight sections of the road provide the first glimpse of the lake and the jagged, snow-capped peaks of Mount Odin on the eastern fringes of Monashee Provincial Park. The descent takes a short break at Km 175 where Highway 31 joins Highway 23, creating a need for a decision. To the south lies Nakusp, 49 km away on a paved highway. Another 93 km will take the backroad traveller back to Kaslo for another visit to the bakery.

Northwest of the junction, the road continues for two km to the ferry slip at Galena Bay. After an indeterminate wait and a 20 minute crossing, the traveller can continue 50 km north to Revelstoke and the Trans-Canada Highway--with the opportunity for a few more stops along the way.

Gerrard Dedication Plaque at East end of Trout Lake, north of Lardeau, BC, Canada. © Murphy Shewchuk

Goldstream River, north of Revelstoke, BC. This was the site of a gold rush in 1866.
© Murphy Shewchuk

CHAPTER 21

Big Bend Highway 23: Revelstoke to Mica Creek– and beyond

STATISTICS

For map, see page 252.

Distance: 150 km, Hwy 1 at Revelstoke to Mica Dam crest.

Travel Time: Three to four hours.

Condition: Paved highway, sections may be temporarily closed in winter.

Season: Year around.

Map: BC Highway Map.

Backroad Mapbook: Kootenay Rockies BC.

Communities: Revelstoke and Mica Creek.

Special Note: There are no fuel or grocery sources north of Revelstoke.

The Big Bend Highway was called a lot of things–most of them unprintable in a family book, but for nearly forty years it was a major link in the British Columbia automobile transportation route from Alberta to the Pacific Coast.

Selkirk Mountain Range

The Columbia River begins at Columbia Lake south of Fairmont Hot Springs and works its way north past Golden to the "Big Bend" at what was once known as Boat Encampment. The river then winds south to the 49th parallel defining British Columbia's Selkirk Range from the Rocky Mountains on the east and the Monashee Mountains on the west. If you look closely at a map of the interior of British Columbia, northern Idaho and Montana, you may notice that the Columbia and Kootenay rivers surround the Selkirk Range, creating a huge inland island. Before man-made bridges and waterways, the only dry crossing to this "island" was near present-day Canal Flats where the Columbia and Kootenay Rivers are only a few km apart.

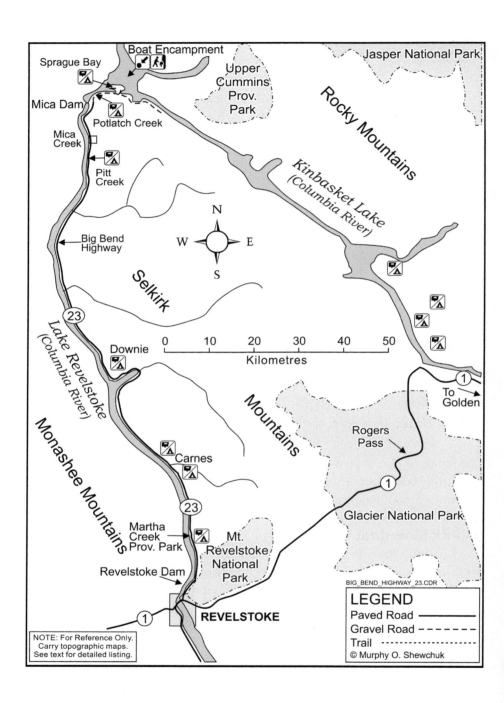

Boat Encampment

Sprague Bay

Jasper National Park

Mica Dam

Upper
Cummins
Prov.
Park

Potlatch Creek

Rocky Mountains

Mica
Creek

Kinbasket Lake
(Columbia River)

Pitt
Creek

N
W E
S

Big Bend
Highway

Selkirk

23

Lake Revelstoke
(Columbia River)

Downie

0   10   20   30   40   50
Kilometres

To
Golden

Mountains

Rogers
Pass

Carnes

23

1

Monashee Mountains

Martha
Creek
Prov. Park

Mt.
Revelstoke
National
Park

Glacier National Park

Revelstoke Dam

1

REVELSTOKE

BIG_BEND_HIGHWAY_23.CDR

NOTE: For Reference Only.
Carry topographic maps.
See text for detailed listing.

LEGEND
Paved Road ——————
Gravel Road – – – – –
Trail ··················
© Murphy O. Shewchuk

Mount Dunkirk and Kinbasket Lake, north of Mica Creek, BC. © Murphy Shewchuk

David Thompson, Astronomer and Surveyor

The first general map of the region was made by David Thompson in 1813 and 1814 while he was in the employ of the North West Company. It was the result of 20 years of exploration beginning in 1792. A sextant and magnetic compass were Thompson's tools; canoe and foot were his transportation; and friendly natives were his guides. While it may be considered sparse and inaccurate by today's standards, Thompson's maps contained a surprising amount of detail.

David Thompson and his crew spent the winter of 1810-1811 at what he called "Boat Encampment" at the mouth of the Canoe River and the "top" of the Columbia River's big bend. They had crossed the Rocky Mountains via Athabasca Pass and in the spring of 1811, after building new boats, descended the Columbia to the mouth at the Pacific Ocean.

Boat Encampment became an important fur trade depot on the trade routes from the Columbia River eastward via Athabasca Pass to Hudson's Bay.

Big Bend Gold Rush

When news of gold in the rivers of British Columbia reached San Francisco and New York in 1857 the fur trade was waning. The initial exodus was to the Fraser River gravel bars north of Hope, but the gold fever race for the Mother lode continued up the Fraser River into the Cariboo and eastward into Boundary and Kootenays.

News of gold strikes in the Big Bend Country in the fall of 1865, prompted a miner migration from the Cariboo and other districts to the west.

The steamer S.S. *Marten* was the first to run from Savona at the west end of Kamloops Lake to the north end of Seymour Arm on Shuswap Lake. The ship was built at Whitfield Chase's Shuswap Ranch of local whipsawed lumber. Its machinery was brought to Savona via a brand new wagon road and the ship was sailed down to Savona where the hardware was installed. On her inaugural voyage, S.S. *Marten* left Savona at 5:00 p.m. on May 26, 1866. She spent the night in Kamloops and reached Seymour City at the head of Seymour Arm at 6:00 p.m. the next day.

Miners rode the steamboat from Savona to Seymour City then tramped north up the Seymour River and east up Ratchford Creek and over the divide to the Columbia River. Other gold seekers came up the Columbia, also via steamboat, from Washington Territory; a few others trekked around the Selkirks, down the Columbia from Wild Horse Creek, where there had been another small rush.

The mining district was not at the Columbia River's bend itself, but nearby on the southward course to today's Revelstoke, along several streams including Downie Creek, Goldstream River, French Creek, McCulloch Creek, Carnes Creek, and Gold Creek. All the excitement proved to be relatively short-lived, however, and the rush had largely ended by the fall of 1866. The exodus did last through the later 1860s, but by the end of the decade the boom was over.

Rogers Pass bypassed the Big Bend

In 1881, barely a decade after the Big Bend Gold Rush, Albert Bowman Rogers discovered the pass through the Selkirk Mountains that bears his name. Prior Canadian Pacific Railway surveyors had favoured a route from Jasper through the Yellowhead Pass and then south to the coast. When the railway was built through the Rogers Pass in 1884, it took the traffic off the Columbia River, and the Big Bend route fell into disuse.

Big Bend Highway

The CPR's monopoly on east-west transportation wasn't appreciated by the growing number of post WWI automobile owners. In 1926 the predecessor

Revelstoke Dam, north of Revelstoke, BC. © Murphy Shewchuk

to the Trans-Canada Highway was completed between Revelstoke and
Golden via the Big Bend Highway. As anyone who drove it can attest,
"highway" was definitely a misnomer. But despite numerous complaints
and broken vehicles, it continued to be an important part of the link across
British Columbia until 1964 when the Rogers Pass route was opened.

Columbia River Treaty

It may be a coincidence, but the Columbia River Treaty also came into
effect in 1964. The agreement included a series of dams on the Columbia
River system that began with Duncan Dam in 1967, followed by Hugh
Keenleyside Dam in 1968 and Mica Dam in 1973.

The first two dams didn't have a serious impact on the Big Bend
Highway, but construction of the Mica Dam certainly did. Getting men and
equipment 150 km north of Revelstoke to build one of the world's largest
earthfill dams meant major improvements of the old road were required.
When construction was completed and the dam gates closed, the rapidly
rising waters of what is now Kinbasket Lake inundated the community of
Boat Encampment and much of the Big Bend Highway between the top
of the "Bend" and Golden. While the rising water closed the road, the

Antique Truck at the BC Interior Forestry Museum, north of Revelstoke, BC. © Murphy Shewchuk

powerhouse began to produce the rated 1,800 megawatts for the provinces electric grid. With the expansion completed in 2015 and 2016, output was nearly doubled to 2,805 megawatts.

Revelstoke Dam

Taking reuse and recycle to the extreme, BC Hydro built a second dam downstream from the Mica Dam to reuse the water stored in Kinbasket Lake by creating Lake Revelstoke. The five turbines in the Revelstoke Dam powerhouse are capable of producing 2,480 megawatts with room for another 500 megawatts of generating capacity. With an impoundment that backs all the way up to the foot of Mica Dam, the 175-metre-high Revelstoke Dam and Lake Revelstoke prompted more rebuilding and rerouting of the Big Bend Highway.

Big Dam Road

Although the two huge man-made lakes created by the Mica and Revelstoke dams have inundated hundreds of km of road, the 545 square km of new lakes also created new recreation opportunities (and challenges).

With the junction of the Trans-Canada Highway and Highway 23 on the east side of Revelstoke at Km 0, head north for four km to junction to the

Lake Revelstoke, near Mica Creek north of Revelstoke, BC. © Murphy Shewchuk

Revelstoke Dam Visitor Centre. It's a 1.5 km drive down the hill to the dam with a short stop at the security gate. Security is important to BC Hydro and bags, purses, cell phones and cameras are prohibited in the visitor centre. The centre includes extensive information on the hydroelectric system and local First Nations. Check for current hours and entry fees.

BC Interior Forestry Museum

The same junction will take you to the BC Interior Forestry Museum. In addition to the outside display of antique logging equipment, the museum has an extensive display of vintage chainsaws. Open May to October–check for current hours and entry fees.

It's a short drive north to the first view of Lake Revelstoke and a few minutes more to the Five Mile Boat Launch–the first of many along the lake which were created as the road was rerouted during various phases of dam construction.

According to BC Hydro, as release water from Mica dam provides almost three-quarters of the inflow into the reservoir, the Revelstoke power plant operates as a run-of-the-river plant, with normal maximum fluctuations in the reservoir level of 4.5 metres.

Martha Creek Provincial Park

Martha Creek, at Km 17, is the only official park on the Revelstoke reservoir. It offers 25 campsites, a boat launch and a beach and picnic area. Drinking water is available. The facility is usually open early May to late September on a first-come, first-served basis.

If the park campground is full (as it can be on a long weekend), Wadey Recreation Site, near Laforme Creek is only 7.5 km farther north. It also has a boat launch and a network of campsites in the trees.

Carnes Creek Recreation Site

Although not as highly developed as the park campground, the Carnes Creek Rec Site at Km 36 offers the advantage of more campsites, some spectacular views and an interesting "wilderness" trail within the south campground that the junior set will have fun exploring. The rec site roads are paved, partly the result of a major washout and highway reconstruction in 1999-2000. The rec site is split by Carnes Creek with access to the northern section another three km farther up the Big Bend Highway.

Carnes Creek was one of the creeks worked over during the Big Bend gold rush. With a trail and forest road heading upstream, there may be opportunities to search for the gold that the miners missed.

Downie Creek

There are numerous side roads to explore north of Carnes Creek. Some lead up to the Keystone Snowmobile Area and Keystone Basin while others provide access to the lake and what are known as dispersed use rec sites. These may have a picnic table, a rudimentary boat launch and little else. But on a summer long weekend the limited facilities do little to dissuade the avid camper and boater.

Downie Creek Forest Road, near Km 66, provides access to a variety of trails to the east of the main Columbia River valley. According to the Forest Service, the Downie Creek Rec Site near Km 73 "has the best boat launch on Lake Revelstoke."

Goldstream River Forest Road, at Km 92, also provides access to a wide variety of recreation opportunities including kayaking. According to the Forest Service, there is an 18-km marshy section of the river suitable for kayaking. I'm not a kayaker so check it out for yourself with information from Forest Service office in Revelstoke or the Recreation Sites and Trails BC website http://www.sitesandtrailsbc.ca/.

Pitt Creek Rec Site, near Km 139 also offers camping and a boat launch.

Mica Dam, north of Mica Creek, BC. © Murphy Shewchuk

Mica Creek

The community of Mica Creek (Km 145) is primarily a residential base for Mica Dam BC Hydro workers and contractors. There is eco-tourism in summer and heli-skiing in winter, but other services are limited. Plan to bring all the fuel and supplies you'll need for exploration of the area when you leave Revelstoke.

Mica Dam, at Km 150, was the first of the Columbia River Treaty dams in British Columbia to produce electricity. It came online in 1973 with an installed capacity of 1,740 megawatts. There is no public access or visitor centre at Mica Dam.

Kinbasket Lake

Highway 23 ends at the crest of Mica Dam, but the Forest Service Roads continue northeast to the top of the Big Bend and then southeast along the south shore of Columbia Reach.

There are also at least two BC Rec sites on Kinbasket Lake. The first is at Potlatch Creek, 2.5 km from the dam. It is a relatively small site with 17 campsites and a boat launch. The fluctuating levels of Kinbasket Lake mean launching any boat could be tricky.

Sprague Bay Rec Site, 16 km from the dam, has a "multi-season" boat launch ramp and an open camping area.

Boat Ramp at Sprague Bay Recreation Site on Kinbasket Lake, north of Mica Creek, BC.
© Murphy Shewchuk

Boat Encampment Trail

Although not clearly marked, there is a half km long trail that winds northwest from the Sprague Bay rec site to a bronze plaque commemorating the historic Boat Encampment site. The trail starts across the entrance road from the boat launch ramp and initially follows what appears to be an old skid road before winding through the trees. It's an easy walk, but sturdy boots will be an asset.

While they may require some serious exploring, there are numerous other "informal" recreation sites that use old routings of the Big Bend Highway and Forest Service Roads to access the lake and various trails in the surrounding mountains.

It is important to note that this is a "wilderness" area. There is no cell phone service and there certainly isn't anyone patrolling the area for lost or stuck tourists–not necessarily a negative.

Additional Information

Columbia Forest District Map

http://www.for.gov.bc.ca/dco/dcomap.htm

Revelstoke Dam Visitors Centre

Tel: 250 814 6697 (peak season) 250 814 6600 (off season)

BC Interior Forestry Museum

5205 HWY 23 North,

Revelstoke, BC, Canada

Mailing Address:P.O. Box 419,

Revelstoke, BC, V0E 2S0

Web: bcforestrymuseum.ca/

Recreation Sites and Trails BC

Web: http://www.sitesandtrailsbc.ca/

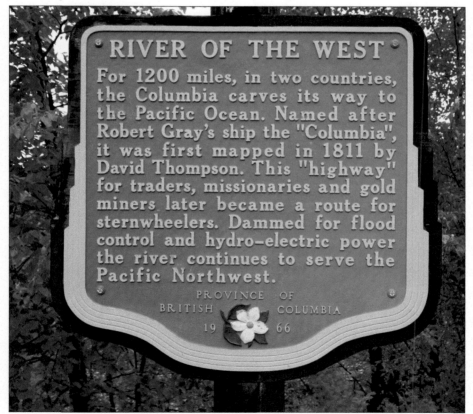

River of the West stop-of-interest sign at the BC Interior Forestry Museum, north of Revelstoke, BC.
© Murphy Shewchuk

Ice in a hollow near First Footsteps Trail at the summit of Mount Revelstoke, near Revelstoke, BC.
© Murphy Shewchuk

CHAPTER 22
Mount Revelstoke Road: Meadows in the Sky Parkway

STATISTICS

For map, see page 264.

Distance: 24.5 km: Trans-Canada Highway to Summit parking area.

Travel Time: Driving time approximately one hour depending on vehicle, etc.

Condition: Paved road with over a dozen switchback corners.

Elev. gain: 1350 metres.

Season: Usually early July to late September.

Backroad Mapbook: Kootenay Rockies BC.

Map: British Columbia Highway Map.

Communities: Revelstoke.

Alpine Hiking for the Casual Adventurer

There are very few places in the Kootenay-Columbia region where you can drive to the 1,830-metre (6,000-foot) elevation of a mountain top on a paved road and enjoy a walk on maintained trails through subalpine meadows. The Meadows in the Sky Parkway in Mount Revelstoke National Park is one of these.

There are, however, a few restrictions. The road to the summit is not maintained in winter. The usual snow-free season is early July to late September. Parks Canada advises that trailers and motor coaches are not permitted. Dual axle recreational vehicles (RVs) are not permitted. While there are no restriction on the length of RVs please note that parking options are limited for longer RVs. Trailer parking is available 0.5 km up the Parkway from the Trans-Canada Highway interchange (watch for signs indicating the Nels Nelsen Historic Area).

If you aren't in a hurry, there are at least half a dozen roadside

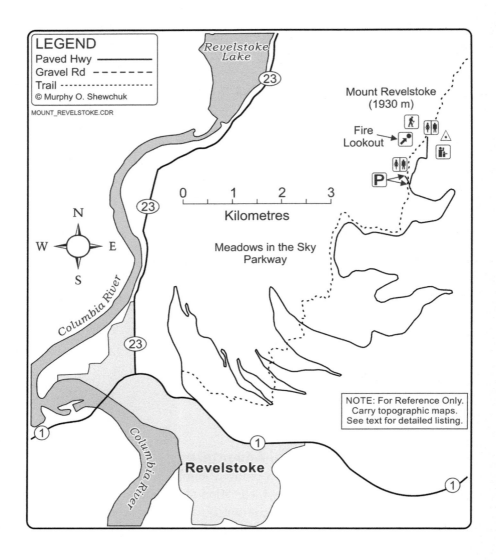

Revelstoke Lake

Mount Revelstoke
(1930 m)

Fire
Lookout

0   1   2   3
Kilometres

N
W   E
S

Meadows in the Sky
Parkway

Columbia River

NOTE: For Reference Only.
Carry topographic maps.
See text for detailed listing.

Columbia River

Revelstoke

viewpoints along the lower two-thirds of the road. If you are challenging
yourself by pedaling your bike to the top, you may appreciate a welcome
break along the way.

Easy Strolls and Longer Hikes—and Plenty of Photo-Ops

You might want to bring along your hiking poles and, most certainly, your
camera. Sturdy boots, a warm jacket and hat are also a good idea. We
hiked the summit trails in mid-July, and there was still some snow on the
trail up to the fire lookout. The summit trails were otherwise open and

View of Selkirk Range northeast of Mount Revelstoke, near Revelstoke, BC. © Murphy Shewchuk

the wildflowers were abundant in the shaded areas and almost over in the south-facing meadows.

The RV parking area is a short walk to the Summit Shuttle Bus stop at Balsam Lake where you can get a ride up to the summit trails. If you are energetic, you can hike the one-km trail up to the upper Shuttle Bus stop before your subalpine meander.

Many of the trails at the summit will take about half an hour plus photo stops. If you are interested in longer, more challenging trails, Parks Canada has an online brochure that lists over a dozen trails in the area ranging from 15 minutes to several hours.

The Revelstoke Online Trail Guide (https://revelstoketrails.com/) is a good place to check out the rest of the region. To quote the website: "Revelstoke is truly an 'adventure' hiker's paradise. You will not see hordes of tourists pulling up to the trailheads in tour buses, or the invasion of weekend hikers from the city. In fact, with the exception of the Mount Revelstoke and Glacier National Park trails, you are not likely to encounter anyone at all on your adventure."

View of subalpine meadows and Revelstoke Lake from North Parapet on Mount Revelstoke, near Revelstoke, BC. © Murphy Shewchuk

Mount Revelstoke Campground

The latest news at the time of writing is that Parks Canada is planning a 50-site campground to be located near the start of the Meadows in the Sky Parkway. It is scheduled to be open in time for the 2019 visitor season.

~⋐⋙⋗~

Additional Information

Revelstoke Online Trail Guide

Web: https://revelstoketrails.com/

Parks Canada

Web: http://www.pc.gc.ca/eng/pn-np/bc/revelstoke/index.aspx

Indian Paintbrush wildflowers on Mount Revelstoke, near Revelstoke, BC. © Murphy Shewchuk

Gardner Creek Falls, Hot Springs Road northeast of Nakusp, BC, Canada. © Murphy Shewchuk

Highway 23—Revelstoke to Nakusp: Ferries, Hotsprings & Waterfalls

STATISTICS

For map, see page 270.

Distance: 105 km: Revelstoke to Nakusp.

Travel Time: Two to three hours—depending on ferry schedules.

Condition: Paved two-lane highway plus Upper Arrow Lake Ferry.

Season: Maintained year around.

Map: British Columbia Highway Map.

Backroads Mapbook: Kootenay Rockies BC.

Communities: Revelstoke & Nakusp.

If you are interested in a trip that includes a free ferry, several hotsprings, and mountain scenery, Highway 23 south of Revelstoke could fit that bill. You can start by leaving the Trans-Canada Highway (Highway 1) on the western outskirts of Revelstoke and following Highway 23 south for 48 km to Shelter Bay. Upper Arrow Lake separates the Monashee and Selkirk Mountain ranges and Highway 23 presents some spectacular views of all three.

Visit an Old Farm

Blanket Creek Provincial Park, approximately half way between Revelstoke and Shelter Bay, is the first of many provincial parks and recreation areas along the route. Depending on the time of day, you may wish to stop at this 64-unit campground and continue south with the light of a new day to add to your enjoyment. Allow plenty of time, for the beach surrounding a natural pond and walking paths through the old farm and to a waterfall may persuade you to spend an extra day or two.

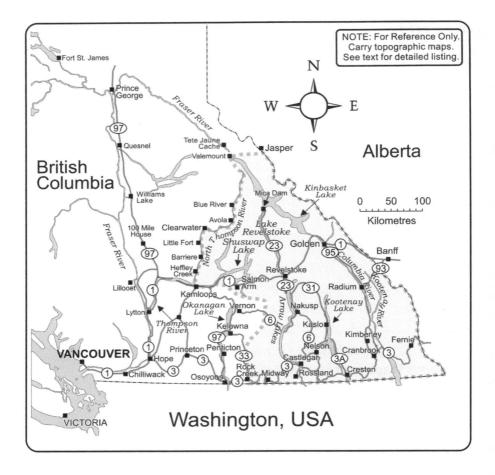

NOTE: For Reference Only.
Carry topographic maps.
See text for detailed listing.

More Camping

If Blanket Creek campground was full or you decided to continue south, BC Parks also has a small campground at the Shelter Bay Ferry landing. With only 17 sites, it could also fill up quickly.

You have at least one more option before taking the ferry across Upper Arrow Lake. Look for Shelter Bay Forest Service Road on the west side of Highway 23 about 1.5 km north of the ferry slip. Eagle Bay Recreation Site is 10.5 km south on the gravel road. It has a beach, boat launch and the usual recreation site biffy and tables. There are only 18 vehicle sites here; but at the time of writing no fees were being charged. Note that it is a "user-maintained" site so bring your own TP and pack out your garbage and junk.

Free Ferry

The Shelter Bay-Galena Bay Ferry (a.k.a. Upper Arrow Lake Ferry), 52 km south of Revelstoke, runs every hour on the hour from Shelter Bay from 5:00 am to 12 midnight. The return trip is every hour on the half hour from Galena Bay, starting at 5:30 am and continuing to 12:30 am. Additional sailings are usually added during the summer months. Check the Upper Arrow Lake Ferry Schedule for updates.

If you reach Shelter Bay between ferry runs or have to wait because of exceptionally heavy traffic on the free ferry, you may appreciate the picnic area near the terminal. You may even consider wetting a fishing line in Upper Arrow Lake.

Hot Springs and Water Falls

After the 30-minute crossing to Galena Bay on the east side of the lake, follow Highway 23 south. Your first major distraction will be Highway 31, approximately two km south of the ferry slip. This backroad could take you north and east past Trout Lake and south to Kootenay Lake, Kaslo and Balfour. We cover it in detail in the "Kootenay Highway 31" chapter. For this description, continue south on Highway 23.

Halcyon Hot Springs

The first of several hot springs is at Halcyon, 13.5 km south of the Galena Bay Ferry landing. The Halcyon Hot Springs Hotel was first developed in the 1880s by a steamboat captain plying the Arrow Lakes. It was expanded considerably in 1898 and underwent a major renovation in 1924. In the winter of 1955, it disappeared in a column of smoke, taking with it its then owner, Brigadier-General F.W.E. Burnham.

When we first visited the area in the 1990s, the Halcyon Hot Springs pool was a wooden structure a short distance up a steep gravel side road. A sign at the start of the access road marked it "Private Property–Do Not Abuse", but the pools were generally considered to be open to the public.

I suspect that Brigadier-General Burnham would be proud of the present Halcyon Hot Springs Resort. It is open year-around with several pools overlooking Upper Arrow Lake. Temperatures range from 42°C (105°F) for the hot pool down to 12°C (55°F) for the cold plunger. Being a coward, I stayed out of the cold plunger. The facility has continued to expand since opening to the public and now offers a restaurant, various accommodations and a campground. Visit http://www.halcyon-hotsprings.com/ for the latest information.

Boats at Eagle Bay BC Recreation Site on Upper Arrow Lake south of Revelstoke, BC. © Murphy Shewchuk

Halfway River Hot Springs

Brigadier-General Burnham might not be so impressed with the downright "rustic" nature of the Halfway River Hot Springs. But if you don't mind a little dust and a steep, it is worth exploring.

The road into the Halfway River Hot Springs starts on the south side of Halfway River about 23 km south of the Galena Bay Ferry landing or 25 km north of Nakusp. (Don't take the road that begins north of the bridge.) When we last visited the area, the gravel road was in generally rough condition and the start of it was somewhat obscured. Follow the forest

Ione Falls, Highway 23 north of Nakusp, BC. © Murphy Shewchuk

service road east into the mountains, keeping generally to the left except for a junction near Km 6.3. This is not a road for motorhomes or RV trailers. A four-wheel-drive vehicle is a definite asset.

The parking area is approximately 11.5 km northeast of Highway 23.

Recreation Sites and Trails BC undertook major upgrading there in the summer of 2016 and have added a 20-site campground plus a change shelter and toilets. A fee of $12.00/night ($6.00/night for seniors) will now be charged to offset the cost of maintenance. Note that cash is required in most recreation sites and remote campgrounds. Visit their website at www.sitesandtrailsbc.ca/ for up-to-date information.

Note that poison ivy is common in the area. The old rhyme "Leaves of three, let them be... Leaves of five, let them thrive!" is worth remembering.

Ione Creek Falls

BC Highways has a rest area at Ione Falls, approximately 27 km south of Galena Bay. The site is on the east side of the highway and the 20-metre

Nakusp Hot Springs pool, Hot Springs Road northeast of Nakusp, BC. © Murphy Shewchuk

(60-foot) falls is clearly visible from the road. The falls is worth a photo-op, particularly in spring or early summer.

Nakusp Hot Springs

The last major diversion on Highway 23 is Hot Springs Road, about 2.5 km north of downtown Nakusp. It is 12 km from the highway to the Nakusp Hot Springs parking lot. The views to south and east are spectacular until you get into the Kuskanax Creek canyon.

Gardner Creek Falls, 8.3 km from the highway, is worth a stop any time of the year, but can be a photographer's challenge in spring or early summer. The original road and bridge was a bit north of the present bridge and the old west end approach presents a safe place to park out of the line of traffic.

Decision Time

Nakusp presents time for a decision. Do you take Highway 6 south and west to Vernon or south and east to Castlegar or Kaslo via Slocan Lake? The Highway 6 chapters describe many of the sights along both routes making the decision more difficult.

Nakusp has a museum, eateries, stores and shops, and a waterfront walk to fill in the time while you are deciding.

Additional Information:
Nakusp Hot Springs
8500 Hot Springs Road PO Box 280
Nakusp BC V0G 1R0
Ph: 250-265-4528
Toll Free: 1-866-999-4528
Web: http://www.nakusphotsprings.com/
Upper Arrow Lakes Ferry Schedule
Western Pacific Marine
Web: http://arrowbridge.ca/ferry.php

Hounds Tooth Spire, Bugaboo Provincial Park. © Murphy Shewchuk

CHAPTER 24

Backroad to the Bugaboos: Exploring the Heart of the Purcell Mountains

STATISTICS

For map, see page 280.

Distance: 45 km: Brisco to Bugaboo Provincial Park

Travel Time: One to two hours.

Condition: Mostly gravel road.

Season: June to November. May be closed in winter.

Topo Maps: Bugaboo Creek 82K/15. (1:50,000)

Howser Creek 82K/10.

Spillimacheen 82K/16.

Backroad Mapbook: Kootenay Rockies BC.

Communities: Brisco & Radium Hot Springs.

A giant field of alpine spires and glaciers, known the world over for their challenging heli-skiing and mountaineering opportunities, lies hidden in the mountains of southeastern British Columbia.

First Mountaineers in 1910

The "Bugaboos", as they are now called, were originally named "The Nunataks" by Conrad Kain and the first group of mountaineers to visit the region in 1910. Who knows what epithets the gold seekers of the late 1800s used to describe this jumble of granitic rock that barred their way across the Purcell Mountains. But when Conrad Kain returned in 1916 to climb the central spire of this granite jungle, the name "Bugaboo" seems to have stuck to the spire, and later to a mountain pass, a glacier and a creek that drains the western portion of what has now become Bugaboo Glacier Provincial Park.

The word bugaboo, according to the battered dictionary that shares my desk, is derived from bugbear and means a fancied object of fear or a false belief used to intimidate or dissuade. For most of us bucket-seat travellers, the Bugaboos are neither fancied nor false, but real objects of awe and inspiration coloured with more than a tinge of downright respect.

While the Bugaboos continue to be the playground of skilled mountaineers and rich helicopter skiers, there is no reason, financial or otherwise, why backroads explorers, fishers and hikers can't enjoy this mountain wilderness to the limits of their abilities.

Good Gravel Road

With the recent major improvements in the road to the Canadian Mountain Holidays (CMH) Bugaboo Lodge, summer access should be easy for all but motorhomes and low-slung automobiles. The main accesses to Bugaboo Creek road are from Spillimacheen and Brisco on Highway 95 between Golden and Radium Hot Springs. Although we have used both routes, our most recent trip into the area was from the southeast via Brisco and thus, to be as accurate as possible, this is the route outlined.

Brisco Road [Km 0] leaves Highway 95 at a tiny community 29 km northwest of Radium Hot Springs. The road is well marked by "Bugaboo Glacier" signs and an information sign outlining the "No Services" nature of the park and surrounding area. Brisco is the last chance to stock up on supplies as none are available at the CMH Bugaboo Lodge or the Conrad Kain alpine hut. Self-sufficiency is the key to enjoyable backroads exploring, particularly in the mountains, and the Bugaboos are no exception.

The road to the Bugaboos crosses the Columbia River and its broad, fertile marshes at Km 2.0, and joins Westside Road at Km 3.4. Turn right (north) at the junction and watch for another side road to the left near km 5.0. If you have a four-wheel-drive vehicle or good traction, take this first junction. If not, stay on the main road for another 1.5 km to another junction and then swing west. Both roads are marked and join about 1.5 km west of Westside Road.

Once away from the Columbia Valley, this backroad follows the Templeton River upstream to Km 19 before crossing over a low ridge and into the Bugaboo Creek drainage system. Keep right at the junction at Km 18.5. The road to the south will take you into the Cartwright Lakes area and variety of small British Columbia recreation sites and hiking trails.

We don't have space to cover the details here, but the *Kootenay Rockies BC* edition of the Backroads Mapbook series provides basic information. The

Bugaboo Falls. © Murphy Shewchuk

Recreation Sites and Trails BC website at www.sitesandtrailsbc.ca/ also has information on the various sites. Check the "Getting There…" chapter for a variety of other map sources.

From the junction at Km 18.5, Bugaboo Road continues west to the Kain Creek Bridge near Km 28 before swinging southwest and into the heart of the Purcell Mountains.

Pioneer Mountaineers

Conrad Kain's name is attached to several features in this area. According to John F. Garden in his well-illustrated book *The Bugaboos—An Alpine*

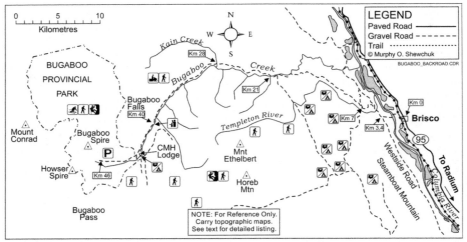

History (Footprint Publishing, Revelstoke), Conrad Kain was an Austrian-born (1883) mountaineer who outgrew his native Alps and came to North America in search of new mountains to climb. Kain obtained employment with Arthur Wheeler as a guide for the Alpine Club of Canada and the Dominion Government surveyors in the Canadian Rockies.

"[The year] 1913 heralded Conrad's most famous climb, that of the first certain ascent of Mt. Robson with Albert MacCarthy and Bill Foster," writes J.F. Garden. "From that summer on Conrad was always in demand."

Conrad Kain found Canada's winters too harsh for his liking and in 1913 he headed south to New Zealand's Southern Alps. For many years he climbed and guided in New Zealand's mountains in their summers and Canada's mountains in our summers.

From Km 21 to the CMH Bugaboo Lodge at Km 44, the road parallels the north then west side of Bugaboo Creek with numerous opportunities for creek fishing. Bugaboo Falls, at Km 40, offers a diversion of a different sort. An easy trail leads a short distance down to the foot of the falls where the mid-morning sun can create a spectacular rainbow in the drifting mist.

Above Bugaboo Falls, the creek and the road meander through a mountain meadow with an important junction at Km 43. Here the road to the park trailhead leads to the right while the road to the lodge and the Forest Service recreation site continues along the creek to the left.

The afternoon sun was impossible to resist when we visited there one Labour Day weekend and we took the rough and narrow road to the right and drove to the park trailhead. Worth noting was the ample supply of chicken wire at the parking lot. Porcupines appear to be the local "wildlife" to watch out for. The chicken wire is wrapped around the base of the parked vehicles and held in place with boulders to keep the porcupines from dining on tires, fan belts and other delicate parts.

After checking our water bottles and loading up a small pack with insect repellent and camera gear, we headed up the trail to Boulder Camp and the Conrad Cain Hut. It was too late in the afternoon to safely complete the five-hour round trip, but we did get far enough up the granite boulder-strewn mountain to appreciate the immense size of the glaciers and the compelling attraction of the Bugaboo spires. While we didn't have the inclination to climb the spires, we did find time to enjoy the cold clear water and the ripe blueberries and huckleberries that grew in the thickets along the mountain streams. A yearling black bear was also enjoying the berries, and when we came tramping along it headed for the timber before I could swing my camera into action.

A Relatively New Intrusion

The coarse grey granite spires of the Bugaboos are a massive, relatively new intrusion into the ancient 1,500 million-year-old metamorphic rocks of the Purcell Mountains. Some 70 million years ago, when the Rocky Mountains were concluding their development, the Purcell Range split open to allow molten magma from within the earth to well up close to the surface. Millions of years of erosion have worn away the weaker surface rock, revealing the challenging spires that jut up to 11,150 feet (3,400 metres) above sea level.

The 1910 expedition, which Conrad Kain was part of, had also arrived at the foot of the Bugaboo glacier on September 2, but it had taken them three days of bushwacking and trail-clearing to get the same distance we had traversed in an hour. His reports led an ever-increasing stream of mountaineers to challenge and beat the spires, usually with great difficulty and occasionally with the loss of life.

"Located as they are directly in the westerly storm tracks of moisture-laden Pacific air, the Spires receive a fair share of snow," writes J.F. Garden. "Two Austrian-Canadians, Hans Gmoser and Leo Grillmair, took note of this liberal snowfall and the obvious beauty of the area. During the winter of 1963-64 they set in motion their dream to make a livelihood in the Bugaboos."

CMH Bugaboo Lodge

Back at the junction at Km 43, the road to the left leads to Bugaboo Lodge and mining/logging roads on both sides of the south fork of Bugaboo Creek.

Hans Gmoser's first Bugaboo Lodge was built in 1968. It has been expanded and renovated several times since then, but the original stone fireplace still forms an attractive focus to the interior of the building. Under Gmoser's supervision, the Bugaboos and Canadian Mountain Holidays became synonymous with the ultimate in heli-skiing.

Although the Bugaboo Lodge is primarily geared for group tours with advance reservations, it can provide a room when space is available, or a fine meal, but advance reservations through their Banff office—(403) 762-7100—is essential to avoid disappointment.

Bugaboo-Septet Recreation Site

The backroad crosses Bugaboo Creek approximately 500 metres south of the CHM Lodge driveway. An old log cabin sits on the northwest bank of the creek and a rustic BC recreation site, with room for half-a-dozen vehicles, is located in the trees behind the cabin.

On one visit to the area the recreation site was too busy for our liking (three vehicles) so we nosed our way up the east side of Bugaboo Creek, parting the new growth with our windshield as we followed an old logging road south toward Bugaboo Pass. For our VW van, the road ended in a washout near the seven-km point. We back-tracked to a wide log landing with a roaring stream nearby and cooked our evening meal as the last rays of the sun turned the glacier-clad Quintet Peaks to gold.

This was backroad exploring as it is meant to be. A warm breeze keeping the mosquitoes at bay, the muffled roar of a stream all but drowning out the occasional coyote howl. And most important of all, huckleberry-laced bannock cakes cooking in a frying pan on an open fire.

Bugaboo Provincial Park Trails

BC Parks advises that inexperienced or ill-equipped climbers or hikers should forego a visit in favour of less demanding areas.

Parking Lot to Conrad Kain Hut: Length 5 km, suggested time 2 1/2 hrs, elevation change 700 m. The trail follows the northern lateral moraine of Bugaboo Glacier. The trail is very steep and strenuous. Extreme caution should be exercised along its route. Strong reliable footwear must be worn.

CMH Lodge to Cobalt Lake (Blue Lake): Length 5 km, suggested time 2-3 hrs, elevation change 884 m. Trail switchbacks up steep grade to open ridge and view of Cobalt Lake. A marked route then descends to lake. Open meadow area at high point excellent for wandering.

Routes lead from Conrad Kain Hut to climbing destinations. The route from the Hut to Malloy Igloo (shelter located at Malloy Glacier) traverses a distance of approximately 13 km. Elevation change 762 m. Only roped parties should attempt the trip as several glaciers have to be crossed.

Please keep to designated trails. Shortcutting, switchbacking and trampling meadows destroy the plant life and soil structure which keep rain and snow melt from eroding trails.

Additional Information:

Canadian Mountain Holidays
Box 1660
Banff, Alberta T1L 1J6
Toll Free: (800) 661-0252
Phone: (403) 762-7100
Web: http://www.canadianmountainholidays.com/
Recreation Sites and Trails BC
Web: www.sitesandtrailsbc.ca/
Bugaboo Provincial Park
Web: http://www.env.gov.bc.ca/bcparks/explore/parkpgs/bugaboo/

KVR Trestles under reconstruction after 2003 forest fire at Myra Canyon above Kelowna, BC.
© Murphy Shewchuk

CHAPTER 25
Historic Railways:
Rail to Trails Introduction

American and Canadian Railway Rivalry

The completion of the Northern Pacific Railway (NPR) across the US in 1883 connected Minneapolis in the east to Portland in the west. It ran through Helena, Sandpoint and Spokane, south of British Columbia's Kootenay-Columbia region. The Canadian Pacific Railway (CPR) was completed two years later with the last spike being driven at Craigellachie in 1885. It ran from Montreal, across Ontario and the Prairies through Calgary, Golden and Revelstoke before continuing to the Pacific Coast at Port Moody. It crossed the northern section of the Kootenay-Columbia region with crossings of the Columbia River at Golden and Revelstoke.

Neither railway directly served the area richest in minerals, but both were accessible via trail and waterway. The Columbia River and integrated lakes such as the Arrow Lakes, supplied the CPR. The Kootenay River and its integrated lakes served the NPR. Both major rivers disregarded international boundaries and flowed generally north-south in great loops as they found their way from the Rockies to the Pacific.

Paddlewheel Steamers Filled the Gaps

In the competition to carry the rich ore to smelters and bring in supplies to the new communities springing up at the mines, steamboats were imported in pieces or built on the spot.

The first of the steamers to ply the Upper Columbia River was the *Duchess*, launched in Golden in 1886. According to its 27-year-old Captain F.P. Armstrong she was "a pretty crude steamboat." The 74-foot-long hull was built from salvaged lumber: the upper deck "resembled an outhouse hit by a hurricane." Her engines weren't much better, having worked for nearly half a century in a St. Lawrence River ferry. Coincidentally, the same Captain F.P. Armstrong, piloted the *Nowitka* on its final voyage on the Columbia in 1920. In the interim, this very same Captain Armstrong established a network of steamers, barges and tramways that provided service from Golden to Fort

Steele. The NPR wasn't asleep at the switch. It employed steamers to transfer rich galena ore via the Kootenay River to its tracks at Jennings, Montana and then carried the bounty to smelters in Montana and Washington. In 1893, the steamer *Annerly* made her maiden voyage to Fort Steele via the Kootenay River, setting up competition with Captain Armstrong.

Steamers were the queens of the waterways and a major link in the Kootenay transportation chain until the completion of the major railway lines and World War I. The SS *Moyie,* the only survivor of the glorious Kootenay paddlewheel era sits on shore at Kaslo, serving as a much-photographed tribute to her kind. She was built in 1898 and retired in 1957 after nearly 60 years of service.

Much more information is available in Art Downs' book, *Paddlewheels on the Frontier.*

Railway Explosion

Between 1890 and 1893, 11 railways were incorporated in the Kootenay-Columbia Region. Several of these never made it past the charter stage, but enough of them did to set the stage for railway service and rivalry that was to last nearly half a century.

Columbia and Kootenay Railway and Navigation Company

Railroad construction on the Boundary Subdivision began in 1890 when the Canadian Pacific Railway (CPR) chartered the Columbia and Kootenay Railway and Navigation Company (C&K) to extend BC's southern mainline from Kootenay Lake at Nelson to the Columbia River at Castlegar. Service began in 1891 between Nelson and Sproats Landing (across the Columbia River from present-day Castlegar). Completion of this line provided transportation of ore from Nelson north on paddle wheel steamers over the Arrow Lakes and Columbia River to the CPR mainline at Revelstoke. A short extension of the C&K from Sproats Landing to Robson allowed for the construction of a rail barge slip.

Destination Sandon

Prior to the construction of the two main railways noted below, a network of railways and steamboat services were developed to serve the silver mining boom in the Sandon area. The mid 1890s saw the construction of the Nakusp & Slocan Railway from Nakusp on Upper Arrow Lake to Roseberry and New Denver on Slocan Lake and then up to Three Forks and Sandon. It used water transport on Arrow Lake to connect to the CPR at Revelstoke.

Steam Locomotive: photo courtesy of the Nicola Valley Museum & Archives.

During that same period, The Kaslo and Slocan Railway was built into Sandon from Kaslo on Kootenay Lake. Steamers carried freight to and ore from Kaslo via Kootenay Lake and river to the Great Northern Railway at Bonners Ferry in the United States.

In this same general area a short-lived Kootenay and Arrowhead Railway was built from Lardeau on Kootenay Lake to Gerrard on Trout Lake in 1902. Steamers were used to carry freight to and ore from the mining camps at the west end of Trout Lake.

C&W: Castlegar to Midway

In 1890 gold and copper were discovered near Rossland. The Columbia and Western Railway (C&W) was chartered to run from the smelter in Trail to Penticton. This line was completed to Robson in 1897. Hydro-electric power was transmitted from the Bonnington Dam a distance of 52 km (32 miles) to Trail in 1898. On April 2, 1898, surveyors led by a man named Rice reached Grand Forks with slashing crews following close behind them. By September 24, six railroad construction camps between Cascade and Grand Forks employed 250 men. A portable sawmill, operated by McPherson and Stout, supplied rail ties and timbers and

KVR Water Tank at Brookmere, BC. © Murphy Shewchuk

W.H. Fisher supplied 70,000 rail ties from a site north of Niagara (north of Grand Forks).

C&W Purchased by CPR

In the midst of this construction activity, the Columbia and Western Railway was purchased from mining developer Fritz Heinze, along with the Trail smelter by the CPR in 1899.

The Boundary Subdivision line was constructed from the Columbia River at Robson to Midway, a distance of 202 kilometers (125 miles), during the two years 1898-1899. Total cost of this section of railroad was approximately $5 million. Despite the low temperatures and heavy snow of the winter of 1898-99, the railway construction was rushed as fast as human labour could do the job. Railway grading was completed within a year and on September 18, 1899 the first official train arrived in Grand Forks. On September 23, regular passenger service commenced and on October 11, 1899, the first shipment of ore from Boundary country (from the City of Paris Mine) was delivered to the Trail smelter. On November 25, 1899 passenger service extended to Greenwood. By 1900 the railroad had reached Midway with a branch line from Eholt to the copper-rich area of Phoenix.

Dangerous Work

Construction and maintenance of this railroad required great effort and was often times extremely dangerous. On January 11, 1900 two men were killed by flying rock. With regards to maintenance, on February 4, 1900, for instance, 100 men were sent out to shovel drifts.

Canadian control in Southern British Columbia

By reaching the Boundary District, the CPR had scored a major victory against its American railroad competitors in its bid to re-establish Canadian control in southern British Columbia. American communities along the Kettle River and tributary valleys south of the international boundary found it easier to ship via CPR than to use the long and rough wagon roads leading to J.J. Hill's Great Northern (GN) railroad in Washington State.

The "victory" wasn't permanent. Fierce rivalry between the US and Canadian railroads included considerable legal maneuvering and occasional skirmishes between construction crews such as the "Battle of Midway." According to Dan Langford in *Cycling the Kettle Valley Railway:* "It was in November 1905, in the little town of Midway ... that the battle between railway rivals ... was to come to physical blows." The VV&E construction

KVR Railway Bridge across Coldwater River near Brookmere, BC. © Murphy Shewchuk

crew "inadvertently" crossed a small part of CPR land. Before the dust settled "tracks were torn up, shovels and picks clanged against one another, and shots were fired. Miraculously no one was killed."

Branch lines were built at various locations, diverting traffic from one side of the border to the other.

Bridge across the Columbia River

Barges at first joined the C&K and C&W railways between Robson and West Robson. The bridge across the Columbia River was completed in 1902, completing the last link in a continuous rail line between Nelson and Midway. This line was renamed the Boundary Subdivision in 1910. Grade revisions were made in the early 1940s and late 1960s to accommodate the construction of dams at Brilliant and Labarthe. Trackage was added to West Midway following the abandonment of the Carmi Subdivision (Kettle River Railway) in 1978 to serve the sawmill there.

The Historic Kettle Valley Railway:
Three Mountain Ranges and 500 Km

The Kettle Valley Railway, a subsidiary of the Canadian Pacific Railway, was constructed in 1910-1916 to provide an all-Canadian railway route between the Boundary region in the southern interior of British Columbia and the

BC coast near Vancouver. The 500 km (300 mile) long railway commenced at Midway, at the western terminus of the CPR's Columbia and Western Railway.

It ran westward across three mountain summits (the Monashee Mountains, the Interior Plateau, and the Cascades Mountains), and through three deep valleys (the Okanagan, the Tulameen and the Coquihalla), to the Fraser River Valley. It established an uninterrupted rail communication from the Kootenays to the Coast by connecting with the CPR mainline near Hope.

Served Mining Centres

In running westward from Midway, the Kettle Valley Railway passed through the mining centres of Beaverdell and Carmi; crossed over the Okanagan Highlands to Penticton in the Okanagan Valley; over Trout Creek Canyon to West Summerland; and then crossed the Thompson Plateau to Princeton in the Similkameen Valley. It then ascended the

KVR Steam Locomotive during railway construction: photo courtesy of the Nicola Valley Museum & Archives.

Tulameen and Otter valleys through Coalmont and Tulameen to Brookmere and Brodie Junction in the North Cascade Mountains. At Brodie, the rail line first branched northwards down the Coldwater River Valley to Merritt where it joined an existing CPR branch line (the Nicola Branch). From Merritt the grade led westward to the CPR mainline at Spences Bridge in the Thompson River Valley. At Brodie, the railway was also built southwards along the Coldwater and Coquihalla Valleys to connect, via the narrow Coquihalla Pass, with the CPR mainline at Odlum in the Fraser River Valley, near Hope. The Kettle Valley Railway headquarters was at Penticton in the Okanagan Valley.

Over Half a Century

The Kettle Valley Railway served the Kootenay Mining Region of the southern interior of British Columbia for 60 years, and for many of those years operated both as a freight and passenger railway. The KVR served the Okanagan and Similkameen for another 16 years before freight service ended in 1989 in the face of severe competition from trucking companies. Sections of the railway were abandoned piecemeal as freight traffic declined: the Coquihalla section in 1961, following a severe washout; the Midway to Penticton section, in which the Myra Canyon is located, in 1978; and the last operating section, Penticton to Merritt, in 1990. After each abandonment, the railway tracks, a number of the steel bridges, and most of the ancillary railway structures (stations, section houses, freight sheds, engine houses and turntables, tools sheds, and the telegraph line, etc.) were demolished, and the rail yards and sidings obliterated. Earlier, following the dieselization of the Kettle Valley Railway in 1953-54, the coaling towers and almost all of the water tanks of the steam locomotive era were removed. However, a large number of the most significant bridges, tunnels, trestles, rock cuts and embankments, and the rail bed, with many short gaps, survive today within the former right-of-way of the 500-km-long railway.

Destination Sandon

Prior to the construction of the two main railways previously noted, a network of railways and steamboat services were developed to serve the silver mining boom in the Sandon area. The mid 1890s saw the construction of the Nakusp & Slocan Railway from Nakusp on Upper Arrow Lake to Roseberry and New Denver on Slocan Lake and then up to Three Forks and Sandon. It used water transport on Arrow Lake to connect to the CPR at Revelstoke.

During that same period, The Kaslo and Slocan Railway was built into

Style of 1890 Steam Locomotive: photo courtesy of the Nicola Valley Museum & Archives.

Sandon from Kaslo on Kootenay Lake. Steamers carried freight to and ore from Kaslo via Kootenay Lake and river to the Great Northern Railway at Bonners Ferry in the United States.

In this same general area a short-lived Kootenay and Arrowhead Railway was built from Lardeau on Kootenay Lake to Gerrard on Trout Lake in 1902. Steamers were used to carry freight to and ore from the mining camps at the east end of Trout Lake.

Tracks are Gone but not Forgotten

For the most part, the tracks were lifted when the mining booms subsided. In some cases the rail grades reverted to Nature. In other cases they became part of the provincial highway system. In recent years many of the grades that haven't been converted to roads have been resurrected as part of an ever-growing rail-trail network. Examples of these can be found all across southern British Columbia and in the northern US states. In the BC side of the boundary they seem to be the most prolific in the Kootenay-Columbia region.

Probably most notable are the C&W and KVR rail trails, but no less significant to local residents is the Galena Trail near New Denver and the Slocan Valley Rail Trail from Slocan Lake to South Slocan. These are looked after by relatively small local groups.

The Kimberley to Cranbrook rail-trail, one of the few that is paved, is under the stewardship on the North Star Rails to Trails Society.

Most of these trails are on land that has reverted to the province. Some of them are part of the Trans Canada Trail and others are spur lines maintained to serve local recreation interests.

Trails in Transition

I have attempted to provide a brief description of the two major rail trails in the following chapters and touched on several of the other trails throughout this book. However, no book can ever be truly up-to-date in an environment of constant change.

Some of this change is caused by the vagaries of the terrain that has challenged road and railway builders for well over a century. Other changes have been prompted by the evolution in transportation that sometimes pits Off Road Vehicle and ATV users against cyclists.

Most of the change can be considered positive as local trail advocates work to settle differences and raise funds to repair and improve the rights-of-way long abandoned by the glorious days of the steam locomotive. In other cases such as the 40+ km Cranbrook to Wardner Chief Isadore Trail, local groups have established a trail that utilizes bits of old railgrade, abandoned logging roads and new construction to build something they are proud of.

In light of the admission that this isn't the definitive resource, I suggest that you check closely with each community you visit to see what trails are available. Community brochures and websites are a valuable resource.

The Mussio Ventures Ltd. Backroad Mapbook series provides a lot of information on a larger scale. The same company has developed the BRMB Navigator app for both iPhone & iPad and Android devices. It permits a much closer view of the terrain plus the ability to follow your meanderings on your phone or tablet. More information on the apps is available at http://brmbnavigator.com/ .

The Trails BC website at www.trailsbc.ca is also a valuable resource. The Great Trail, formerly the Trans Canada Trail, at https://thegreattrail.ca/ has information, interactive maps, and, as I write this, a trail app for iPad.

Happy exploring!

Carlyle on the C&W Rail Trail Nursery Trestle east of Grand Forks, BC. © Murphy Shewchuk

CHAPTER 26
Columbia & Western Railway Trail: Castlegar to Midway

STATISTICS

For map, see page 298.

Distance: 162 km: Castlegar to Midway

Travel Time: Cycling: Three to five days.

Condition: Mostly gravel railway grade with some rough sections. A few paved sections through communities.

Season: June through September. Prepare for snow at higher elevations.

Backroads Mapbook: Kootenay Rockies BC.

Communities: Castlegar, Christina Lake, Grand Forks, Greenwood, Midway.

Colourful History

While the present cycling route runs from the Hugh Keenleyside Dam, about 10 km north of downtown Castlegar, the history of the Columbia & Western Railway links back to the smelter at Trail and mines at Rossland.

The discovery of gold-copper ore in the West Kootenay district in 1890 led to a mining boom. Within five years, almost 2,000 claims were staked nearby. Shipping the ore by wagon and paddle-wheel steamer and rail to the smelter in Montana proved costly. Fritz Augustus Heinze, one of the three "Copper Kings" of Butte, Montana, decided to build a smelter at Trail and a railway to the Rossland mines.

Fritz Heinze also chartered the Columbia and Western Railway (C&W) to run from the Trail smelter to Penticton, in the Okanagan Valley. The line was completed to Robson on the Columbia River in 1897. By September 1898, construction was well on the way to Grand Forks. In the midst of the frenetic activity, mining developer F.A. Heinze sold the C&W Railway and the Trail smelter to the Canadian Pacific Railway (CPR). Under the auspices of the CPR, the rail line was completed from Robson to Midway by 1900, at

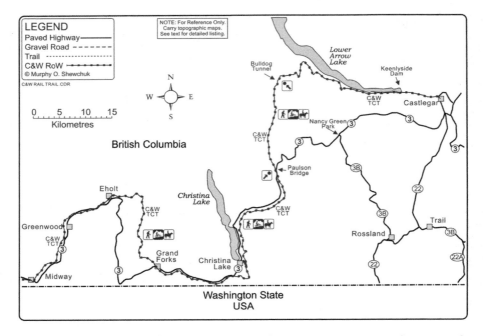

a cost of approximately $5 million. Branch lines were constructed to several locations including one from Eholt to copper-rich Phoenix. The bridge across the Columbia River at Castlegar was completed in 1902, completing the last link in a continuous rail line between Nelson and Midway.

By reaching the Boundary District, the CPR had scored a major victory against its American railroad competitors in its bid to re-establish Canadian control in southern British Columbia. American communities along the Kettle River and tributary valleys south of the international boundary found it easier to ship via CPR than to use the long and rough wagon roads leading to J.J. Hill's Great Northern (GN) railroad in Washington State.

After the completion of the Kettle Valley Railroad linking Midway to Hope through Penticton and Princeton and over the Coquihalla Pass in 1915, Nelson had become only a day's travel by passenger train from Vancouver and ten hours from Penticton.

More Recent Adjustments

The Columbia & Western Railway was renamed the CPR Boundary Subdivision in 1910. Grade revisions were made in the early 1940s and late 1960s to accommodate the construction of dams at Brilliant and BC Hydro's Hugh Keenleyside Dam near Labarthe. Trackage was added to West Midway following the abandonment of the Carmi Subdivision (Kettle River Railway) in 1978.

The End of an Era

Highways, including the Hope-Princeton, stripped the railways of some of their freight traffic. Airlines and automobiles did the same to the passenger traffic. The Coquihalla section of the KVR, between Hope and Brodie, was abandoned in 1961. The 210 km of track between Midway and Penticton were abandoned in 1978. The last train between Okanagan Falls, south of Penticton, and Spences Bridge on the CPR mainline, ran in 1989. Rails were removed between Midway and Castlegar in 1990. Many of the spur lines have since become roadways or have reverted to Nature.

The Start of a New Era

The CPR initially transferred ownership of much of the C&W Railway grade to the Trans Canada Trail Foundation which turned it over to Tourism BC. By 2006, decking and railing of all trestles between Grand Forks and Castlegar had been completed. Bulldog Tunnel had been improved and numerous culverts replaced and washouts repaired.

Nature continues to strain the resources of the various stewardship groups. However, the railgrade is generally considered passable from Castlegar to Princeton with a few detours through various communities. At the time of writing, the Trails to the Boundary Society was installing km signposts along much of the route from Fife to McCulloch.

Points of Interest along the C&W Rail Trail

The Castlegar Museum has been designated as Km 0 of the rail trail. The initial route is along city streets and Arrow Lakes Drive to Km 8.8 and the start of the 540 metre climb to the Bulldog Tunnel Station. With an average grade of 1.75 percent from the trailhead to Tunnel Station, (elev. 960 metres) the 31 km can be a steady slog, particularly if you have loaded panniers.

There are plenty of scenic views, bridges and tunnels along the way that can serve as photo-ops and excuses to catch your breath. There are numerous viewpoints to "shoot" Lower Arrow Lake, starting with the dam. The longest bridge on this section is the McCormick Creek Bridge near Km 17. It is a steel structure 125 meters long and 57.9 meters high.

Bulldog Tunnel

There are several see-through tunnels, but the Bulldog Tunnel, at Km 38.4, is definitely not see-through. At 912 metres it was the longest tunnel on the Boundary Subdivision and the longest railway tunnel built in southern British Columbia.

Cyclists on the C&W Rail Trail north of Grand Forks. © Murphy Shewchuk

A good bicycle lamp is essential if you are to navigate this tunnel safely. In addition to the length, it curves near the west end resulting in total darkness. When you do see "light at the end of the tunnel" the bright spot can make vision even trickier. In my ride through the tunnel, I used a 12-volt high-intensity lamp mounted on my bike. Others wearing headlamps seemed to have more problems as they wobbled around rocks on the tunnel floor.

The Bulldog Station area is relatively flat, but the grade continues to climb up to 1,220 metres elevation near Farron before beginning a steady descent to the Kettle River and Cascade at Km 90. The 158-metre-long Highway 3 Paulson Bridge passes high over the rail grade near Km 61. The beautiful blue arch sits 84 metres above McRae Creek and the trail.

Paulson Tunnel, a km farther along, is 111 metres long and may also deserve a good light. There are numerous photo-ops of Christina Lake as the trail emerges from the McRae Creek canyon. A large ore bin at Fife (Km 82) served a local lime quarry. A rather steep road down the hill will take you to Highway 3 and the east end of the community of Christina Lake.

Christina Lake has been the holiday destination of thousands for a century and a half. If you need advice, bike repairs, parts or a little sympathy, WildWays Adventure Sports (1925 Highway 3) is certainly a good place to stop. If you are looking for a campsite, we have stayed at the Schulli Resort on Bakery Frontage Road numerous times.

Santa Rosa Road (Km 87) is an alternate, paved road down to Christina Lake. If you have taken the earlier detour, it is a way back up to the trail. See the Cascade Highway chapter for a potential backroad route from Christina to Rossland via Santa Rosa Road and the Old Cascade Highway.

Kettle River Bridge

The 153.9-metre-long steel bridge across the Kettle River was re-decked in July, 2003 as a joint military exercise with the CME and British and New Zealand troops. At 440 metres, the Kettle River crossing is the lowest elevation point on this section of the C&W. From here west it is a steady climb up the Kettle River to Grand Forks.

Pioneer AC Generating Plant

It is another km to Highway 395 and the general area of the Cascade Station and Cascade City. The waterfalls on the Kettle River gave the community its name and also provided energy for the Cascade Powerhouse hydroelectric plant located here. It began operation in 1902 as one of the first 3-phase, 60-cycle alternating current electrical generating

Hugh Keenleyside Dam on Lower Arrow Lake, near Castlegar, BC. © Murphy Shewchuk

plants in the world. The AC generators were based on the original Nikola Tesla design and produced 3,000 kilowatts or 4,000 hp.

Another railway bridge crosses over to the north side of the Kettle River near the top of the Cascade Gorge. Then the trail continues west through Gilpin Grasslands Provincial Park. The park was established in 2007 to protect the delicate grassland ecosystem and habitat for numerous blue listed species including bighorn sheep. There aren't any services and motor vehicles are limited to the highway and Gilpin Forest Service Road.

Nursery Trestle

The C&W Trail runs between the Kettle River and the south side of Highway 3 to the Nursery Trestle (Km 107) where it crosses to the south side of the river. It skirts the edge of the river to 68th Avenue then follows 2nd Street into Grand Forks. There is a campground located in City Park at 7162 5th Street.

The city of 4,000+ has a wide variety of services and an excellent museum.

Climbing North

The trail winds through Grand Forks city streets before crossing Highway 3 near Columbia Drive and on to the rail trail again. Before beginning the steady climb 26 km north to Eholt Station it might be worth a stop at the old railway station (7654 Donaldson Drive). While many communities have turned their historic stations into museums, this one is a pub. I will vouch for the fine dining and friendly staff.

With an average grade of 1.6 percent to Eholt, you could be looking for a few other places to rest. In addition to photo-ops of the city and Granby Valley, there are historic buildings and tunnels at Km 123 and 127.6. Both of these tunnels are long enough to require a headlamp.

Eholt Station was also the junction of a spur line to the Phoenix mine site. Some sections of the Phoenix spur are now used as cross-country ski trails. See the "Phoenix Road" chapter for more information.

Cold clear water from a trailside spring. © Murphy Shewchuk

Carlyle at Cascade Gorge Bridge over Kettle River—C&W Rail Trail. © Murphy Shewchuk

Greenwood

From Eholt Station the rail trail begins a steady descent to Greenwood, crossing to the south side of Highway 3 near Km 138. The trail passes through farm fields on the way to a second highway crossing at Greenwood (Km 145) where it also crosses over to the west side of Boundary Creek.

If you are interested in a break or a place to stay, Deadwood Street can take you back across Boundary Creek to the city centre where there are plenty of options. With about 700 residents, most visitors would hardly consider this a "city". However, Greenwood is proud to proclaim that it is Canada's smallest city. It was established in 1897, during the copper mining boom, also making it one of British Columbia's oldest cities.

Copper was king here for a couple of decades starting in the 1890s. In 1918 copper went into a tail spin and most of the people left, but some of the heyday buildings were left and are now part of a rejuvenated Greenwood.

Downhill to Midway

The Rail Trail follows the west side of Boundary Creek for about a km before crossing back over. On the way it passes the site of the original Anaconda

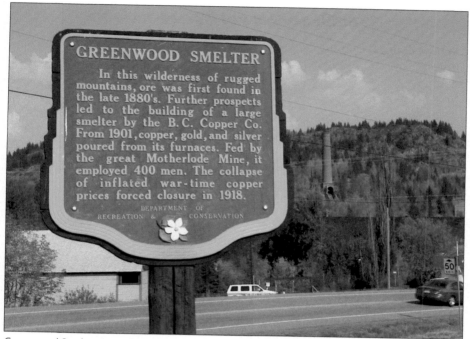

Greenwood Smelter stop-of-interest sign at Greenwood, BC. © Murphy Shewchuk

smelter. If you look up the hill to the northwest, you may be able to see the smelter smoke stack. The 36-metre-high stack was built in 1904 and has stood as mute evidence of the colourful history of the Boundary for over a century.

The rail trail crosses back over to the west side of Boundary Creek before reaching Boundary Falls (Km 153). There was also a short-lived smelter and hydroelectric plant here.

For the remainder of the 15-km run from Greenwood to Midway, the trail clings to the edge of the hillside; sometimes well above Highway 3 and the creek.

Midway

Midway (Km 162) was Mile 126 on the Columbia & Western Railway and Mile 0 of the Kettle Valley Railway. The railway station still stands and the nearby depot has been converted to a museum and visitor information centre. There is camping and services in the village.

Notes:

Note 1-From railway historian Joe Smuin: "Employee Time Tables, while useful, can sometimes lead one a bit astray on the exact mileage of stations. This information is obtained from my copy of the Boundary Subdivision

Castlegar-Midway Mileage Table

Station Boards Note 1	Miles May, 1914	Km Converted	Point of Interest	C&W Trail km Note 2
Nelson	0	0		
Castlegar	25.73	41.41		0
Robson West	27.40	44.1		
Westley	30.32	48.8		
			Keenleyside Dam	
			C&W Trailhead	8.8
Labarthe	32.41	52.16		11.0
Shields	39.12	62.96		21.5
Coykendahl	43.64	70.23		28.7
Tunnel	50.40	81.1		39.7
Porcupine	55.08	88.6		46.6
Farron	57.98	93.3		51.6
			Verigin Monument	53.0
Paulson	62.44	100.48		59.3
			Paulson Overpass	60.9
Coryell	66.35	106.8		65.7
Wade/Lafferty 7	0.52	113.49		72.6
Christina	73.20	117.8		
Fife	76.88	123.7		82.2
			Santa Rosa Road	86.8
			Kettle R. Bridge	89.1
Cascade	81.81	131.66	Hwy 395 X-ing	90.2
Billings	82.83	133.30		91.8
Gilpin	87.06	140.11		98.4
Cuprum	93.40	150.31	Wind through	
Grand Forks city	108.9			
Grand Forks	94.74	152.47		111.3
West End	95.89	154.32		112.1
East Granby	96.69	155.60		
Fisherman	100.34	161.48		120.3
Hodges	105.36	169.56		128.2
Eholt	108.71	174.95		133.7
Hwy 3 X-ing				137.9
Hwy 3 X-ing				145.2
Greenwood	117.32	188.80		147.5
Anaconda	118.5 est.	190.70		
Boundary Falls	121.03	194.77		153.2
Midway	126.57	203.69		162.3

Boundary Creek Bridge near Greenwood. Courtesy of the Trails to the Boundary Society.

Condensed Profile, which probably will be just about the most accurate source available to anybody now.

"One caveat ... these mileages can fool you because they aren't always determined at the same place from one station to the next. If there was a platform or shelter building, often the station mileage would reflect the mileage of that point. However, at places where there was no shelter or platform, in early years, the Station Name Board would be situated at the mid-point of the siding–if there was a siding. You can't automatically assume that there was a platform/shelter/station building at every station. In later years, Station Name Boards were placed on the section foreman's house and the station mileage calculated to be at the sign on the section house. This is why sometimes station mileages in later years have a slight difference from the earlier mileages. The station didn't go anywhere ... just the Station Name Board.

"Also be aware–if you aren't already–that railroaders use the term 'station' interchangeably. They may be referring to what is properly the 'station building.' Otherwise, the station was usually considered to be between two designated switches or mileages–depending upon location.

"I appreciate that this is a laborious explanation, but I know only too well how confusing all this can get when you are trying to reconcile the written records to what you are seeing on the ground and they just don't jive."

Note 2: Columbia & Western Trail km references are adapted from *Cycling the Kettle Valley Railway* by Dan & Sandra Langford (Rocky Mountain Books). *Cycling the Kettle Valley Railway* is considered by most to be the "bible" for rail grade travellers. Langford's km references are used by the Columbia and Western Trail Society and Grand Forks Community Trails Society as well as the Trails to the Boundary Society for their km boards along the route.

～⌒≈⌒～

Additional Information
Columbia & Western Trail Society
Web: http://www.columbiaandwestern.ca/
Grand Forks Community Trails Society
Web: http://www.gftrails.ca/
Kootenay Columbia Trails Society
Web: http://www.kcts.ca/
Trails BC: Boundary Region
Web: http://www.trailsbc.ca/tct/boundary
Trails to the Boundary Society
Facebook: https://www.facebook.com/trailstotheboundary
Trans Canada Trail–The Great Trail
Web: https://thegreattrail.ca/

Poison Ivy on rock bluffs near Kettle River, Christina Lake, BC. © Murphy Shewchuk

Little Tunnel on KVR north of Naramata, BC. © Murphy Shewchuk

CHAPTER 27

The Great Trail (TCT)–
Midway to Penticton:
The Kettle Valley Railway
Carmi Subdivision

STATISTICS

For map, see page 312.

Distance: 213 km—Midway to Penticton.
Travel Time: Variable.
Condition: Variable.
Season: Best in dry weather. Sections used year around.
Backroad Mapbook: Thompson Okanagan, BC.
Communities: Midway, Rock Creek, Beaverdell, Carmi, Kelowna, Naramata, Penticton.

A Critical Period in British Columbia History

The late 1800s and early 1900s were a period of intense railway competition and track laying in BC's Boundary District. However, it wasn't until June, 1910 that construction began on the Kettle Valley Railway under the stewardship of Chief Engineer Andrew McCulloch. The rails reached Beaverdell in July, 1912 and Hydraulic Summit (McCulloch Lake) in December, 1913. In the meantime, construction started at the Penticton end of the grade in September, 1912. By the end of 1913, most of the grading work was completed. Work continued on the Adra (Spiral) Tunnel and the numerous trestles of the Myra Canyon throughout 1913 and 1914. According to Barrie Sanford in *McCulloch's Wonder: The Story of the Kettle Valley Railway*, "... on October 2, 1914, not far from the 4,178 foot summit of the railway, the last spike on the Penticton-Midway section was driven at West Fork Canyon Creek bridge." The steel rails had met at what is now known as the Pooley Creek Trestle in the heart of the Myra Canyon.

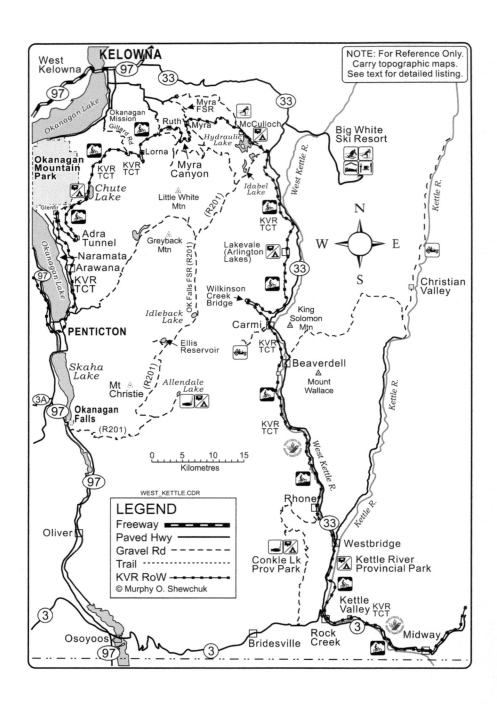

NOTE: For Reference Only.
Carry topographic maps.
See text for detailed listing.

LEGEND
Freeway
Paved Hwy
Gravel Rd
Trail
KVR RoW
© Murphy O. Shewchuk

0   5   10   15
Kilometres

WEST_KETTLE.CDR

The Great Trail, Formerly the Trans Canada Trail

Today the Trans Canada Trail follows much the same route as the former KVR, except for a detour around the Boundary Sawmill (formerly Pope & Talbot) in the western outskirts of Midway and around some development near Rock Creek. While the grade is rising up the Kettle River Valley between Midway and Rock Creek, the climb is minimal as the trail winds through farms and ranches and along the river. Be prepared to dismount to open and close gates and use caution when crossing cattleguards. Also be prepared for a few rough sections although plans are underway to clean up the railgrade.

The general consensus among cyclists is that fat tire mountain bikes may be the transportation of choice on the rail grade due, in part, to motorized use on sections of the trail. I would like to add that a strong, bright bicycle headlamp could be a life-saver in a tunnel or if your trip ends up running into darkness. Inexpensive helmet headlamps may not have the sight distance or battery life.

It is also worth noting that while the trail follows rivers and crosses numerous creeks, clean drinking water may be in short supply during the summer months. A good micro filter pump and appropriate chemical treatments can reduce the risk of diarrhea or worse. Mountain Equipment Co-op (MEC) offers a variety of options.

Forest Fire Damaged Sections of Rail Trail

From Rock Creek, the grade swings north up the West Kettle River. The climb increases slightly, occasionally reaching 0.8 percent as it winds through forest parkland and the occasional farm. A major forest fire in August, 2015 destroyed numerous homes and scorched the forest adjacent to the rail grade. Fortunately the railway bridge at Kettle River Recreation Area and most of the 114-campsite campground was spared.

The valley narrows at Westbridge and the forest parkland becomes more predominant. The grade gets a bit steeper, regularly reaching 1.0 percent on the steady climb to Beaverdell.

Blythe-Rhone Road

A couple of missing bridges near Rhone mean that the trail traveller is forced to take Blythe-Rhone Road for about seven km before returning to the rail grade. The distance change is minimal and there was the benefit of being able to take a break at Paul Lautard's cyclist's rest stop. For more than a decade Paul often came down from his nearby house to greet travellers and

The Trans Canada Trail five km west of Midway. Courtesy of the Trails to the Boundary Society.

fill them in on the history of the region. Paul recently retired to Midway (he turned 94 in September, 2016) and sold the property. The latest report is that the water pump there is no longer operational; however, water may be obtained at Little Dipper Hideaway, approximately three km farther north.

According to George and Frauke Delisle, owners of the Little Dipper Hideaway, they also offer camping and limited accommodations in their B&B and a small rustic log cabin. They also can supply a supper with plenty of advance notice. (Phone 250-446-2213.) Note that they only accept cash and do not handle credit cards. Cell phone coverage can be limited so it is wise to plan ahead.

Spectacular Canyon

Bull Creek Canyon, seven km north of the rest stop, is one of the more spectacular canyons on the West Kettle River. In September the pools are like mirrors, but in May or June, you can hear the roar long before you see the canyon. The rail grade crosses the river on a steel bridge a few hundred metres up from the canyon mouth. Note the "M 29.8" and "16-10-56" marks on the southeast side of the bridge.

About one km north of the bridge the rail grade becomes a logging road although there are signs of efforts to limit motorized traffic. Km markers will signal your northward progress as the steady climb continues. On one trip along the route, I cycled from Rock Creek north to Beaverdell and found my energy beginning to flag on the steady straight sections.

Beaverdell

The railway grade disappears under a gravel road and it is difficult to determine where it is on the final approach to Beaverdell. Finally the route is blocked by industrial development. The only way through is to go right (east) on Beaverdell Station Road for a couple hundred metres to a Y-junction marked by a wooden kiosk and information signs. If you are continuing north without a stop in Beaverdell, take the rough road north through the trees. If, however, it is time for a break, follow the pavement as it loops southeast to Highway 33 and the heart of the community.

There are restaurants, accommodations, and an RV Park and campground. At the time of writing the RV Park/Campground was up for sale so it may be wise to search "camping at Beaverdell" for up-to-date information.

Wilkinson Creek Loop

North of Beaverdell, the railway begins a steady one percent grade that takes it through Carmi and up Wilkinson Creek to a yellow steel bridge. The original railway bridge was removed from the site after the rails were lifted in 1979. The gap remained for over 20 years, forcing trail users to make a long detour or ford the creek–a particularly dangerous activity in high water. As part of a major rail-trail improvement project, the bright yellow 24-metre prefabricated steel span was lifted into place by a crane in November 2001.

The rail grade makes a 10-km loop up Wilkinson Creek before returning to the West Kettle River Valley a hundred metres higher than where it started. The grade continues north along the west side of Arlington Mountain, past the Lakevale station and the Arlington Lakes. There is a 23-campsite BC Recreation Site on Lower Arlington Lake. The site is maintained with a $12.00 camping fee from early May to mid-October. Note that it is wise to carry cash as few of the recreation site operators can handle credit cards. The foundation of a large water tank adjacent to the rail grade is a reminder of the historic significance of the area.

When we last cycled the grade, the Cookson speeder or tool shed at Mile 70.6 (Km 113.7) was one of the few remaining buildings along the route. It and a similar building near Wilkinson Creek make good photo subjects in the afternoon sun.

There is a resort farther north at Idabel Lake that offers suites and lakefront cottages if you are getting a bit tired of pedalling and camping. It can be a busy place in summer so it is wise to check ahead.

KVR Bridge over Kettle River–Kettle River Provincial Recreation Area. © Murphy Shewchuk

Okanagan Highland

The relentless one percent climb continues to Mile 74.7 (Km 120.2) before levelling off at Summit Lake. If you are keeping track, this amounts to 50 km of steady climbing (over 450 metres elevation gain) since the outskirts of Beaverdell–ample reason to consider doing this section in the reverse direction.

There are BC Recreation Sites at McCulloch Reservoir and Hydraulic Lake with similar features to the Arlington Lakes site.

The summit also marks the division between the Regional District of Kootenay Boundary and the Regional District of Central Okanagan. The southwest section of the rail trail is part of the Regional District of Okanagan-Similkameen.

The grade is now making a steady arc as it passes north of McCulloch Reservoir and starts its southward passage to Penticton. However, if you are expecting a downhill coast, you will be disappointed. The elevation difference between Summit Lake and Chute Lake (Mile 106.5 or Km 171.4) is a mere 56 metres.

Myra Canyon Trestles

The historic Myra Canyon section of the Kettle Valley Railway corridor, just 40 minutes from downtown Kelowna, is a major attraction and a major part of the Trans Canada Trail.

Steel rails were laid through this steep-walled rocky canyon in the early 1900s, and the line was completed in 1914. They were removed in the 1980s because the railway was no longer used. However, the intricate steel and wooden trestles spanning creeks and cuts in the canyon remained behind, a legacy of the visionaries who created this transportation link. Those historic artifacts were considered an engineering marvel in their day, and are still awe-inspiring today, with the highest reaching 55 metres (180 feet) from its base to the wooden ties. In all, there are 18 trestles—16 wooden and two steel—and two tunnels in this 12-km stretch of the old railway bed.

A Bit of History

The Kettle Valley Railway (CPR) carried freight and passengers through the Myra Canyon from 1915 until passenger service ended in 1964 and the last scheduled train went through in 1973.

In June 1973 the Kettle Valley Railway section in the Myra Canyon, with its wood-frame trestles, tunnels, rock cuts, and awe-inspiring mountainous terrain, was used by the Canadian Broadcasting Corporation (CBC) as a location for filming a segment of Pierre Berton's *National Dream* television film on the construction of the CPR through the mountains of British Columbia. The province purchased the rail corridor from the Canadian Pacific Railway in 1990.

Myra Canyon Trestle Restoration

In 1993, following both death and injury to persons falling from the trestles, the community formed the Myra Canyon Trestle Restoration Society. The members coordinated an upgrading of the trestle crossings and construction of 1.2 metre high handrails to prevent people from falling to the rocks far below. In two years there were donations of thousands of metres of lumber, an estimated 80,000 nails and more than 10,000 hours of volunteer labour. They constructed a one-metre (three-foot) wide board walkway, complete with handrails, across each of the trestles. From corporations to kids, everyone got involved to create a safe walking and cycling corridor at this 1,250-metre (4,100-foot) elevation of Kelowna's southeast slopes.

As a result, the trestles became a cornerstone of the Provincial Rails to Trails network, a vital link along the Trans Canada Trail, as well as a significant tourism asset attracting as many as 50,000 visitors a year.

Myra-Bellevue Protected Area was established on April 18, 2001 as part of the Okanagan-Shuswap LRMP. In January 2003, the Myra Canyon section (from Mile 84.5 to Mile 90.5) of the Kettle Valley Railway was designated a National Historic Site. In May of 2004, the Protected Area was reclassified as a Provincial Park.

Okanagan Mountain Park Fire

Early on Saturday morning, August 16, 2003, a bolt of lightning struck a tree near Squally Point in Okanagan Mountain Park. An extremely dry summer and plenty of fuel, coupled with high winds, quickly spread the fire into the city of Kelowna. It destroyed over 230 homes before spreading up the mountainside to the former Kettle Valley Railway right-of-way. On September 3, the Okanagan Mountain Park wildfire entered the Myra Canyon area and, despite heroic efforts by firefighters and water bombers, it destroyed 12 wooden trestles and damaged two steel trestles.

Soon after the fire was put out, various politicians announced intentions to rebuild and, on August 26, 2004, BC Premier Gordon Campbell and Canadian Senator Ross Fitzpatrick announced a $13.5-million partnership between the provincial and federal governments to rebuild the historic Myra Canyon trestles. Work began on Trestle #18 in October, 2004 and it was completed by year-end. Work continued over the next several years until the trestles were reopened in late 2007.

Bellevue Trestle

After a convoluted set of loops through the Myra Canyon, the KVR grade crosses Bellevue Creek Canyon over one of the longest bridges in the system. According to Joe Smuin in *Kettle Valley Railway Mileboards*, the 65-metre-high, 238-metre-long (780 foot) steel bridge was constructed in 1946-47, replacing an 885-foot wood frame trestle. Due to the hard work of the firefighters and the vagaries of the fire storm, this trestle escaped the Okanagan Mountain Park Fire unscathed.

Unfortunately, the same can't be said for the rest of the rail grade to Chute Lake. While wildflowers, grass and shrubs are growing out of the charcoal and ashes, the reminder of the summer of 2003 will be visible for a long time. I don't want to suggest that this should be viewed in a negative way, for the new growth brings back wildlife such as deer that had very little forage in an old-growth environment.

Paul Lautard, former host of the Cyclist's Rest Stop, at the cenotaph at Rhone, south of Beaverdell, BC. © Murphy Shewchuk

Chute Lake Resort

Chute Lake Resort barely escaped the 2003 conflagration that devoured much of Okanagan Mountain Park. That it still stands to serve trail travellers and those escaping the heat of the valley is a testament to the persistence of the water bomber pilots. The resort is open year-around and offers rooms in the lodge, cabins, camping and a small RV park. And, after a hard day on the trail, the licensed dining room can be a very welcome site. Again, it is wise to check ahead during the busy summer season. (Phone: 250-493-3535.)

Chute Lake also marks the end of the relatively flat crossing of the upland plateau and the beginning of a steep (by railway standards) 44 km descent to Penticton. With much of the grade rated at 2.0 to 2.2 percent, extra engines were needed to climb it and working brakes were a definite asset on the way down.

For today's cyclists, a fat tire bike with good working disk brakes may also be an asset.

Rock Ovens

The KVR grade initially cuts across the mountainside on a southwest direction before gradually swinging south and then southeast. Signs mark the start of

Rock Oven Regional Park approximately nine km from Chute Lake.

According to several sources, including Bob Gibbard of nearby Glenfir, these ovens were used by the railway construction camp cooks during 1912 and 1913, when baking for the hungry, hardworking crews. The regional park was established to protect these unique ovens as relics of an important part of our past. Although we only managed to find a few complete ovens on our trips down the KVR, the signs suggest that there are nearly a dozen such locations between Chute Lake and Naramata.

Adra Tunnel

Watch for the foundation of a railway water tank near Km 181.7 (Mile 112.9) and the extra wide right-of-way of the passing track of Adra before reaching the 489-metre (1,604 foot) Adra Tunnel. The tunnel carves a 217-degree curve within the mountain. A weak spot in the roof near the mid-point is slowly caving in. At last check, the tunnel had been barricaded and a hiking/biking trail bypasses it. The Elinor Lake Road, near Km 180.6, can also be used to get down to the next level of the right-of-way.

After the tunnel bypass, the right-of-way now traverses the mountainside in a northwesterly direction. Watch for a wide spot in the grade near Km 186.5 just before it enters a rock cut. If you've found the right wide spot, you have lots of room to get off the grade and follow a fairly well-used trail up the hillside to several fine specimens of the rock ovens that once served the railway construction crews. (If you bypassed Adra Tunnel via Elinor Lake Road, back-track a few hundred metres up the railway grade.)

Little Tunnel

A little more than five km farther down the hill, the KVR grade makes another switchback loop at Glenfir. There is an opportunity here to take Chute Lake Road up or down the hill. There is also a pit toilet near the trail. Although the scenery has been quite spectacular, it becomes even more so as the grade edges southward along the cliffs. The Naramata (Little) Tunnel, at Mile 122 (Km 196.3) is one of the most photographed landmarks on this section of the KVR. The view to the south takes in Naramata, Penticton, Okanagan Lake and Skaha Lake.

Major work is underway to make this section of the KVR grade user-friendly. There are trail head maps, benches, pit toilets and bike parking throughout the ride to Smethurst Road.

Smethurst Road, approximately 4.5 km south of the tunnel, is your next opportunity to leave the railgrade. If you are interested in a break much closer to the KVR, there is a short trail down to the Hillside Estate Winery at Km 208. The grade crosses Naramata Road a few hundred metres later and then winds through the orchards to McCulloch Trestle across Randolph Draw.

McCulloch Trestle

According to Joe Smuin, Randolph Creek was originally spanned by a 300-foot-long timber frame trestle. This was later replaced by a concrete culvert and still later, due to unstable soil, a steel culvert. The steel culvert was removed some time after the trains quit running, leaving a 90-metre-wide gap in the grade. In keeping with the tradition of the former railway trestles in this region, the local community decided to build a timber bridge over the valley. Unlike the original heavy timber trestles, which relied on abundant quantities of large timbers, this new bridge was built from glued-laminated Douglas fir using state-of-the-art technologies including computer numerically controlled (CNC) machining and high strength connectors. Because the new bridge did not need to carry the weight of a freight train, the new design, coupled with the reduced load, meant that the amount of timber required was much less.

Downtown Penticton

The Trans Canada Trail (KVR grade) skirts the west side of Mount Munson as it continues through the orchards and vineyards. It enters Vancouver Place at Km 212.2 and, a couple hundred metres later, Vancouver Avenue. A right turn down Vancouver Avenue and another right turn on Lakeshore Drive should take you to the Trans Canada Trail pavilion in Rotary Park. If my calculations are correct, you will have travelled approximately 213 km since leaving Midway.

Additional Information:

Beaverdell RV Park
5880 Hwy 33
Beaverdell, BC V0H 1A0
Phone: 1-877-399-4341
Fax: 250-766-0470
E-mail: info@beaverdellrvpark.com

Chute Lake Resort
9540 Chute Lake Road Naramata,
BC V0H 1N1
Information: info@chutelakeresort.
com
Reservations: reservations@
chutelakeresort.com
Phone: (250) 493-3535
Fax: (250) 496-4017 (summers)

Idabel Lake Resort
800 Idabel Lake Road Naramata, BC
V0H 1N0

Phone: (250) 765-9511
Toll Free: 1 855 765 9511
E-mail: info@idabellakeresort.com

Little Dipper Hideaway
Box 27, Westbridge, BC
Canada, V0H 2B0
Phone: (250) 446-2213
E-mail: littledipperhideaway@gmail.
com

The Great Trail (a.k.a. Trans Canada Trail)
Web: https://thegreattrail.ca/

Trails BC: Boundary Region
Web: http://www.trailsbc.ca/tct/
boundary

Trails to the Boundary Society
Facebook: https://www.facebook.
com/trailstotheboundary

KVR Distance Table—
Midway to Penticton

Reference	Distance (km)	KVR Mileage	Elevation (metres)
Midway KVR Station	0	0	575
Rock Creek Fairground			
Jim Blaine Memorial Park	17	10.5	600
Rock Creek Station	18.8	11.7	
Kettle River Park Trestle	25	15.5	610
Westbridge	33	20.5	626
Rhone (Cyclists Rest)	40	24.7	650
Bull Creek Canyon	47	29	704
Bull Creek Canyon Trestle			
(West Kettle River)	48	29.8	705 Taurus Water
Tank Foundation	50.7	31.5	716
Tuzo Creek	61.5	38.2	762
Dellwye	63.6	39.5	770
Beaverdell (Welcome Kiosk)	68	43	790

Downtown Beaverdell	69		787
Carmi Station	46.4		
Carmi Information Kiosk	74.2		
Wilkinson Creek Bridge	81.3	50.5	908
Lois Speeder Shed	86.9	54	951
Lakevale Stn – Arlington Lake	98.2	61	1060
Cookson Speeder Shed	113.7	70.6	1182
Road 201 Crossing	118.7		1240
Summit Lake Gazebo	121.2		1248
Rec Site	122.2		1260
McCulloch Lake Resort	122.5		1260
McCulloch Station	123.1	76.5	1256
Myra Station / Myra FSR	135.2	84	1258

Myra Canyon Trestles—18 Trestles between Myra and Ruth stations.

Ruth Station	146.8	91.2	
Little White FSR	148		
Bellevue Trestle	155	96.3	1226
Lorna Station	97.5		
Gillard Creek	158.7		
Gillard Creek FSR	159.4		
Lebanon Lake	166.4		
Old Chute Lake Road	169.2		1202
Chute Lake Resort	171.4	106.5	1192
Rock Oven # 11	180.3		
Elinor Lake FSR	180.6		
Water Tank Foundation	181.7		
Adra Tunnel Bypass	182.9		
Adra Tunnel	183.5	114	
Rock Ovens	186.5		
Glenfir Loop – Chute Lake Rd	192		
Naramata (Little) Tunnel	196.3	122	
Arawana water tank (gazebo)	202	125.5	
Hillside Estate Winery	208		
McCulloch Trestle (Randolph Cr)	209.6		
Vancouver Place (Penticton)	212.2		
Vancouver Avenue	212.4		
TCT Pavilion – Rotary Park	213.2		

Information Sources

Alpine Club of Canada
201 Indian Flats Rd
PO Box 8040 Stn Main
Canmore AB T1W 2T8
Tel: 403-678-3200
Email: info@alpineclubofcanada.ca
Web: http://www.alpineclubofcanada.ca/

BC Parks General Information
Web: http://www.env.gov.bc.ca/bcparks/

Beaverdell RV Park
5880 Hwy 33
Beaverdell, BC V0H 1A0
Phone: 1-877-399-4341
Fax: 250-766-0470
E-mail: info@beaverdellrvpark.com

Bugaboo Provincial Park
Web: http://www.env.gov.bc.ca/bcparks/
explore/parkpgs/bugaboo/

Canadian Mountain Holidays
Box 1660,
Banff, Alberta T1L 1J6
Toll Free: (800) 661-0252
Phone: (403) 762-7100
Web: http://www.
canadianmountainholidays.com/

Chute Lake Resort
9540 Chute Lake Road Naramata, BC V0H 1N1
Information: info@chutelakeresort.com
Reservations: reservations@
chutelakeresort.com
Phone: (250) 493-3535
Fax: (250) 496-4017 (summers)

Columbia & Western Trail Society
Web: http://www.columbiaandwestern.ca/

Creston Valley Wildlife Management Area
PO Box 640
Creston, BC V0B 1G0
Web: http://www.crestonwildlife.ca/

Elk Valley Bighorn Outfitters
Anna Fontana
Box 275,
Cranbrook, BC V1C 4H8
Tel: 250.426.5789
Email: fontanabighorn@telus.net

Freshwater Fisheries Society of BC
http://www.gofishbc.com/

Grand Forks Community Trails Society
Web: http://www.gftrails.ca/

Great Divide Trail Association
http://www.greatdividetrail.com/

Idaho Peak Shuttle
306-Fourth St. Silverton, BC V0G 2B0
Cell (250) 505-4368
Web: http://idahopeakshuttle.ca/

Kootenay Columbia Trails Society
Web: http://www.kcts.ca/

Little Dipper Hideaway
Box 27, Westbridge, BC
Canada, V0H 2B0
Phone: (250) 446-2213
E-mail: littledipperhideaway@gmail.com

Bull Canyon on Kettle River north of Rhone, south of Beaverdell, BC. © Murphy Shewchuk

Nakusp Hot Springs Resort
8500 Hot Springs Road PO Box 280
Nakusp BC V0G 1R0
Phone: 250-265-4528
Toll Free: 1-866-999-4528
Web: http://www.nakusphotsprings.com/

Needles/Fauquier Cable Ferry
Western Pacific Marine
Web: http://arrowbridge.ca/ferry.php

Parks Canada: Mount Revelstoke Park
Web: http://www.pc.gc.ca/eng/pn-np/bc/revelstoke/index.aspx

Phoenix Mountain Alpine Ski Society
Box 2428, Grand Forks, BC V0H 1H0
Office phone: 250-442-5870
Mountain phone: 250-444-6565
Fax: 250-442-5090
Email: skiphoenix@gmail.com
Web: http://www.skiphoenix.com/

Recreation Sites and Trails BC
Web: www.sitesandtrailsbc.ca/

Revelstoke Online Trail Guide
Web: https://revelstoketrails.com/

Sandon Historical Society
PO Box 137,
New Denver, BC V0G 1S0
Phone: (250) 358-7920
Email: sandonmuseum@netidea.com

The Great Trail (a.k.a. Trans Canada Trail)
Web: https://thegreattrail.ca/

The Prospector's Pick
PO Box 308,
New Denver, BC V0G 1S0
Phone: (250) 358-2140
Email: sandon.bc.canada@gmail.com
Web: http://www.sandonbc.ca/index.html

Trails BC: Boundary Region
Web: http://www.trailsbc.ca/tct/boundary

Trails Society of British Columbia (Trails BC)
Email: trailsbc@trailsbc.ca Web: http://www.trailsbc.ca/

Trails to the Boundary Society
Facebook: https://www.facebook.com/trailstotheboundary

Bibliography

Akrigg, G.P.V. & Helen B. *1001 British Columbia Place Names*. Vancouver, BC: Discovery Press, 1973.

Akrigg, G.P.V. & Helen B. *British Columbia Chronicle, 1847-1871*. Vancouver, BC: Discovery Press, 1977.

Barlee, N.L. *Gold Creeks and Ghost Towns*. Surrey, BC: Hancock House Publishers Ltd., 1988.

Barlee, N.L. *Lost Mines and Historic Treasures of British Columbia*. Surrey, BC: Hancock House Publishers Ltd., 1989.

Blake, Don. *Valley of the Ghosts: The history along Highway 31A, BC* Kelowna, BC: Sandhill Publishing, 1990.

Bowering, George. *Bowering's BC, A Swashbuckling History*. London, England. Penguin Books Ltd., 1996.

Burbridge, Joan. *Wildflowers of the Southern Interior of British Columbia and adjacent parts of Washington, Idaho and Montana*. Vancouver, BC: University of British Columbia Press, 1989.

Cannings, Sydney and Richard Cannings. *Geology of British Columbia: A Journey through Time*. Vancouver, BC. Greystone Books, Douglas & McIntyre Publishing Group, 1999.

Christie, Jack. *Inside Out British Columbia*. Vancouver, BC: Raincoast Books, 1998.

Donnelly, Al. *Greenwood British Columbia Heritage Comes Alive*. Other details unknown.

Donnelly, Al. *Stories from Boundary Creek*. Greenwood, BC: Published by Al Donnelly, 2014.

Downs, Art. *Paddlewheels on the Frontier*. Surrey, BC: Foremost Publishing Co. Ltd., 1971.

Edgewood History Book Committee. *Just Where is Edgewood?* Published by the Edgewood History Book Committee, 1991.

Garden, John F. The *Bugaboos: An Alpine History*. Revelstoke, BC: Footprint Publishing Co. Ltd., 1987.

Hill, Beth. *Exploring the Kettle Valley Railway*. Winlaw, BC: Polestar Press, 1989.

Jacobsen, Larry. *Jewel of the Kootenays: The Emerald Mine*. West Vancouver, BC. Gordon Soules Book Publishing Ltd., 2008.

Langford, Dan & Sandra. *Cycling the Kettle Valley Railway*. Calgary, AB. Rocky Mountain Books, 1997, 2002.

Mussio Ventures & Trails BC. *Trans Canada Trail: The British Columbia Route.* New Westminster, BC: Mussio Ventures Ltd., 2001.

Nanton, Isabel and Mary Simpson. *Adventuring in British Columbia.* Vancouver, BC: Douglas & McIntyre, 1996.

Neering, Rosemary. *A Traveller's Guide to Historic British Columbia.* North Vancouver, BC: Whitecap Books, 1993.

Sanford, Barrie. *McCulloch's Wonder: The Story of the Kettle Valley Railway* North Vancouver, BC: Whitecap Books, 1977.

Sanford, Barrie. *Steel Rails and Iron Men: A Pictorial History of the Kettle Valley Railway.* North Vancouver, BC: Whitecap Books, 1990.

Shewchuk, Murphy O. *Backroads Explorer Vol. 2 Similkameen & South Okanagan.* Surrey, BC: Hancock House Publishers Ltd., 1988.

Shewchuk, Murphy O. *Coquihalla Trips & Trails.* Markham, ON: Fitzhenry and Whiteside Limited, 2007.

Smuin, Joe. *Canadian Pacific's Kettle Valley Railway.* Port Coquitlam, B. C., 1997.

Smuin, Joe. *Kettle Valley Railway Mileboards: A Historical field guide to the KVR.* Winnipeg, MB: North Kildonan Publications, 2003.

Steeves, Judie and Murphy Shewchuk. *Okanagan Trips & Trails.* Markham, ON: Fitzhenry and Whiteside Limited, 2006, 2013.

Strong, Janice. *Mountain Footsteps: Selected Hikes in the East Kootenay.* Calgary, AB: Rocky Mountain Books, 1994.

Turnbull, Elsie G. *Ghost Towns and Drowned Towns of West Kootenay.* Surrey, BC: Heritage House Publishing Company Ltd., 1988.

Turner, Robert D. *Steam on the Kettle Valley Railway: A Heritage Remembered.* Victoria, BC: Sono Nis Press, 1995.

Turner, Robert D. *West of Great Divide, An Illustrated History of the Canadian Pacific Railway in British Columbia, 1880-1986.* Victoria, BC: Sono Nis Press, 1987.

Williams, David R. *"…The Man for a New Country" Sir Matthew Baillie Begbie.* Sidney, BC: Gray's Publishing Ltd., 1977.

About the Author

Murphy Shewchuk has been writing and illustrating articles and books since the mid-1960s. He first started with technical articles for Canadian Electron magazine. In 1971, his work took him to Kamloops, BC, where he began a weekly Outdoor Scene column for the *Kamloops Sentinel*. From the column, he moved to features in *BC Outdoors* magazine and many other magazines.

More than 400 of his magazine articles and 2,000 of his photographs have appeared in such publications as *Adventure Travel, BC Outdoors, Camping Canada, Canadian Geographic, Field & Stream, MotorHome, Photo Life, Skyword, Western Living,* and *Westworld.*

He has also written and illustrated 13 other books including: *Exploring Kamloops Country; Fur, Gold & Opals; Exploring the Nicola Valley; Cariboo; The Craigmont Story; Backroads Explorer Vol 1: Thompson-Cariboo; Backroads Explorer Vol 2: Similkameen & South Okanagan; Okanagan Country: An Outdoor Recreation Guide; Coquihalla Country: A Guide to BC's North Cascade Mountains and Nicola Valley; Okanagan Trips & Trails: Coquihalla Trips & Trails* and *Cariboo Trips & Trails.*

In addition to his life-long interest in writing, photography and exploring the mountains of western Canada, Murphy has been a workshop speaker at writer's conferences across Canada and in the U.S.A. His writing and photography has received awards from the Outdoor Writers of Canada and the Macmillan Bloedel newspaper journalism competitions. In 1989, he was given the Allan Sangster Award for Outstanding Service to the Canadian Authors Association. In 2008, Murphy Shewchuk was selected as the winner of the British Columbia Heritage Award.

Shewchuk now lives in Merritt, BC with his wife Katharine. He currently serves on the board of the Nicola Valley Museum Archives Association and is also an active member of Trails BC, the organization involved with the Trans Canada Trail in British Columbia.

Acknowledgments

My first "real" taste of the Kootenay-Columbia region was in the late 1950s when, as a teenager, I hitched a ride with some friends to visit relatives in Manitoba. We bounced along the Big Bend Highway between Revelstoke and Golden going east. The label "highway" as in "Big Bend Highway" would hardly stand up to today's scrutiny. We rode a Kootenay Lake ferry or two coming back. This brief glimpse of the mountains of eastern British Columbia suggested the rest of BC was equally as rugged as my home in the Coast Range.

Half a Century of Outdoor Writing

After high school, my work took me across the country, but eventually brought me back to British Columbia. It was during the early 1970s that I met Margaret "Ma" Murray, the feisty editor of the *Bridge River – Lillooet News*, and began writing outdoor material for her paper. After a move to Kamloops, I developed an outdoor column for the *Kamloops Daily Sentinel* and then branched out to articles for Art Downs' *BC Outdoors* magazine and a host of other magazines and books.

The mountains and my friends helped foster my appreciation for the outdoors and my editors helped influence how I presented my views about my surroundings. My readers have also encouraged me with suggestions and feedback; however my greatest appreciation goes to the outdoor enthusiasts, historians and fellow writers who have been free with their information and advice over the past half century. The list is long, but those who have helped with this book include members of Trails BC and the Trans Canada Trail organization. Some have retired and moved on to other things, but those who are still active with Trails BC as this goes to press include Ciel Sander of Greenwood and Al Skucas of Cranbrook. Special thanks go to Clive Webber of Victoria who maintains the Trails BC website, a valuable resource for myself and all trail users. Sarah Meunier, Trans Canada Trail Coordinator living at Castlegar has also been a great help. Special thanks to Chris Newel – North Star Rails to Trail; Al Skucas – Trails BC Rockies Region and Terry Nelson – Fernie Trails Alliance for supplying the material

for the chapter on the Kimberley-Cranbrook-Fernie trails.

I would especially like to thank my wife Katharine for her hours of note-taking and expert advice on the flora and fauna of the region.

Murphy Shewchuk

INDEX